The Changing Population of Britain

Edited by
Heather Joshi

Basil Blackwell

Copyright © Centre for Economic Policy Research 1989

First published 1989
Reprinted 1990

Basil Blackwell Ltd
108 Cowley Road, Oxford OX4 1JF, UK

Basil Blackwell, Inc.
3 Cambridge Center
Cambridge, Massachusetts 02142, USA

British Library Cataloguing in Publication Data

A CIP catalogue record for this book is available from the British Library.

Library of Congress Cataloging-in-Publication Data
The Changing Population of Britain.
  Bibliography: p.
  Includes index.
  1. Great Britain—Population.   I. Joshi, Heather.
HB3583.C46   1989   304.6′0941   88–16740
ISBN 0–631–16409–X
ISBN 0–631–16515–0 (pbk.)

Typeset in 10 ½ on 12 pt Garamond
by Colset Private Limited, Singapore
Printed and Bound in Great Britain by
T.J. Press (Padstow) Ltd, Padstow, Cornwall

Contents

Preface

The study of population is vital. It is vital in that it is concerned with the vital events of birth and death and other momentous transitions in people's lives. It is vital for informing forecasting and decision in both public and private sectors. It is also vital, as this book shows, in the sense that it is a very lively branch of social science in Britain. These essays survey the latest research on the causes and consequences of demographic change in contemporary Britain. They are intended to bring the findings of such work to those interested in the study of our society but who do not have access to the specialist and disparate literature in which the scholarly material is published. They also underline the importance for future policymaking of research into demographic change.

The contributors have been assembled under the joint auspices of the Centre for Economic Policy Research and the British Society for Population Studies. Both organizations have among their other objectives the common purpose to promote the dissemination of research on the contemporary British population.

Since its inception in 1983, CEPR's research programme in Human Resources since 1900 has recognized that population change is an important part of the story of the long-run development of the British economy and social structure. The Centre has brought together economists, historians and demographers in about equal numbers as Research Fellows in this pro-gramme. In addition to the contributions to this book, Research Fellow's work is disseminated through CEPR's Discussion Paper series as well as the meetings, seminars and workshops which it organizes and reports in its Bulletin.

The British Society for Population Studies was founded in 1973, having its origins in the Population Study Group of the Royal Society. It has since become the main forum in the United Kingdom for the discussion and dissemination of research on human populations. Besides the topics addressed in this book, its members' interests span historical demography and the demography of the developing countries, fields in which British demographers have made outstanding contributions. The society organizes several afternoon and day meetings each year which are held in London, and an annual residential conference held elsewhere in Britain.

In both 1985 and 1986, the BSPS annual conferences addressed questions about the results and direction of research on the contemporary British population. The papers for the 1985 conference were published, at the time, as OPCS Occasional Paper No. 34: *Measuring Socio-Demographic Change in Britain*, though in a limited edition. Revised versions of most of the papers presented to the Society's 1986 Conference in Norwich on *Population Research in Britain* will be appearing in a volume edited for the Oxford University Press by John Hobcraft and Mike Murphy.

To widen the audience for its work, the BSPS joined forces with CEPR to hold a series of lunchtime lecture meetings during 1986 and 1987. The eight lectures in the series were specifically intended to highlight findings of demographic research relevant to policymakers and to attract an audience from Whitehall and other non-academic institutions. It is upon material presented in this series that this book is based. Each chapter has been extended to include background information useful to the non-specialist reader and references to the scientific literature. The book also contains two extra chapters which cover topics which were not treated in the lecture series itself. These are chapter 8, by Tony Champion on the Spatial Distribution of Population, and chapter 11, by Ian Diamond and Sue Clarke on the Demography of Britain's Ethnic Minorities. The editor is particularly grateful to these contributors for having written these chapters at short notice.

The editor also wishes to express heartfelt appreciation to all of the other contributors for the effort involved in presenting their original lectures and in converting their material in to a form suitable for this book; to the staff at CEPR, particularly Paul Compton and Michele Low, for help at all stages of organizing the lecture series and this volume; to Nicole Price for her assistance in preparing this manuscript and to Sue Owen for producing the graphics. The graphs are all original, and have been generated from the data sources indicated.

Thanks are also very much due for the financial assistance which has made this project possible. The cost of putting on the lectures was met by grants to CEPR from the Department of Health and Social Security, the Central Statistical Office, BSPS, the Population Investigation Committee and the Simon Population Trust. The last two donors have also contributed to the expenses of producing this book.

This financial support is all the more essential since research on population issues in Britain is heavily dependent upon funding from grants – 'soft money' as opposed to the 'hard money' of permanently funded university posts. For all its international reputation, demography is a curiously underfunded discipline within the social sciences in Britain. There are no more than 15 full-time academic positions funded by the University Grants Committee of which five have been established since 1980. Between 1978 and 1986, the ESRC funded five additional posts at one of its Designated Research Centres, the Centre for Population Studies located at the London School of Hygiene. These funds were intended to support research into the causes and consequences of population change in Britain. A substantial portion of the research reviewed in this book had its origins in this funding. ESRC support to population studies continues, though on a reduced level and time scale. For example, the editor gratefully acknowledges the funding, by the ESRC, of her own post which has made it possible for her to edit this book. Acknowledgement of particular research grants are made in each chapter as appropriate.

The understanding of contemporary change is a never-ending task. Yet it is far from certain whether, in the 1990s, there will be sufficient researchers to pose questions of data whose supply also seems jeopardized. Meanwhile it is hoped that this account of Britain's changing population in the 1980s will reach and interest a far larger audience than the small band who are professionally concerned with monitoring and interpreting demographic developments. As will be clear from the contributions to this book and its bibliography, population studies touch on a wide range of topics across the whole field of social science, and have applications to the concerns of policy-makers in Whitehall, town halls and the private sector. This is quite apart from their intrinsic interest, which the contributors to this book hope to share with its readers.

1 Population Matters

John Hobcraft and Heather Joshi

Overview

Births, deaths, marriages and divorces, and migration are crucial to everyone's lives. These events and their effects on the formation, attrition and dissolution of households and on the growth of population are of great cultural, social, economic and biological salience. Demography, the study of human population, has its origins in the works of Graunt and Petty in the seventeenth century and of Malthus in the late eighteenth and early nineteenth centuries. As an academic discipline demography has relatively few exponents in Britain though, as this book shows, it is of relevance to a number of branches of social science as well as being a subject of interest in its own right.

The relatively small group of demographers working on British population come from a wide range of backgrounds; in addition to training in demography, they are drawn from sociology, psychology, anthropology, human biology, economics, statistics, geography, and even mathematical physics. In this small community there are ample opportunities for interdisciplinary exchange, which is crucial to any successful study of demographic behaviour. Most demographers have a fairly strong background in quantitative skills, a strength found lacking in some other fields by the ESRC's review of 'New Horizons' in British social science (ESRC, 1987), in which demography emerged with flying colours. These quantitative skills have enabled substantial use to be made of results from large and complex national surveys.

Good research on most subjects begins with imaginative formulation of questions that require answers. Considerable skill is then required to use existing information in new ways in order to answer such questions; otherwise results either become trivial or never appear. We believe that recent research on British demography combines these qualities of imaginative research design with skilful implementation and analysis, in the best traditions of empirical social research. Moreover, the questions posed and answers obtained are often of considerable relevance to contemporary policy issues, as well as providing new insights into human behaviour. This volume draws together the fruits of such research, and purposely hides the underlying complexities, in order to bring the results to wider attention.

The population of Great Britain numbers around 55 million people in the mid-1980s.[1] It had doubled over the century to 1975; since then its overall size has been almost at a standstill. The 1985-based official projections suggest that the British population will pass the 57 million mark around the turn of the century, peak at about 58 million around the year 2025, and fall back again very slowly to reach its current level again in the third quarter of the twenty-first century. The changes described in this book are thus mainly changes in structure rather than in size. These concerns include changes in the age composition of the population, its grouping into households and families, its geographical distribution and its ethnic composition. Changes in demographic structure are associated with changes in social and economic structure both as cause and effect. The contributions to this book trace some of the complex relationships between the housing and education systems, the labour market, and the climate of beliefs and values on the one hand, and processes of family formation and breakup on the other. In some instances demographic factors are important in widening the gap between the advantaged and the disadvantaged within the social structure. Migration tends to leave the less advantaged people behind, in the inner city cores, and in the North of the country generally. The distinctive demographic characteristics of people living in council housing – earlier childbearing, higher divorce rates and lower migration – tend to compound their relative educational and economic deprivation.

The family has always been the focus for much social interaction, and it plays an important role in the socialization of the young and in the care of the elderly. Yet traditional family functions are changing in Britain as a result of demographic changes. The consequences of these demographic changes are far-reaching. Divorce has become the greatest source of single parent families, and this has significant implications for the incidence of poverty and the workings of the benefit system. Divorce is also a prime reason for movements out of the owner-occupied sector of the housing market. The ramifications for the family networks and child care are also considerable.

Fluctuations in fertility in the past also have many important consequences for policy today (see Hobcraft, 1985; Ermisch, 1983 and 1985). The high levels of fertility of the 1960s placed severe pressure on maternity services,

---

[1] This total consists of England, (47 million), Scotland (5 million) and Wales (3 million). The fourth country of the United Kingdom, Northern Ireland, has a further one and a half million inhabitants. In general the geographical coverage in this book does not extend to Northern Ireland for which comparable statistical information is often lacking or not easily accessible.

primary and secondary schooling, higher education, and the job and housing markets. The precipitous decline in birth rates during the 1970s has created equally severe strains, although of a different nature, on these services. Falling birth rates, combined with out-migration from the inner cities, have meant that maternity services in urban areas have been significantly under-used. Major urban teaching hospitals have in effect been oliged to 'import' mothers for treatment. Population decline has also had major ramifications for the funding of these hospitals.

Similarly, the combined effects of fertility decline and migration have severely reduced school rolls in inner-city areas, with important consequences for the provision of teachers and for school closures. These fertility fluctua-tions also have profound implications for the debates about the provision of places in higher education during the 1990s and about the future of pension provision and the State Earnings Related Pension Scheme (SERPS) in the first half of the next century.

Population forecasts prepared in the post-war period have often proved incorrect. At the peak of the baby boom in the mid-1960s, official pro-jections led to expectations of a poplation of 73 million for Great Britain by the turn of the century. This contrasts with a 1983 projection of about 56 million. The 'crash' plans for major new cities that were developed in the late 1960s have proved unneccessary and most recent forecasts suggest that fertil-ity is likely to stay at or just below replacement levels until the end of the century.

Official projections for Britain, until 1983, assumed that fertility would return to replacement level before the end of the century. The 1985-based projections have lowered the long-term level of fertility to two children, just below replacement level. In contrast, for most other European countries, projections assume continued low fertility, or even a small further decline. Indeed in some countries of Europe, such as West Germany and Italy, concerns about widespread childlessness and about prospects of population decline have emerged, which parallel those expressed in the 1930s. Current and projected fertility levels in the United Kingdom are among the highest in Western Europe.

Unlike some countries facing more precipitous rates of population decline or ageing, there is little call, or need, for an explicit official population policy in Britain. There is, of course, a very stringent policy of immigration control, whose operation is described in chapter 11. Official policy on birth control is liberal. Since the 1970s contraceptive services and advice are freely available even to the unmarried. Access to abortion was liberalized in 1967 though the law does not extend to abortion on demand. Government policy is to enable people to prevent unwanted births. Indirectly, many other public policies may affect private decisions about whether or when births are wanted, as well as affecting the other sources of population change, migration and mortality.

These questions, as well as those of the impact of demographic changes on policy, are addressed in the following chapters.

Fertility and the Family

As described by William Brass in chapter 2, there have been striking variations in the level of fertility in Britain during the nineteenth and twentieth centuries. British demographers have, since the turn of the century, sought to explain both medium-term fluctuations and the long-term trends in fertility. The sustained fertility decline from the 1870s to the 1930s, for example, led to considerable concern about a likely long-term decline in the population of Britain, exemplified by Enid Charles's book *The Twilight of Parenthood*. In the most extreme projection the population of England and Wales was forecast to fall below ten million in the early part of the twenty-first century, and there were discussions of the consequences of such developments for the age structure of the population. This concern about imminent population decline underlay the setting up of a Royal Commission on Population in 1944.

Subsequent developments in fertility proved to be quite different; they included a brief but substantial post-war surge in births, a sustained baby 'boom' during the late 1950s and early 1960s, followed by a dramatic baby 'bust', beginning in the late 1960s and accelerating in the early 1970s. Since 1977, overall fertility levels have been fairly stable, although illegitimate fertility has risen and there are signs of rising fertility levels for women in their thirties.

In chapter 2, William Brass presents his own interpretation of recent fertility trends and prospects. He challenges the impression given by the conventional measure of current fertility rates that fertility has been below 'replacement' for most of the 1970s and 1980s. He provides an alternative index of the underlying tendencies, the Total Quantum Fertility Index, which puts fertility around the 2.1 mark for most of the period since 1972.

Unfortunately, Brass's Quantum Index cannot be directly calculated from birth registration data, which do not record the length of time since a woman's previous birth (nor how many previous births there were, in the case of illegitimate births). In the absence of better data, imputations are necessary to construct this Index, so its value will remain somewhat speculative. In addition to the underlying developments that this index is designed to uncover, there are short-term variations in birth rates which reflect changes in the timing ('tempo' in the terminology adopted in chapter 2) which can cause marked fluctuations in the level of births from year to year without there being any great change in completed family size for successive generations. These variations can nevertheless have big effects on the course of the age structure for years to come. Their consequences need to be anticipated, and are all the more difficult to accommodate, the more rapid and substantial are the swings.

The future course of fertility will always defy certain prediction, but anticipation of the future is enhanced by an improved understanding of influences on current trends as well as an improved measurement of what is actually taking place. As Brass suggests, fertility levels are influenced by a wide variety of social and economic factors, and forecasting fertility involves more than just mechanical projections. Some social and economic indicators could be interpreted as suggesting that fertility in Britain will remain constant or even fall slightly. These indicators include higher levels of female participation in further education and paid employment, rising divorce rates, and high levels of unemployment, leading to smaller family sizes. Moreover, since around 1970, more effective methods of contraception have become readily available and access to abortion has become easier, helping to reduce unwanted births. On the other hand, we may see a noticeable rise in fertility at the higher ages, as those women who kept their options open in the late 1970s and early 1980s decide to have children in their late twenties or thirties. This tendency is already apparent in Sweden and evidence of postponed childbearing exists in England and Scotland.

Alongside the trend to later childbearing over the 1970s came other changes in the structure of the British family, discussed by Kathleen Kiernan in chapter 3. Later childbearing was a consequence of later marriage, although there was also a trend towards earlier sexual relations before and outside marriage. Cohabitation, both before and between marriages, has become increasingly common during the last decade and the recent increase in illegitimacy rates may herald a move towards increased childbearing by cohabiting couples, a change which has already been observed in Scandinavia. This change has probably been retarded in Britain by the nature of the housing market, which affords only very limited opportunities for private rented accomodation. This contrasts with Denmark, where a more fluid housing market is associated with children leaving home much earlier.

Since the 1969 Divorce Reform Act, which became effective in 1971, there has been an unprecedented rise in divorce rates and, *if rates current in 1984 are maintained*, about a third of all marriages may end in divorce. Higher risk of divorce has been linked to early marriages, and both to childlessness and to early or compressed childbearing within marriage. The high divorce rates have also been associated with increased remarriage, but they have nevertheless become the principal source of Britain's very rapidly growing contingent of one-parent families. There were estimated to be about one million such families in 1986, double the number in 1966. Nine out of ten such lone parents are women. One-parent families, along with pensioners and the unemployed, include a significant proportion of Britain's most impoverished people.

In chapter 4 John Ermisch presents some new results of research into the economic and demographic background of women who become and remain lone mothers. Increased experience of paid work appears to raise the chances of a woman divorcing, other things being equal, but it also increases the chances of her remarrying. It thus appears that as the population of one-parent families increased over the 1970s and 1980s it was also becoming more diverse, with more families spending relatively short spells before reconstituting. There was also a growing core of the most economically and psychologically vulnerable mothers remaining for long periods dependent on Supplementary Benefit for financial support. The growth in the numbers of children spending at least some of their childhood under these circumstances must be a cause for concern.

Along with the rise in divorce, there has been a concomitant rise in the occurrence of remarriages, especially for men. The requirement that remarried men contribute to the support of two families causes considerable strain to some of these second marriages, although inability or failure to meet these obligations undoubtly causes even more serious poverty among women heading lone-parent families with young children, given their persisting disadvantages in the labour market.

The role of women in the economy is discussed in chapter 10 alongside the question of ethnicity in chapter 11, on the grounds that both sex and race are among the accidents of birth that still generate social and economic advantages for individuals in contemporary Britain. Heather Joshi introduces her findings from the MRC Survey of the 1946 birth cohort which suggest that the labour market treats men more favourably than their female contemporaries. This is the case, even though the Equal Pay Act has been brought into force, and after allowances have been made for family responsibilities lowering the rate of pay received by those women who had taken them on. Chapter 10 is therefore also very much concerned with the family. It is argued that women's role in the family has a clearly detectable impact upon women's role in paid work, and that influences in the reverse direction, from female employment to family formation and dissolution are occurring perhaps more slowly than is sometimes supposed.

Female wage rates did rise relative to those of men in the early 1970s, probably as a result of equal opportunities legislation along with the raising of the school leaving age and incomes policy. These higher wage rates have probably contributed to higher rates of female labour force participation and may have contributed to lower fertility levels, although debate continues over the direction of causation. Higher wage rates have increased the opportunity costs to women (in terms of forgone income) of reducing their labour force participation in order to provide child care or other caring activities. This has important implications for women's roles as unpaid carers, and may be associated with increasing use of child-minders and moves towards sheltered housing schemes and institutional care for the elderly. The tendency toward increased female labour force participation may also have contributed to rising divorce rates by strengthening female independence and autonomy, a process which chapter 10 argues is still far from complete.

A complete account of the complex changes occurring within the British family must clearly extend beyond the consideration of economic factors. Changes in contraceptive technology and attitudes to the physical and social relations between the sexes should also be brought into account. John Simons (1986a) has brought sociological insight to examining how changes in the climate of cultural values effect attitudes towards the family and reproduction. There is still much need to improve our theory and understanding of the role of social attitudes and values in the rearing as well as the bearing of successor generations. Moreover, we lack good theory about the value placed on other people's children by the community, as expressed in the balance of public and private provision for children.

Population Structure and Change

Falling birth rates tend to increase the share of the aged in the population, and the ageing of a population is often depicted as if it entailed the problems of growing old faced by an individual and as if the individual was a burden on relatives or society. In chapter 5, Pat Thane takes an optimistic look at the consequences of such changes in the age structure. It is well known that the old, and especially the very old, have been becoming steadily more numerous since the 1950s. It is less well known that there will be a lull in the growth of the numbers of pensionable age in the 1990s. Thane argues that this lull presents an opportunity to reassess the presumption of elderly dependency and to plan sensibly for the twenty-first century when the numbers of elderly are set to increase considerably, especially when those born in the 1960s reach retirement age. The reappraisal of the State Earnings Related Pension Scheme in the 1980s partly arose from the fact that neither the rate of economic growth nor the level of fertility maintained the values that had been expected when the scheme was drawn up in 1975, but its concern with the burden of old age may have distracted attention from the need to rethink, as Thane advocates, the institution of retirement.

There have been substantial declines in mortality among those aged about 45 to 64 in many other developed countries, largely because of the reduced incidence of heart disease. The recent and belated launch in the United Kingdom of the World Health Organization's 'Health for All' programme emphasized that we are now the laggards in Western Europe, with mortality risks being especially high in Scotland and Northern Ireland. If serious attention is given to public and preventive health in the United Kingdom these age groups may well experience considerably lower mortality by the turn of the century, and this will swell the numbers of the elderly still further. It is hard to predict the implications of mortality decline for the joint survival patterns of husband and wife (where they have not already divorced); knowledge of joint survival patterns is necessary to project numbers of lone elderly, the most vulnerable group. Nevertheless, it is almost certain that the ratio of dependents to those in employment will increase considerably and it is likely that the demand for caring will rise sharply. Such care has traditionally been provided by daughters, but increased mobility, increased and prolonged female labour force participation, and smaller family sizes suggest that this may not continue to be the case. This will entail a further move towards sheltered housing for the elderly. Demographic simulation models of kinship and household structure can help considerably in assessing the likely combined impact of these changes.

Young adults are another group in the population who are of particular concern for policy formulation. Those aged 16–24 in the mid-1980s were almost all born in the 1960s, and 20–24 year olds were born into especially large birth cohorts. As these cohorts reached the minimum school-leaving age in 1978–82, they placed additional burdens on the higher education sector and were the first to experience the consequences of the reductions in university funding after 1981, as Ian Diamond discusses in chapter 6. Those who are teenagers in the late 1980s are experiencing to an even greater degree the effects of reduced opportunities for higher education. These opportunities are already extremely limited, by European and North American standards, and have recently been reduced even further on the grounds that those born slightly later will be less numerous and so demand fewer places. Diamond argues that many young people, particularly those from disadvantaged backgrounds, are still not fulfilling their educational potential. The falling cohort size presents an opportunity to increase access to higher education and to equip the labour force of the twenty-first century with the skills that could at least compensate for their relatively small size. Chapter 6 also discusses the role of demography in forecasting school rolls, and explores the procedures which identify, and in some cases unwittingly perpetuate, local pockets of educational disadvantage.

The entry of the large cohorts of the 1960s into the labour market has also exacerbated structural unemployment problems, and this age group had suffered in a predictable manner. In addition, recent work by Moser and others (1984, 1987) has shown that unemployment brings increased risks of mortality and morbidity, and, as discussed by Mike Murphy in chapter 7, the unemployed also tend to be forced out of owner-occupation and to have higher fertility. Those who are employed among the 16–24 age-group in the 1980s, in conjunction with their slightly older peers, are placing very great pressure on the housing market. This has driven up house prices and consequently delayed cohabitation, marriage and childbearing.

Recent research has elucidated other important links between the housing market and demographic behaviour. Research by Fox and Goldblatt (1982) indicates that tenure in local authority housing is associated with substantially higher mortality risks. Such tenure is also associated with significantly higher fertility levels: only some of this differential fertility can be attributed to the regulations governing the allocation of local authority housing, as Mike Murphy has demonstrated. These differences in demographic behaviour by housing tenure have been shown to be at least as strong as those associated with social class, and they persist in the face of controls for social class. Thus, chapter 7 points to housing provision as a determinant as well as an outcome of demographic change. Murphy argues that the housing stock has failed to match the changes in demographic structure. He also points to the difficulties of reaching target levels of owner-occupation among such growing categories of households as single-parent families and other families with unemployed earners.

Processes of social polarization are also revealed in chapter 8 on the changing spatial distribution of Britain's population. Tony Champion draws attention to two dimension of redistribution of the population: the continued drift from the North to the South and the flight from the Inner Cities.

The changing regional distribution of population reflects employment decline in the North and employment growth in the south. This geographical divergence in economic prosperity, which has also revealed a mismatch between employment and housing markets, has been exacerbated by a disjunction between government policy on housing, planning and the economy. These trends have also resulted in political polarization, manifest in the Parliamentary elections of 1987, where there was a swing against the Conservative Party in the North, especially in Scotland, but increased support in the South.

The drift away from city centres is a trend which has, by contrast, slowed in the 1980s. Inner cities, nevertheless, present enormous social, economic and planning problems, which were once again highlighted as a priority by the Government returned in 1987. Differential migration only serves to exacerbate and may even cause some of these difficulties. Markedly reduced employment opportunities and shrinkage of the local authority rate base make funding of the existing social infrastructure, such as roads, schools and hospitals, progressively more difficult. A gradual 'residualization' of these areas, through selective migration, brings about concentrations of disadvantaged groups, including the elderly, the unemployed, ethnic minorities and one-parent families. The residualization of many ethnic minorities in such areas militates against understanding and acceptance of cultural diversity in Britain. Residualization also places strains on social services, benefit structures, and the conventional social fabric in the inner cities.

As discussed by John Hobcraft in chapter 9, population estimates, along with indicators of areal deprivation, play a major role in regional resource allocation procedures, particularly through the Grant-Related Expenditure Assessment for local authorities and the Resource Allocation Working Party (RAWP) procedures for health authorities. Yet these procedures are based on very limited information and little effective effort has been made to incorporate alternative indicators into the process.

Extensive evidence is available on the tendency toward 'undercounting' in Census returns, and Britton and Birch (1985) have provided evidence showing less complete enumeration for inner London in the 1981 Census. In the United States, litigation has resulted in major demands to adjust for the effects of Census undercounts before Census figures are used as a basis for allocating resources. In Britain, a rough and ready adjustment procedure is already used to adjust for Census undercounts in inner London, by broad age groups. But such crude adjustments are not properly reflected in many other Census-based indicators, such as ethnic composition or numbers of lone-parent families. Many further problems arise through lack of timeliness in indicators based upon the 1981 Census, which will not be updated until after a 1991 Census. For example, the number of lone-parent families has been increasing steadily in recent years, with consequent implications for local authority expenditure. Yet estimates of the expenditure needs for lone parents use static measures from the 1981 Census. A means of updating these estimates at a local authority level is clearly needed.

What is also needed is improved understanding of the diverse circumstances which generate local indicators of social problems. Besides the marital breakup stressed in chapter 4 and 10 as sources of the growing number of one-parent families, there is also a growing minority of such families headed by never-married women, among whom those of Afro-Caribbean origin are over-represented. Kaufman (1984) has shown a strong positive association between illegitimacy levels in London boroughs and the proportion of the population which is of West Indian origin. The origins of this within Caribbean culture are clear, with stable childbearing unions commonly occurring with or without regular cohabitation. An understanding of the cultural background to such demographic issues is needed by those working on this topic.

Cultural diversity notwithstanding, the research on Britain's ethnic minorities reviewed by Ian Diamond and Sue Clarke in chapter 11 points to demographic assimilation. This process is taking place faster than any equalization of the economic opportunities facing the Black, Brown and White British. Fertility levels of the ethnic minorities are converging on those of the white community. The ethnic minority population is still growing, but is unlikely to pass 7 per cent of the national total. If the demographic dynamics behind this process of stabilization were more generally appreciated, fears of swamping which feed racial prejudice and discrimination might be more effectively countered.

Conclusion

The new findings summarized in this book draw heavily on a wide range of nationally representative data dources. In addition to the classic sources of vital registration and the decennial Census, long the staple of demographic research, increasing use has been made of survey data, both of a cross-sectional and a longitudinal nature. Many of the findings presented derive from government sponsored surveys, including the General Household Survey, the Family Formation Survey and the Labour Force survey. These are very rich data sources, and it is cost-effective for them to be used as secondary sources in academic research. But there are other reasons for a shift towards secondary analysis which are to be regretted. In particular, the dearth of research funds in the social sciences in the late 1980s has made it extremely difficult to fund nationally representative surveys with a research focus. As a result of considerable ingenuity, demographers often obtain important insights from secondary data sources, but there are many important research questions which cannot be tackled without new, in-depth information.

An area which receives a great deal of attention in the studies presented here is the use of longitudinal data sources. These sources include true prospective studies such as the National Survey of Health and Development or the one per cent Longitudinal Study, and rich retrospective histories collected in cross-sectional surveys, such as the Women and Employment Survey. Demographers have stayed close to the forefront of applying recent methodological advances to the analysis of these data sources. Quite clearly the analysis of social change must incorporate a time dimension and quite often involves a complex interplay between several processes and between different levels of aggregation. Techniques to permit such complicated analysis are increasingly being developed and demographic research has become much richer through intelligent use of these approaches.

Ultimately the substantive conclusions presented in this volume rest heavily upon rich data sources and imaginative exploitation or analysis of these. But it is essential that such methodological issues remain subordinate to the goals of understanding and accounting for demographic change. Demographic change is the common thread which runs through all the issues touched on in this volume. Population studies serve as a focal point for discussion of these topics, bringing together the insights of many disparate disciplines, which range far beyond demography itself. As this volume makes clear, there is no doubt of the importance and policy relevance of these population issues: population does indeed matter.

2 Is Britain Facing the Twilight of Parenthood?

William Brass

Dismal Prospects or Dismal Forecasting?

The future size and composition of populations are of critical concern to policymakers. Since the configuration of the future emerges relatively slowly from that of the past, along paths whose characters are well defined, forecasting depends on the elucidation of population dynamics. A plausible case can be made that this activity is the core of the science of demography. There is no doubt that practitioners in other professional disciplines see the uses of the subject in these terms. Thus forecasting or projecting the populations of the future is an integral and indeed central concern of demography and not a peripheral issue. It is, therefore, particularly unfortunate that the record of success in the operation is so poor, and the exposition of the nature and bounds of uncertainty unsatisfactory.

Superficially it appears rather easy to discern what has happened, given adequate statistical data. The trends in population growth, birth and death rates can be measured and extrapolated with greater or less caution into the future. But both experience and more sophisticated analysis demonstrate that the outcome can be seriously misleading. Once 'common sense' procedures are abandoned, the necessary progression is to complex measurements and indicators. Interpretation begins to depend on a technical knowledge of how the measurements are constructed. When there is a strong consensus among specialists – on the concepts and procedures which are of most value – a coherent scheme of result and exposition is developed. If agreement is poor, there is confusion, a concentration on esoteric features and a failure to explain the significant issues. The latter is a sustainable description of the present state of population forecasting.

It is now widely claimed by politicians, social scientists and demographers that many developed countries, particularly in Europe, are entering on a period of substantial population decline (see, for example, Macura and Malacic, 1987). An inevitable concomitant is population ageing with rising proportions of old dependents and relative reductions of the young and energetic in the labour force. Most commentators regard the prospect with dismay – for economic, social, psychological and patriotic reasons – although it should be noted that the scientific literature is by no means in agreement on the consequences of the population size and composition changes (National Research Council, 1986; Ermisch and Joshi, 1987).

The aim of this chapter is to examine the evidence on whether Britain is likely to experience a notable population decline in the imminent future, with particular attention to the use of relevant indices and their interpretation. Although some references will be made to the conditions in other developed countries the conclusions for Britain should not be lightly generalized. Thus at the level of analysis pursued here, European populations are not closely similar but display major divergences. An important source of confusion has been a tendency to assume that what holds true for (say) Sweden, often regarded as a pace setter, or the Netherlands, with social similarities, also applies to Britain.

The Importance of Births in Population Forecasting

Of the components in forecasts, the number of births is the cause of most uncertainty; mortality trends are comparatively regular and deaths before the reproductive age span is completed are now statistically uncommon. In 1986 only about 3 percent of female deaths occurred at under 45 years. Thus mortality reduces negligibly the chances of childbearing. It is true that variations in the incidence of deaths at higher ages change the rates and hence the population growth, not always in ways expected. In Western Europe this has led to higher growth than previously forecast and in Eastern Europe to lower. These effects have important consequences for the population composition, particularly the numbers of the old and the very old, but in comparison with the impact of fertility variations, the influence is small.

There are no automatic bounds to the growth implication of migration and it is obvious that population declines could be offset neatly by sex–age selective immigration. Whether this would be economically, socially and politically feasible is a valid issue which will not be discussed. Usually the possibility of population decline is considered in terms of native stocks. Although Britain has experienced periodic migration flows in and out the net effect on growth in the longer run has been small.

The nature of the determinants sketched out here is simply illustrated by figure 2.1 which compares the numbers of persons by single years of age in England and Wales at the census of 1981 with the sizes of the birth cohorts from which they come. The area between the birth and census number graphs represents the cumulated deaths up to the ages in 1981 and a small

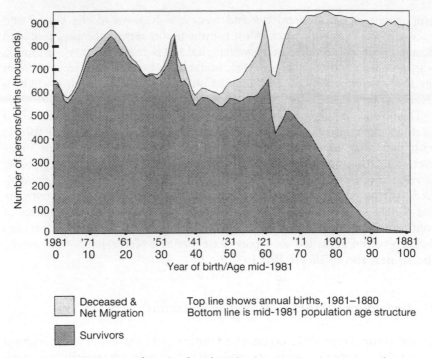

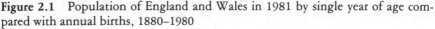

Figure 2.1   Population of England and Wales in 1981 by single year of age compared with annual births, 1880–1980

Source: Birth Statistics. Historical Series FM, No. 13 and Population Estimates, 1981

component of net migration. The census profile follows closely that of the births up to ages in the sixties, the large swings in the latter being reflected almost exactly in the former. Variations in the death and migration component are lost in the movements of births.

Over the past fifty years in Britain the number of births per year has fluctuated hugely from 700 thousands in the 1930s to a postwar bulge of one million in 1947; a drop to 750 thousands in the early 1950s was followed by the baby boom years of the mid-1960s, again with around one million. Thereafter a steep decline began to the 630 thousands of 1977. It was this fall which led to the claims that fertility would decrease to such a low level that population decline and age imbalance would follow (Harlem Brundtland, 1983; Debré, 1978).

The Total Fertility Index

The numbers of births depend heavily on the proportion and age distribution of women in the reproductive period. To allow for this the Total Fertility

Index was devised as the conventional summary measure of childbearing performance. Firstly, the rates of births in the year per woman at each age are calculated. Summation over all ages gives the average number of children born per woman if these rates persist for a birth cohort as it moves through the reproductive span. On these assumptions, Total Fertility Index can be regarded as the average final family size implied by childbearing in the year. A value of 2.1 for Total Fertility means that each women would be replaced on average by one daughter in the next generation. The need for slightly more than two children per woman to give one replacement daughter is explained by the sex ratio at birth (a lower proportion of females than males) and the allowance for the girls who die before they reach equivalent ages to their mothers. Total Fertility of 2.1 would be sufficient in the long run to keep a population with low mortality at a constant size. The Total Fertility Index in Britain was about 1.7 in 1977 although it rose a little subsequently and was 1.8 in the mid-1980s. Many European countries show more dramatic shortfalls from replacement, for example the 1.38 of Denmark and 1.33 of the Federal German Republic (1983). If these low fertilities continued the population would soon be in rapid decline.

Lessons from the Past?

The title of this chapter has implications beyond the simple question. *The Twilight of Parenthood* was the original name of a notorious book by Enid Charles published in the mid-1930s, later re-issued as *The Menace of Under-Population* (1936). In it she argued that the populations of Western Europe and indeed the United States were certain to experience a rapid decline in the near future. The view was popular among demographers at the time. It was the major theme of the second General Conference of the International Union for the Scientific Study of Population held in London in 1931. The evidence cited was the fast fall in the total fertility in most of Western Europe and also in the United States. For example the total fertility of England and Wales reached a minimum of 1.72 in 1933 when the replacement rate was 0.74, comparable with the 1.66 and 0.79 of 1977. Because mortality was reduced in 1977, a higher replacement could be achieved with a lower total fertility. Some commentators refused to accept the inevitabiliy of the downward trend and saw the low birth rates as a temporary fluctuation. In a short unsigned review of the London Conference under the title 'Population Prophecies' in the *Lancet* in 1933, C. P. S. Blacker wrote 'The First World Population Congress was held at Geneva in 1927, when the world was in the middle of a boom, and the dominant note was optimistic.' In 1931, 'doubtless in response to the prevailing economic depression the dominant note was pessimistic. . . . At the 1931 Conference the emphasis was laid not upon the dangers of over-population in Western Europe but upon the appalling prospects of an imminent depopulation in this area.' Blacker supports the view of Hankins (1932, p. 188), 'There seems to be no reason to doubt the possibility of a restoration of the birthrate when and if the cultural opportunity develops', and reprimands those 'who seem to regard human vital statistics, represented by curves in plotted charts, as inevitably destined to continue in the directions they have already taken, as do the curves made by the heavenly bodies in space' (Blacker, 1933, p. 480). Of course, Blacker's scepticism proved correct. The analogy with the present is obvious. 1927 and 1933 could be replaced by 1971 and 1977 with little alteration in wording. Much of what has been said about the likely continuance of the low fertility and downward trend has no more substantiation than in the 1930s. There was more excuse then because the phenomena had not been encountered before. It is not inevitable that the falsification of the hugely erroneous forecasts of the past will occur again for the future. However, to engender a degree of credibility, the evidence on current and likely fertility trends must be more precise and convincing.

Some respectable population scientists believe there is such evidence and the significant demographic measurement must, therefore, be considered more closely. But demographers have no claims to be prophets although too often they have been forced into the role. Experience of the past shows that sharp, significant and unanticipated changes can take place from the interaction of external events and social responses. Wars and, indeed, the ending of wars are the most obvious examples. A more subtle illustration is the baby boom of the 1960s when the Total Fertility Index rose greatly in many developed countries, for example to 2.93 in 1964 in England and Wales. There is no agreement on the exact determinants of that rise despite the acceptance that certain factors, such as earlier marriage in a climate of optimism about economic recovery from the war, were important. Such sharp changes in direction cannot be predicted with any reliability of size or timing and probably not at all. The best a population scientist can do is to seek current indicators, which on the basis of past experience, behave most regularly over time and whose relation to social and economic forces can be sensibly interpreted.

Appropriate Indicators

The number of births per year, the crude birth rate and the Total Fertility Index are not satisfactory indicators for this purpose. In the longer perspective each contains transient components which are a consequence of the timing of births rather than variations in the ultimate family size.

Distorting Effects of Birth Timing

Two main timing effects can be distinguished. One is short-term period fluctuations in response to temporary, economic and social 'perturbations' such as housing prices, claims of the health risks of particular forms of contraception and changes in abortion laws. The birth outcome usually extends over a few years, producing ripples in the rates which confuse the recognition of the initiation of significant trends. The second timing effect comes from systematic alterations in the distribution of births over the reproductive period of women. The simplest illustration comes from first births. In England and Wales, the mean age of women at first birth fell from 25.5 years (women born in 1920) to 23.9 years (women born in 1940) in strong association with earlier marriage. In 1960 (say) the 1920 to 1940 birth cohorts of women were in the main reproductive ages of 20 to 40 years. The proportion of first births at the younger ages had gone up for the later cohorts in accordance with the lower mean age but there was no compensating decrease in 1960 for the earlier cohorts who had entered childbearing at higher ages. The Total Fertility Index in 1960 was thus pushed upwards relative to what it would have been if there had been no changes in the age of first birth. These effects are not confined to first births but extend to all orders. Thus the mean ages of women at their fourth birth were 32.5 and 29.4 years for the cohorts of 1920 and 1940, a reduction twice as large as that for first births because intervals between births had shortened notably.

If the timing changes are consistent in direction over a considerable period, as in the illustration, the Total Fertility Indices are an unreliable guide to the ultimate family size and the corresponding replacement measures are equally misleading. The assumption that the fertility rates by age of woman in a year can be added to give a sensible measure for the final family size is unsound. If after a period of consistent change the distribution of births over the reproductive period of the women stabilizes, the Total Period Fertility Indices will gradually come into agreement with final family sizes. If, however, a swing in the opposite direction occurs (as in England and Wales for cohorts born after the early 1940s) the Total Fertility Indices begin to be biased downward relative to the final family size. It is convenient to use the general term *tempo* to describe birth timing of the kind described and *quantum* for fertility levels without tempo distortions.

These effects of the changes in birth tempo are spread over many years, well beyond the range of the movements which itself may be considerable. With good data over a long span the trends in the quantum of fertility can be disentangled from those of tempo, but when rapid changes are in operation the estimation of 'real' current trends is difficult. Thus in 1977, when period total fertility in England and Wales was at its lowest, only slightly more than one half of the women born in 1952 had become mothers by age 25 years compared with over 60 percent at the same age of those born in 1942. Was the forecast that the 90 percent finally achieving motherhood for the 1942 cohort would be reduced proportionately to 75 percent for the 1952 cohort a sensible one at that time? In fact 80 percent of the women born in 1952 had become mothers by the age of 33 years, with a likely addition of 3 or 4 percent by the end of the reproductive age span. In other words there had been a significant redistribution of first births by age of woman.

Cohort Total Fertility

The limitations of the Total Fertility Index for the measurement of trends have been known for at least 40 years as a result of the re-analysis of the 1930s experience. There are methods for eliminating or reducing the distortions from tempo changes. The simplest is the use of cohort (or generation) total fertility indices (the average births per woman over the reproductive span for a group born or married in the same year). With the increase in illegitimacy, calculations for marriage cohorts are becoming less attractive. The completed cohort measures are not distorted by a redistribution of births over the reproductive period since there is automatic compensation for a movement of a birth from one age to another. Cohort measures are not immune to timing fluctuations due to short term social and economic influences. A reduction in births due to adverse conditions at marriage is not necessarily made up when the hindrances are removed.

The average births to women of completed childbearing vary less than the period Total Fertility Indices. In England and Wales, the women born around 1935 achieved an average final family size of just over 2.4 compared with a period total fertility of 2.7 to 2.9 in the baby boom years of 1960 to 1967 when most of their children were born. Part of the discrepancy can be explained by the childbearing outside the highest fertility time span but a substantial contribution comes from the tempo bias. Following the maximum, cohort total fertility gradually fell but the women born in 1945 had 2.20 births on average, still comfortably above the 2.1 replacement level. But the later cohorts experienced considerably lower birth rates at the earlier ages of reproduction. How much was due to birth redistribution and what might be the effect of social and economic fluctuations can only be determined with certainty in the future. Extrapolation can be made in several different ways. Survey evidence on how many children women expect to have is one source of information. On the basis of the expectations reported in the General Household Survey for 1979–1983 there would be little, if any, further fall in the cohort total fertility indices in Britain up to the women born in 1960–64. Because of the appreciable non-response it is likely that these expectations are biased upwards. Werner (1986a) has estimated the likely size of the biases.

His adjusted measures are, however, only marginally below the 2.1 replacement gauge. Of course family size intentions reflect the conditions of the present; they may change or not be achievable. In the context of arguments about a flight from parenthood, however, they can hardly be ignored.

In the criteria for useful guides to forecasting put forward earlier it was suggested that indicators 'whose relation to social and economic forces can be sensibly interpreted' should be sought. Over the range of world conditions the Total Fertility Index may resonably be held to fall within the definition; for low fertility, developed countries where movements of a fraction of a birth in the average completed family size are important, it is less useful. In these populations large families form only a small part of the total and the choice of no or one child as opposed to two has a major impact on the deviation of fertility from replacement.

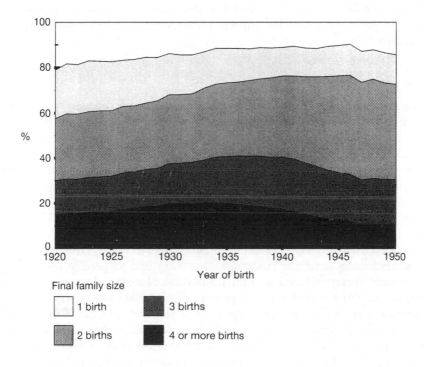

Figure 2.2   Proportions of women in England and Wales, born 1920–50, attaining different orders of births by the end of the reproductive age span
Source: Werner and Chalk (1986)

The Importance of Birth Order

Figure 2.2, based on data from Werner and Chalk (1986), shows the percentage of women in England and Wales having first to fourth births by the end of childbearing for cohorts from 1920 onwards. It can be easily seen that the movements in average completed family size were a result of complex changes in the distribution of births per woman. Childlessness decreased up to the 1945 cohort but then began to rise; families of two children became steadily more popular. Following the cohort of 1935 there was a reduction in the proportions going on to three or more births but there are indications that stability might have been reached. The high completed family size for cohorts of the mid-1930s came when the trends reinforced each other. Since then the movements for higher birth orders have had opposite effects from those at lower. The social and economic concomitants of childlessness and (say) four or more births are so different that measures which decompose total fertility seem necessary for any examination of trends in the context of forecasts.

The Parity Progression Ratio

The most convenient set of measures for this purpose is the parity progression ratios, i.e. the proportion of women who, having had an nth birth go on to an $(n + 1)$th by the end of childbearing; say, where $n = 2$, for example, the proportion of women who have had two who go on to have three. These are not a recent invention (Henry used them brilliantly in 1953) but developments in both problems and data sources have lead to an upsurge in their investigation and application. Returning to the England and Wales birth cohorts of women, the parity progression ratio for first to second births had risen to a level of about 85 percent for those born in the mid-1930s and then remained constant. The second to third and third to fourth ratios after falling appeared to be steadying at around 40 percent and 35 percent respectively. The most uncertain trend is in the proportion of women becoming mothers which reached a maximum at 90 percent for the 1945 birth cohort but then clearly began to decrease. Marriage rates at younger ages have fallen steeply but there has been a large rise in illegitimacy. Since birth orders are not registered for illegitimate children the estimation of childlessness becomes less firm. The allowance for tempo biases in extrapolating the first births for the younger cohorts to the end of childbearing is uncertain. However, Kiernan (1986c) has reported that 90 percent of the women in the 1958 birth cohort sample, surveyed at age 23 years in the National Child Development Study, expected to have children, a level between the reported and adjusted General Household Survey measures. If the expectation is achieved and the cohort trends in parity progression ratios to the second birth and above continue in the future, the average completed family size will remain above the replacement 2.1. In fact some increase in childlessness seems certain, but leading to a cohort fertility only marginally lower.

Parity Progression for a Time Period

The reason that the time period total fertility has remained such a popular measure despite the problems of interpretation is its characteristic of being up to date. The latest information on childbearing comes from the age specific fertility rates of the most recent year and it seems sensible to combine these in overall indices. If time period measures which eliminate tempo biases and retain the advantages of parity progression ratios could be constructed they would be ideal as a basis for forecasting. There is much work in progress on this topic but still problems of data availability and the empirical advantages of alternative procedures. An attractive approach is the calculation of the rates at which women are having $(n + 1)$th births in a year by the duration of time since the nth. The combination of these over all durations gives the proportion moving from the nth to $(n + 1)$th over the reproductive period, that is the parity progression ratio implied by the duration–specific rates of the year. The series of ratios for different birth orders can then be put together as if for a cohort to give the resulting average completed family size. This measure is in fact another period total fertility index, similar in fundamental idea to the traditional index but constructed differently (see Ní Bhrolcháin, 1987). It can be demonstrated that the tempo bias is not completely eliminated in this measure but is substantially reduced. It may turn out to be an effective diagnostic tool but study is hindered by the paucity of suitable data; the calculations require a knowledge of the interval to the last birth and the order for each registered birth.

Analogous but more indirect estimates of time period parity progression ratios can be arrived at by the specification of the distribution of durations from the nth to the $(n + 1)$th birth. As an example when n is two, the proportions of third births taking place in the next calendar year, the next again and so on are defined. These are applied to the number of second births occurring in the preceding year, the one before etc. to give the resulting births; addition over the series provides the total third births expected if all women went on from a second to a third birth. The ratio of the observed to the expected births is then as estimate of the corresponding parity progression ratio, that is the proportion of women who continue to the third birth. The difficulty here is the specification of the proportions by duration, although the outcome is not greatly sensitive to the exact formulation if the variation in the average duration over time is approximately reproduced. In principle the specification of the proportions by duration, particularly for the first births, faces the same difficulties as extrapolation of measures for incomplete cohorts to the end of the reproductive period. There is, therefore, some degree of fuzziness in the measures for the most recent period when the average intervals between births (and the age at birth for the first) are changing sharply.

A Tempo-Adjusted Series for England and Wales

Brass (1983) has devised a method for specifying the distributions of durations to next birth based on a model representation of Farahani (1981) where only one measure, dependent on the mean duration, has to be determined. This is estimated for England and Wales in different time periods from the rates at which married women are going from their first to their second births. Then, as explained above, the period parity progression ratios and corresponding total fertility are calculated. The latter is called the Total Quantum Fertility Index to distinguish it from the conventional measure. The comparison of these measures with the cohort indices can only be made in a broad way because the latter average over time period fluctuations and trends in addition to eliminating tempo effects. For example, the sharp increase in births which occurred over 1979–81 at all birth orders is strongly present in the period total fertilities but smoothed out in the cohort measures. It is obvious, then, that the time period series will be the more erratic. When account is taken of this the consistency of cohort and time period parity progression ratio levels and trends is impressive, as is illustrated in table 2.1. There is a discrepancy in the ratios for zero to first and first to second births with the time period values a little higher for the former and lower for the latter. These deviations are obviously due to the difficulties of adjusting the birth orders for illegitimacy. The discrepancies effectively cancel in the proportions going from zero to two births and in the composite total fertilities.

The conclusions from the tempo adjusted time period measures are similar to those from the cohort values but supplement them in valuable ways. If, as is normal, the cohort measures are roughly equated to the calendar year when the women are aged 27 (the mean age of mothers at the birth of their children) the time period calculations include more recent data. This is, of course, the major reason for the use of period total fertilities in the first place. The trends in the latter support the view that the parity progression ratios from one birth to two and upwards are showing no signs of a decrease. Indeed there was a definitive rise in the progressions for three births and upwards bringing them back in the mid-1980s to the levels of early 1970s. Some indications of an increase in childlessness appear, but of a very modest size.

A Comparison of the Indicators

Figure 2.3 compares the time period total fertilities as calculated in the traditional and tempo adjusted ways and also the cohort measures over the

Table 2.1 Comparison of parity progression ratios per thousand for birth cohorts and time periods[a]

Cohort years of birth	Parity progression				Time period	Parity progression			
	0 to 1	1 to 2	2 to 3	3 to 4		0 to 1	1 to 2	2 to 3	3 to 4
1931–33	861	804	555	518	1958–60	883	760	533	506
1934–36	885	828	555	489	1961–63	925	803	561	526
1937–39	886	847	543	455	1964–66	950	812	548	485
1940–42	890	857	516	416	1967–69	926	801	495	418
1943–45	892	854	458	378	1970–72	936	843	479	393
1946–48	885	849	418	353	1973–75	898	837	380	301
					1976–78	893	886	381	309
1949+	Require a substantial amount of forecasting				1979–81	952	899	438	364
					1982–84	917	822	410	345

[a] The cohort measures are equated approximately to the time period when the women are aged 27.

Source: Werner and Chalk (1986) for the cohort measures and author's estimates for the time period values.

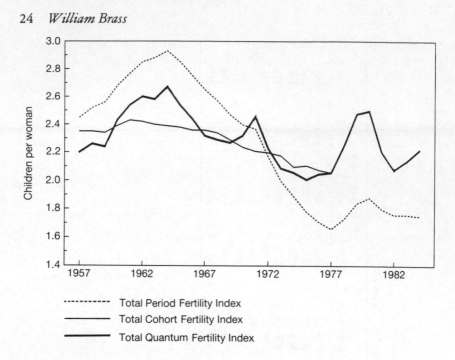

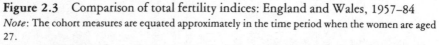

Figure 2.3   Comparison of total fertility indices: England and Wales, 1957–84
Note: The cohort measures are equated approximately in the time period when the women are aged 27.
Source: OPCS (1987a) for the Total Period Fertility Index: author's estimates for the Total Quantum Fertility Index

years 1957 to 1984. Most of the necessary comments have already been made and only the salient features are now emphasized. A substantial part of the trends upwards and downwards in traditional Total Fertility Index is due to changes in the ages at which the women have their births. When the resulting distortions are removed, the baby boom of the early 1960s and the slump around 1977 appear much less dramatic. Apart from the sharp temporary upsurge in 1979–80 the level of fertility has remained remarkably constant since about 1972 with an average value rather close to the replacement 2.1. There then may be a marginal fall with an increase in childlessness but the trends give no support to the belief that the effects on births and population growth will be other than modest.

Looking Forward

It would be unwise to rule out the possibility of another baby boom in the 1990s although it is not suggested that this is highly likely. If the parity progression ratios and cohort final family sizes remain at the present level and ages at births have the same distribution, the numbers of births will increase in the 1990s because the proportion of women in the most fertile ages will be considerably higher. A reversal of the trends towards later marriage and longer birth intervals would induce tempo effects as in the early 1960s which would swell the totals. The changes in social behaviour required would be comparatively modest in the context of the variations over the past thirty-five years.

Socio-Economic Extrapolations

Much of the argument for an approaching severe population decline has been social theorizing, which is not only legitimate but necessary in any assessment of future prospects. But the theorizing should be constrained by a close inspection of developing trends and relationships – and this strand has often been superficial. One line of thought has been the assumption that 'more advanced' populations serve as a guide to the future behaviour of others. But in Britain the reduction in traditional time period marital fertility measures since 1970 has been less in the higher social classes and the movements have not had a consistent gradient with class status (Werner, 1985). It appears that tempo effects have not been the same in all classes but the data to elucidate this are not available. It is true that fertility rates in several European countries are much more below replacement than in Britain. But examination reveals variability rather than uniformity except at the most superficial level. In Britain, whatever criteria are used, the minimum fertility was in the mid-1970s. Since then there has been a significant recovery. Trends in France, both overall and in the family build-up as shown by the parity progression ratios, have been similar to Britain but with slightly greater buoyancy. Other countries have experienced notable fertility recoveries in the 1980s, most interestingly Sweden, which has often been picked out as the leader in the social changes in marriage and the family which are intimately related to the patterns of reproduction. In Italy on the other hand falls have continued, most distinctively in the first two parity progression ratios, with consequent rapid rises in childless and single child couples.

In the selection of the 'more advanced' populations, criteria of the rise of individualism and a resulting transformation of attitudes on the value of children as against personal welfare have been invoked, for example by Lesthaeghe, 1983. But even if these ideas are accepted as relevant their translation into fertility trends specified in size and time during altering economic condition seems insuperable. The influence of past tradition still remains strong as a factor restraining individualism. Thus Simons (1986b) has shown how conservative are British attitudes to children and the family, and the analysis of early childbearing from the follow-up of a sample of persons born in 1946 (The National Survey of Health and Development) reveals remarkable similarities between parents and offspring (Kiernan, 1980b and 1987; Kiernan and Diamond, 1983.)

Conclusions

The balance of social and economic determinants is a fine one and it seems better to rely on a careful and cautious examination of measured trends and family size intentions. The theme is the twilight of parenthood and not what is happening to the family as a stable unit for the production and care of children. Evidence that Britain is facing a revolt from childbearing leading to significant falls in population size and severe age composition disturbance is lacking.

Acknowledgement

Professor Brass describes in this chapter work which he undertook when Director of the ESRC-funded Designated Research Centre at the Centre for Population Studies.

Selected Key Reading

Ní Bhrolcháin, Máire, 1987: Period parity progression ratios and birth intervals in England and Wales, 1941–1971: a synthetic life table analysis. *Population Studies*, 41, 103–125.
Simons, John 1986b: How conservative are British attitudes to reproduction? *Quarterly Journal of Social Affairs*, 2 (1), 41–54.
Werner, Barry 1986b: Trends in first, second, third and later births. *Population Trends*, 45, 26–33.

3 The Family: Formation and Fission

Kathleen E. Kiernan

Introduction

Seemingly significant changes have occurred in recent times to the structure and dynamics of British family life, particularly at the stage of the life cycle when people form and build families. Marriage and childbearing are being increasingly postponed and, perhaps, forgone. The proportion of births born outside wedlock has increased dramatically, from a level around 8 per cent in the mid-1970s to one above 20 per cent in 1986. Childlessness is expected to become more common. Cohabitation has emerged as a widespread form of pre-marital living arrangement and is virtually the norm between marriages. Consensual unions with children may be on the increase. The rate of entry into first marriage has declined dramatically and divorce rates have increased.

These are the aspects of family life that have received widespread attention in recent times. Do these changes signal the fission of nuclear family and the eventual demise of the family in Britain? Before writing the obituary on the British family it might be wise to look beyond some of these selected statistics and examine the evidence in more detail.

Marriage

Marriage is the social event that traditionally heralds the start of a new family and is the component of family life that appears to have undergone the most change in recent times.

From the 1940s up to the beginning of the 1970s the general trend in Britain was towards an increasing overall propensity to marry and for first marriages to occur at increasingly younger ages and over a narrower range of ages. The culmination of this development was the marriage behaviour of the generation born in the 1940s, who passed through their prime nubile ages during the 1960s. It is relative to this generation that the recent changes in marriage patterns appear so dramatic. Young people born since the 1950s have been marrying less at younger ages and it is their behaviour that is reflected in the sharp declines in marriage rates exhibited since around the beginning of the 1970s, and which continue to the present day. Such sharp declines in rates from one year to the next can result from successive cohorts of young people marrying at progressively older ages, or from them exhibiting an increasing proportion never marrying, or from a combination of such postponement and rejection of marriages (for detailed analyses of marriage trends since 1950 see Kiernan and Eldridge, 1985 and Eldridge and Kiernan, 1985).

Women born throughout the 1940s had virtually identical marriage patterns. This generation of women became brides at the earliest average age ever recorded since civil registration started in 1837. The timing of weddings amongst this generation of women was narrowly bounded.

Figure 3.1 charts the marriage patterns for selected birth cohorts, women born in 1946, 1958 and 1964. These data come from marriage registration statistics (OPCS, Marriage and Divorce Statistics). Figure 3.1(a) charts the rate of first marriage per hundred women of each single year of age, figure 3.1(b) the cumulated proportions of each generation who had ever married at each successive age. For women born in 1946, marriages were highly concentrated between the ages of 19 and 23; 60 per cent married at these ages and 80 per cent had married by age 25. The age by which half of the cohort had entered marriage (median age at marriage) was 21.5 years and over 90 per cent of the women had married by age 30. The marriage pattern of the 1946 cohort is typical of the generation of women born during the 1940s (Kiernan and Eldridge, 1987).

From the MRC's National Survey of Health and Development (Atkins et al., 1981) there are detailed micro-data for a sample of the 1946 cohort who have been followed up from birth to the present day. Our analysis of this survey also shows that women with widely differing socio-economic backgrounds all married very rapidly (Kiernan and Eldridge, 1987). For example, unqualified factory workers began to marry at an earlier age than office workers with low level qualifications. These in turn married sooner than highly qualified women in professional occupations. But once a particular group started to get married something like a lemming effect was triggered and they plunged into matrimony rapidly. This suggests that during the 1960s there were strong social norms governing the timing of marriage. Marriage appeared inevitable. All women regardless of background could be expected to have married by their early twenties.

This 1940s pattern of marriage can be compared, in figure 3.1, with that exhibited by cohorts born later. The women born in 1958 and 1964 are followed up to ages 27 and 21 years respectively. These two cohorts capture and exemplify recent changes in marriage patterns. Relative to the 1940s

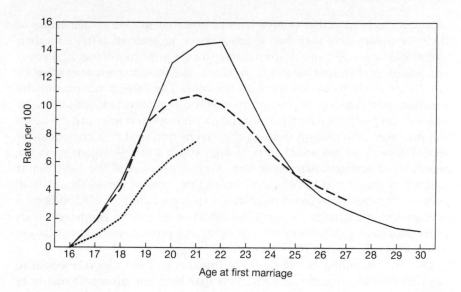

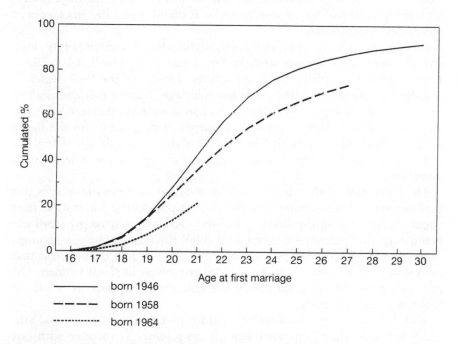

born 1946
born 1958
born 1964

Figure 3.1 First marriages by age at marriage: women born in 1946, 1958 and 1964: (a) rates per year of age; (b) cumulated percentage to each age

cohort, it can be seen that women born in 1958 married to a similar extent in their teens but that they had a much more protracted pattern in their twenties. The median age at first marriage for the 1958 cohort was 22.5 years, one year older than that for the 1946 cohort, and the proportions married by age 30 are likely to be just over 80 per cent. The earliest reaction to the previous early marriage regime of the 1940s cohorts was first seen amongst women who postponed marrying until their twenties. It is not until the 1960s cohorts, who were passing through their teens during the recent economic recession, with its attendant rates of high youth unemployment, that the avoidance of teenage marriage is seen. Only 7 per cent of the 1964 cohort married in their teens as compared with 15 per cent of the 1958 and 1946 cohorts. Extrapolations based on marriage rates prevailing in 1985 indicate a median age at marriage for the 1964 cohort of 24.6 years (some two years older than their predecessors born in 1958) and proportions married by age 30 (in 1994) of just over 70 per cent.

Our understanding of the causes of this change from marriage boom to marriage bust are imperfect. As yet, there have been few attempts to quantify the complex mosaic of cultural and economic forces underpinning these changes (Ermisch, 1983; Lesthaeghe and Meekers, 1987). The focus of this chapter is on the more proximate determinants of changing marriage behaviour: changing sexual mores, contraceptive availability and the emergence of pre-marital cohabitation.

Pre-marital sex is the norm in the 1980s. But when in contemporary times did it become so? The evidence from OPCS surveys (Dunnell, 1979; Bone, 1985) suggests that during the 1950s and the first half of the 1960s less than one-third of women had had sex before marriage. During the latter half of the 1960s the proportion of women who had sex before marriage increased but it was still less than 50 per cent. However, during the 1970s the figure increased dramatically such that by the end of the decade the great majority of young women had experienced sex before marriage, of the order of 80 to 90 per cent.

The latter half of the 1960s could be regarded as the watershed in this development. It was during this period that pre-marital intercourse rates began to rise. During the latter half of the 1960s the contraceptive pill was being increasingly used by married women but this was not the case amongst single women (Bone, 1985). It was not until the first half of the 1970s that the pill was made freely available and used extensively by single women. The pill could be said to have reinforced and enhanced and made safer a trend that was already underway.

The mid- to late 1960s might be regarded as a period when societal attitudes and individual behaviour were in some senses at variance with one another. The disjuncture between increased sexual activity and relatively poor contraceptive availability for the unmarried may be one of the reasons for the upsurge in pre-marital pregnancy rates observed for young women in the 1960s. During the 1960s 1 in 5 brides were pregnant at marriage as compared with 1 in 8 of brides in the mid-1970s and mid-1980s. The proportion of first births born outside marriage also doubled during the 1960s from around 7 to 14 per cent. These unmarried mothers were generally encouraged to have their babies in special mother and baby homes and to place them for adoption. Marriage was very much the normative setting for childbearing. Legal abortion was of course not an option for most young women during the 1960s, as the 1967 Act did not fully take effect until the end of the decade. At the beginning of the 1970s, young pregnant single women were most likely to opt for marriage and much less likely to opt for an illegitimate child or an abortion. By the end of the 1970s, their first choice was an abortion, followed closely by their second choice, and illegitimate child, and getting married was the least popular outcome (Kiernan, 1980a; OPCS Monitor FM1 84/6).

Over a brief period of twenty years, there has been a move from a position where only a minority of women reported having had intercourse before marriage to one where the great majority had such an experience. There has been a shift from a situation where marriage and coitus were inextricably linked, for at least the majority of women, to one where coitus and use of contraceptives prior to marriage has become the norm and pregnancy does not necessarily precipate marriage.

Cohabitation

The increased practice and greater acceptability of pre-marital sex and the increased availability of effective contraception were important preconditions for the emergence on the demographic scene of cohabitation – used here to refer to couples living together 'as man and wife' without having been formally married. Cohabitation at young ages was relatively rare amongst the 1940s generation – probably less than 5 per cent – but was much more common amongst the 1950s generation. For example, analysis (Kiernan, 1986c) of the National Child Development study (NCDS) which has followed up a sample of the 1958 birth cohort showed that by age 23, 19 per cent of women had lived with a partner in a cohabiting union for a period of six months or more. Interestingly the incidence of cohabitation did not vary across social groups. For example, 19 per cent of the women who left school at age 16, the earliest opportunity, had ever cohabited by age 23 and 20 per cent of those who left at age 18 had done so. The analogous proportions for men were 14 and 13 per cent respectively. Cohabitation seems to have been taken up to a similar extent by young people from working and middle class families and those with differing levels of education.

Evidence from the 1984 *General Household Survey* report also shows that throughout the 1970s and 1980s the proportion of cohabiting couples who were not married increased. Only 7 per cent of couples marrying for the first time in the early 1970s had lived together before marriage as compared with 26 per cent of those marrying in the early 1980s. Moreover, the length of time spent cohabiting was relatively short-lived, around one year on average. Up to now cohabitation amongst unmarried young people appears, in the main, to have been a largely child-free, relatively short, transitional form of arrangement preceding marriage.

As more young people choose to cohabit it is possible that young people may decide to cohabit for longer and a minority may choose never to formalize their union. Evidence from small-scale surveys of teenagers suggests that around one-half think it is a good idea to live together – as a trial run – but as yet they do not see it as a more permanent alternative to marriage (Guy, 1983). Time series data from the *General Household Survey* reports suggest that the duration of pre-marital cohabitation is lengthening. The median duration amongst couples marrying for the first time during the 1970s was 10 months, whereas amongst those marrying during the 1980s the median duration was of the order of 13 to 15 months. If pre-marital cohabitation becomes more popular or the duration of pre-marital cohabitation continues to lengthen, then marriage rates at young ages will exhibit further declines.

If pre-marital cohabitation prolongs the period from meeting to the nuptial ceremony then, other things being equal, an increase in cohabitation would lead to a delay in marriage. This was probably an important contributary factor to marriage delays during the 1970s. However, the prevalence of cohabitation was insufficient to account for all the reduction in the proportions of young women married at the prime marriageable ages during, for example, the 1970s. Estimates show that a maximum of 50 per cent of the reduction between 1973 and 1980 in the proportions married at ages 20–24 could be accounted for by cohabitation (Kiernan and Eldridge, 1987).

There can be little doubt that the widespread practice of cohabitation without marriage amongst young people is a new and important development, and it may in due course become an institutionalized part of mating behaviour. Additionally, anecdotal evidence suggests that current taxation laws governing mortgage relief and the substantial increases in the price of homes in parts of Britain during the 1980s may be discouraging couples, particularly in the south-east region, from getting legally married.

It is also instructive to look at the experiences of other Western European countries with respect to changing nuptial pratice. The prevalence of cohabitation in the United Kingdom is much less than in neighbouring continental countries (table 3.1). In 1982, for example, only 6 per cent of British women aged 20–24 were cohabiting as compared to 12 per cent or more in France, West Germany and the Netherlands. Whilst in Denmark and Sweden more

Table 3.1 Percentage of 20–24-year-old women cohabiting in European Countries, 1982[a]

	Percentage	Source
Sweden	44	a
Denmark	42	b
Norway	12	a
The Netherlands	15	a
West Germany	14	b
France	12	b
United Kingdom	6	b
Ireland	1	b

[a] Except in Sweden (1980) and Norway (1977)

Sources: (a) Central Statistical Office's publications; (b) Secondary analysis of Eurobarometer Survey 1982 (Kiernan, 1986a)

young women were cohabiting at these ages than are married, with over 40 per cent cohabiting in the early 1980s. In these two Scandinavian countries having children within cohabiting unions is fairly common. It is also worth noting, as an aside, that British youth, as well as being less likely to cohabit than their continental European contemporaries are also less likely to be living on their own. For example, secondary analysis of Eurobarometer data for 1982 (Kiernan, 1986a) showed that only 6 per cent of United Kingdom women aged 20–24 years were living alone, compared with 17, 23 and 31 per cent of women of the same age in France, West Germany and Denmark respectively. The greater difficulties in obtaining privately rented accomodation in Britain as compared with continental countries may be acting as a brake on setting up independent households.

Britain still has one of the youngest age patterns of marriage in Western Europe. So there is certainly room for further changes if Britain were to follow developments in other countries in Western Europe. As yet there is no concrete evidence that young people are rejecting rather than postponing marriage. For example, analysis (Kiernan, 1986c) of reports on expectations from the 1958 cohort study showed that 90 per cent of the men and women who were single at age 23 expected to marry at some time in the future. But it is highly unlikely that the proportions of young people married before leaving their twenties will be as high as in the 1940s generation.

On the evidence to date, the likely explanation for what has taken place is a shift in the timing of marriage. Young people may be entering marriage at later ages than was common in the 1960s but few as yet have found a permanent alternative to marriage. But marriage trends require careful monitoring as it is not yet known what the impact of unemployment will be, or whether the cohorts who have exhibited later age at marriage patterns will catch up in their thirties. Even though the great majority of young people state that they expect to marry it has been observed that changes in demographic behaviour frequently precede changes in norms. Reported expectations may be better sources of information on the prevailing norms about marriage or parenthood than of likely future behaviour (Westoff, 1986). It is also worth considering developments in other European countries. In France there are indications of the emergence of a core of people who are rejecting marriage (Le Bras and Roussel, 1982). In Sweden and Denmark, where cohabitation amongst young people emerged in the 1960s, cohabitation and marriage are largely indistinguishable. Britain may be just a laggard in these developments.

Marital Breakdown

The institution of marriage and the nuclear family are also under threat from the recently increased propensity to divorce. The divorce rate for England and Wales in 1985 was 13.3 per 1000 married persons as compared with 6.0 per 1000 in 1971 and 2.1 per 1000 in 1961. The rapid increase in divorce has meant that whilst 14 per cent of the couples married in 1959 were divorced by their twentieth wedding anniversary, couples married in 1969 took only 10 years to reach this level, and couples marrying in 1979 only took 6 years. It is estimated that over 1 in 3 (38 per cent) of the marriages contracted in 1979 may have ended in divorce by 20 years of marriage if the divorce rates current in 1984 were to continue, compared with only 7 per cent of marriages contracted at the beginning of the 1950s.

The next chapter deals further with divorce and re-marriage, here the focus is on the group of women who have the highest risk of marital breakdown, namely teenage brides. It is estimated that one in two teenage brides will eventually divorce, if the rates prevailing in 1980–1 were to persist (Haskey, 1983). Given the extent of the risk of marital breakdown amongst teenage brides, it would be useful to know whether women who marry in their teens differ from those who marry at later ages, and whether there are features that distinguish between marriages which survive and those which break down.

Analyses of the life-histories of the MRC's 1946 cohort sample showed that teenage brides as a group have the least advantaged family backgrounds, educational and occupational careers (Kiernan, 1986b). They were also the most likely to have married men with no qualifications and who were in manual occupations. In these respects teenage brides whose marriages had broken down by their early thirties were not very different from those of their contemporaries whose marriages survived. In spite of this similarity, such disadvantaged backgrounds are likely to be the least auspicious for coping with the exigencies and deprivations associated with marital breakdown. It was apparent from this analysis that the parents of these women were unlikely to possess sufficient resources to help their daughters, and the women themselves did not possess the skills and qualifications necessary for obtaining highly paid jobs, which would enable them to support themselves and their children. Their ex-husbands are also the least likely to be able to make a significant contribution to the support of their ex-wives and children.

There were only two truly antecedent factors (amongst the wide range investigated), which clearly distinguished between teenage marriages that survived and those that broke down. Firstly, women who came from a broken family were more likely to experience a broken marriage themselves. This was amongst a generation who had experienced low parental divorce rates. So if divorce begets divorce then the inter-generational transmission of instability in marriage is likely to become a more important issue in the future.

The second and more striking factor was that the neuroticism scores of teenage brides whose marriages had broken down were significantly higher at age 16 than of those whose marriages survived intact into their early thirties. Neuroticism was measured by the short form of the Maudsley Personality Inventory (Eysenck, 1958). This finding was not confined to teenage brides. Women and men who married at older ages and whose marriages broke down were also more likely to have high neuroticism scores in adolescence. Over the last four decades there has been a good deal of controversy as to whether divorced persons have a predisposition to lower psychological well-being or whether the process and events leading up to divorce were contributory factors (Kitson and Raschke, 1981). This study (Kiernan, 1986b), is probably the first to provide unambiguous evidence of predisposing personality factors. There was little evidence that teenage brides from broken families were on average more neurotic than those from intact families. Multivariate analysis showed that the effects of parents' broken marriage and of a higher individual neuroticism score were independent, and the effect due to neuroticism was significantly greater than the effect of having parents whose marriage had broken down.

The other characteristics which distinguished between teenage marriages that broke down and those that survived related to the period after marriage. Our findings and those of others (Murphy, 1985) suggest that the process of family building and the socio-economic context in which it operates act as determinants of marriage breakdown. Among this high risk group, marriage breakdown was more common among couples who started childbearing early, who had four or more children, who were local authority tenants and who had relatively low incomes.

These socially, economically and psychologically vulnerable women are likely to be the lone mothers who are the most visible to the welfare authorities and have to rely on state benefits for much of their income.

Extra-Marital Births

Another development that is making inroads into the conventional nuclear family is the rise in extra-marital childbearing. In 1985 nearly 20 per cent of all births were illegitimate and nearly 30 per cent of first births were born to women who were not legally married (Werner, 1986b).

Since 1976 we have seen a marked rise in the proportion of illegitimate births. In 1976, 9 per cent of all births were out of wedlock, this 'illegitimacy ratio' in 1986 was 21 per cent. For most of this century up to 1960, except for the periods covering the two world wars, the proportion of births which were illegitimate was relatively stable, at between 4 to 5 per cent of all births. It increased during the 1960s, from a level of 5 per cent to reach 8 per cent by 1968, and it remained around this level until 1976, when it again began to increase, slowly at first and then much more rapidly since 1980.

An important issue is to what extent the increasing proportion of extra-marital births reflect an increased propensity to have children outside marriage and to what extent it simply reflects the increased number of single and divorced women in the population. The illegitimacy ratio (the proportion of all births that are illegitimate), which has shown a noticeable rise in recent years, takes no account of the population at risk, in contrast to the illegitimacy rate (the proportion of illegitimate births per 1000 unmarried women). However, this latter measure also has its drawbacks, in that illegitimate fertility rates are not wholly independent of overall fertility levels. Taking the ratio of illegitimate fertility rates to marital fertility rates offsets this problem.

Table 3.2 shows the number of legitimate and illegitimate births by age, age-specific illegitimacy ratios and age-specific extra-marital and marital fertility rates for the years 1975, 1980 and 1985, when the illegitimacy ratios stood at 9, 12 and 19 per cent respectively. The table also shows the ratio of extra-marital to marital fertility rates in the three years. It is apparent that the ratios (shown in the bottom panel and which capture better the propensity to have children outside marriage) increase with age, suggesting a larger disassociation between marriage and childbearing at older ages. The ratio is particularly low for teenage women. The main reason for this is that the fertility rates of the tiny minority of married teenagers are very high (359 per 1000 in 1985), compared with the fertility of the large majority of single women (20 per 1000 in 1985). Between 1975 and 1980 for ages under 30, there was little change in ratio of the illegitimate birth rate to the marital birth rate, suggesting that the increase in proportion of illegitimate births during this period was not due to an increased propensity to have children outside marriage. However, during the period 1980–85 there are indications of such a movement, with noticeable increases at ages under 30 years. The ratio increased by 25 per cent amongst teenage women, albeit from a low

Table 3.2   Number of births and birth rates within and outside marriage, by age of women, 1975, 1980 and 1985, England and Wales

	Year	Under 20	20–24	25–29	30–34	35–39	All ages
Number of births	1975	20.5	16.8	9.8	4.7	2.4	54.9
outside marriage	1980	25.9	26.6	13.5	7.6	3.0	77.4
in 000's	1985	36.9	47.7	24.2	11.3	5.1	126.2
Number of births	1975	43.0	173.4	216.1	83.7	25.8	548.6
within marriage in	1980	34.9	174.9	210.0	122.3	30.8	578.9
000's	1985	20.1	146.3	203.2	114.9	39.3	530.2
Illegitimacy ratio	1975	322.7	88.1	43.6	53.4	83.6	91.0
per 1000 births	1980	425.7	132.0	60.2	58.4	89.7	117.9
	1985	647.7	245.9	106.4	89.7	114.9	192.3
Extra-marital rate	1975	12.8	23.3	30.7	25.5	14.5	17.4
per 1000 single,	1980	13.7	27.8	33.9	26.8	14.5	19.6
widowed and	1985	19.7	35.2	41.8	32.6	16.2	26.7
divorced women							
Marital rate per	1975	307.9	183.2	140.9	62.5	20.6	85.5
1000 married	1980	340.4	210.8	164.6	78.4	23.6	92.2
women	1985	358.8	209.5	168.9	88.1	25.7	87.8
Ratio of extra-	1975	0.04	0.13	0.22	0.41	0.70	0.20
marital rate to	1980	0.04	0.13	0.21	0.34	0.61	0.21
marital rate	1985	0.05	0.17	0.25	0.37	0.63	0.30

Source: OPCS, *Birth Statistics*, FM1 No. 12, Table 3.1

level, and by 31 and 19 per cent respectively amongst those aged 20–24 and 25–29 years.

During the 1980s the number of extra-marital births has increased substantially (by 63 per cent between 1980 and 1985) and the propensity to have children outside marriage would appear to be increasing. As unwed mothers are relatively more likely than married mothers to make calls on social and welfare services, then this increase is of some importance.

What are the characteristics and circumstances of women who have babies outside marriage? Who do they live with? Do they eventually marry? What level of support, financial and otherwise, do they receive from the putative father? These are questions to which there are few direct answers. All that can be done at the present time is to put together disparate clues from vital registration and General Household Survey data.

The variety of contexts within which an illegitimate birth takes place is most easily described with reference to how old the mother is. In 1985, just under a third (29 per cent) of illegitimate births occurred to teenage women, just over one-third (38 per cent) occurred to women aged 20–24 and the remaining 31 per cent occurred to older women.

The method of birth registration provides some clues as to the possible

Table 3.3   Percentage distribution of illegitimate births according to type of registration, by age of mother 1985

| | Age of mother | | | | | |
	16–19	20–4	25–9	30–34	35+	All ages
Sole registration	43	35	30	28	27	35
Joint registration						
different address	24	17	14	11	13	18
same address	33	48	55	61	60	47

Source: Tables 3.9 and 3.10, OPCS British Statistics, 1985

strength of the relationship between the mother and the putative father. Illegitimate births can be registered solely by the mother or jointly by both parents. Additionally since 1983, for a sample of joint birth registrations, OPCS has published information on whether the mother and father were living at the same address (*Birth Statistics* Series).

Table 3.3 shows the estimated proportions of births for 1985, the most recent year for which this information was available at the time of writing, that fell into these three groups, according to age of the mother at the birth of the child. Only one-third of births to teenage women were to couples who might be regarded as being in co-resident consensual unions. The proportion is higher at older ages, nearly one-half of those aged 20–24 and 55 to 60 per cent of the older women. It is known from analyses of General Household Survey data (Werner, 1982; Kiernan, 1983) that teenage women, as one would expect, are predominantly single women having their first child whilst women aged 25 and over bearing illegitimate children were more likely to be separated and divorced women having a second or later born child, and the majority of their previous born children were legitimate.

Prior to the new information on the co-residence of parents there was a general presumption that joint registration implied cohabitation. These more precise data show that this is a reasonable assumption, but that a substantial minority are not cohabiting. If mothers are not living with partners who are they living with? They are most likely to be living alone. Young women in particular also frequently live with their own parents in a three-generation household. Compared to the mid-1970s the proportions of unmarried mothers living with their parents has declined. For example, data from the *General Household Survey* reports show that the proportion of single lone mothers living with their parents declined from 49 per cent in 1973–75 to 43 per cent in 1979–80 and had fallen to 30 per cent in 1983–84, whilst the proportion of single lone mothers living 'alone' increased from 36 per cent in 1973–75 to 48 per cent in 1979–80 and further to 59 per cent in 1983–84. The reduction in the proportions living with parents in the later periods is probably a direct consequence of the Housing and Homeless Persons Act of 1977, which made Local Authorities duty-bound to provide accomodation not only for homeless people but for people threatened with homelessness. Before the Act, Local Authorities only had a duty to provide housing for people who became unforeseeably homeless, and pregnancy did not fall into this category. Never-married lone mothers are also the most rapidly growing group of lone parents on Supplementary Benefit. For example, the number of single lone mothers receiving Supplementary Benefit increased by 90 per cent between 1979 and 1984 (from 89 to 169 thousands) whilst the number of ever-married lone mothers increased by 46 per cent (from 280 to 322 thousands) (DHSS, *Social Security Statistics*, 1980 and 1986).

There is no direct information on the duration of different living arrangements for children born outside marriage. However, analyses from the OPCS Longitudinal Study (Brown, 1986) suggest that circumstances may change fairly rapidly after the birth. For example, amongst children who were registered solely by their mothers during the period 1978–81, nearly 40 per cent were living in a married couple family by the time of the Census in 1981. Married couple families in this context includes both legally married and cohabiting couples who described themselves as married on the census form.

Such visible recent increases in the proportion of illegitimate births may contribute to changing reproductive attitudes, perhaps providing an atmosphere more conducive to childbearing outside marriage. As yet there is a dearth of information on the characteristics and changing circumstances of women who have children outside marriage. There is a need for more longitudinal information on changing living arrangements subsequent to, and perhaps precipitated by, an illegitimate birth.

Again we investigated whether there had been recent upsurges in childbearing outside marriage in other European countries.

Table 3.4 shows that the current levels of illegitimacy in England and

Table 3.4   Illegitimacy ratios (%) in selected countries of Western Europe, 1970–1984

	1970	1975	1980	1984
Sweden	18	32	40	45
Denmark	11	22	33	41
Norway	7	10	15	21
England and Wales	8	9	12	17
France	6	8	11	16[a]
West Germany	6	6	7	9
Netherlands	2	2	4	7
Ireland	3	4	5	8

[a]1983

Source: Vital statistics series of the specified countries

Wales are similar to the levels observed in Sweden in 1970 and in Denmark in 1975. As well as England and Wales two other countries seem to have experienced an upsurge in extra-marital births in recent years, namely Norway and France. It is interesting to relate levels of extra-marital child-bearing to our knowledge on the prevalence of cohabitation in different countries. The story is not totally consistent. Sweden and Denmark have high rates of both unmarried childbearing and cohabitation. Norway and France have relatively speaking medium levels of illegitimacy and cohabitation. The Netherlands and West Germany have low levels of illegitimacy and medium levels of cohabitation, whilst Ireland has low levels of each. But England and Wales appears to be a somewhat atypical case with its medium levels of illegitimacy and a low incidence of cohabitation. To unravel this apparent paradox would require life history data on individuals that would better elucidate the dynamic interplay between cohabitation, childbearing and marriage. The low observed incidence of cohabitation in Britain may in part be due to such unions being more short-lived than in other European countries.

Conclusion

An important key to understanding the trends reviewed in this chapter is the changing value placed on legal marriage. Is the status of marriage losing its traditional significance, as has already occurred to some extent in Sweden and Denmark? Or have marriage norms become less stringent allowing for more flexible family-formation arrangements, as indicated by the trend towards pre-marital cohabitation. Certainly, in Britain in recent times there seems to have been an increased movement towards a more differentiated process of family formation. But some of these changes are so recent that they may not have fully run their course.

The shift towards cohabitation without marriage continues and signs of greater acceptability of childbearing in such unions are emerging. For example, recent changes in Family Law (such as the 1987 Family Law Reform Act) have removed the remaining differences in the legal rights of children born in and outside marriage and the term 'illegitimate' can no longer be used in legal documents. Such modifications are symptomatic of change in societal values.

What will the future bring? Will Britain follow the model of Sweden and Denmark in moving towards childbearing within consensual unions and where the obligations of parents in informal and legal unions are the same? Or will the advent of AIDS reverse the consequences of the sexual revolution in the 1960s and herald a return to more traditional values? The outcome may determine whether the family faces nuclear fission or fusion. Ideational, cultural and economic developments will continue to be critical elements in family dynamics and require careful monitoring.

Acknowledgement

The majority of research reported in this chapter was carried out under ESRC funding when the Centre for Population Studies at the London School of Hygiene was a Designated Research Centre, 1978–1986.

Selected Key Reading

British Society for Population Studies 1983: *The Family*, OPCS Occasional Paper, no. 31.

Kiernan, Kathleen E. 1986b: Teenage marriage and marital breakdown: a longitudinal study. *Population Studies*, 40, 1, 35–54.

Kiernan, Kathleen E. and Eldridge, Sandra M. 1987: Inter and intra cohort variation in the timing of first marriage, *British Journal of Sociology*, 38, 1, 44–65.

4 Divorce: Economic Antecedents and Aftermath

John Ermisch

Divorces more than doubled between 1971, when the Divorce Reform Act came into force, and 1985. If the divorce rates current in the 1980s applied in perpetuity, about a third of all marriages would end in divorce (Haskey, 1983). One of the most important consequences of marital breakdown is the creation of families headed by a mother on her own.

The number of one-parent families has risen by about 60 per cent since 1971, reaching just under a million in 1984 (Haskey, 1986). By 1984, they made up 13 per cent of all families with dependent children, and the primary reason for this large increase is marital break-up: about 70 per cent of the increase is attributable to the growth in the number of divorced and separated mothers. In 1984 about 65 per cent of mothers heading one-parent families were divorced or separated. Although the percentage of lone mothers who have never been married has been increasing (primarily because the baby boom generations reached their teens and early twenties during the 1980s and first marriage rates have declined as discussed in chapter 3), the proportion unwed was still under a quarter.

Families headed by a mother on her own are generally poor. The Family Expenditure Survey shows that, in 1984, the average income of households with children headed by one parent (90 per cent of whom are mothers) was about 40 per cent of the income of two-parent households with children (and no other persons). Even after adjusting for differences in household composition (using 'equivalence scales') their average income was 60 per cent of that of two-parent households with children. Over half (55 per cent in 1984) of one-parent families receive Supplementary Benefit, a rate which has risen from 40 per cent in 1980. Although there is a wide diversity in the circumstances of lone-parent families, the low living standards in a large proportion of them and the possible adverse effects on the future prospects of children spending part of their childhood in these families constitute a major social problem.

While suggestive, these simple cross-sectional comparisons of the economic circumstances of one-parent families with those of two-parent families are apt to be a poor guide to the economic consequences of divorce for a mother. First, they ignore the possibility of remarriage. Analysis by Haskey (1987b) shows that while remarriage rates have fallen in recent years, one third of persons divorcing during 1979 remarried within two and a half years of their divorce.

Second, the economic circumstances of the population of divorced mothers reflect the influences of economic circumstances on the likelihood of divorce and the probability of remarriage, as well as any direct economic consequences of divorce. These two issues are considered in turn.

The Importance of Remarriage

A better way to study the consequences of divorce would be to track the economic circumstances of the *same* individuals before and after divorce and

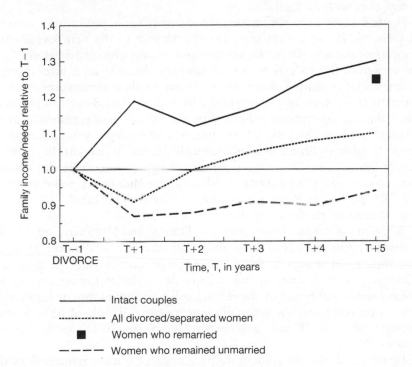

Figure 4.1 Economic circumstances of US women after divorce: family income to needs ratio as a fraction of family income to needs for the year prior to divorce or separation
Source: Duncan and Hoffman (1985)

any remarriage. Data of this type are not available in Britain. Although studies of the financial arrangements following divorce (Eeklaar and Maclean, 1986, and a forthcoming report from the Lord Chancellor's Department) can sometimes provide snapshots of economic circumstances at points of time before and after divorce, they have not followed the individuals over time. An examination of American data (from the Panel Study of Income Dynamics) is, therefore, enlightening. Figure 4.1 shows analysis by Greg Duncan and Saul Hoffman (1985).

Economic circumstances are measured in terms of the *family income relative to 'needs'* of the family to which a person belongs. 'Needs' reflect the composition of the family, with the need standard being the official US government poverty standard. Changes over time are measured relative to the person's economic circumstances in the year *prior* to that in which the marriage dissolved. Functional definitions of marriage and divorce are adopted in the analysis. Marriage includes instances in which unmarried couples live together, and dissolution takes place when residential separation occurs, even without legal divorce.

Figure 4.1 illustrates the importance of remarriage in producing a recovery in economic circumstances after divorce. At least in the first 5 years after divorce/separation, American women who remain unmarried exhibit little recovery from the reduction in their economic circumstances after divorce. Women who remarried, however, attain economic circumstances not very different from those of intact couples by 5 years after divorce/separation. Thus, the marriage market appears to be a better source of economic gain for divorced mothers than the labour market, and evidence from a sample of 'poor' families in Britain is consistent with this conclusion. In the 1978/79 Family Finances Survey, only 11 per cent of lone mothers who did remarry had incomes above the poverty threshold a year later (when followed up in the 1979/80 Family Resources Survey), compared with nearly half (48 per cent) of the lone mothers who did remarry (Millar, 1987).

While this is not shown in figure 4.1, Duncan and Hoffman find that the economic circumstances of men are hardly effected by divorce. There is, therefore, good reason to focus on women when studying the economic consequences of divorce, as this chapter does. The following analysis for Great Britain makes use of the demographic and employment histories of women collected from a nationally representative sample of 5320 women during 1980 in the *Women and Employment Survey* (WES; see Martin and Roberts, 1984).

Figure 4.2 shows the cumulative proportion of women remarried by the number of years since their marriage dissloved. The date of marital dissolution in the WES is the month of the 'end of marriage' reported by women in the survey. While some women may have reported the date of divorce, it appears that the date generally refers to the *de facto* end of

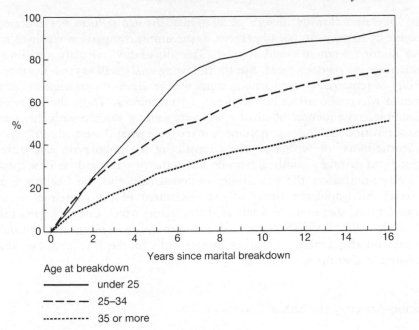

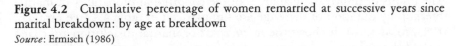

Age at breakdown

———— under 25

– – – – 25–34

············ 35 or more

Figure 4.2 Cumulative percentage of women remarried at successive years since marital breakdown: by age at breakdown
Source: Ermisch (1986)

marriage as assessed by the woman, which generally precedes legal divorce. The analysis focuses on the dissolution of first marriages. The remarriage date reported in the survey is generally the date of legal remarriage, rather than the formation of a new union.

The better economic circumstances for divorced women who remarry takes on added importance because remarriage is common in Britain (as it is in the USA). For instance, figure 4.2 shows that 70 per cent of women aged 25–34 at the end of their first marriage eventually remarry, and 50 per cent do so within 6 years of the end of their first marriage. Even 50 per cent of women aged 35 or older at divorce/separation eventually remarry. Thus, it is very important to take account of remarriage in assessing the economic consequences of divorce in Britain.

A reasonable definition of the expected economic consequences of divorce would be the expected value of income flows (adjusted by needs) associated with remarriage and with remaining unmarried. For instance, if equivalent income of a married woman is taken to be 100 and the equivalent income of a divorced woman is 60 (as the cross-section comparison suggested), the pattern of British remarriage probabilities implies an expected annual income over the 15 years following divorce of 80. Thus, divorce reduces her expected income by 20 per cent, not 40 per cent, as the simple comparison of a divorced and married women would suggest. This illustrative calculation assumes remarriage is a random event. But the following analysis shows that the probability of remarriage varies among women in relation to characteristics of a woman which also affect her economic circumstances. Thus, the expected economic consequences of divorce will vary among women with different characteristics, making it important to investigate what these traits are.

Furthermore, the economic characteristics of the population who suffer most from divorce – mothers who do not remarry – depend on how these characteristics affect the probability of remarriage and the likelihood of divorce. An important aspect of the assessment of the consequences of divorce must, therefore, be analysis of the factors which cause a higher risk of divorce and which affect the speed of remarriage. The present research focuses on this aspect. It studies divorce risks in the first marriage and remarriage after the first divorce.

Factors Affecting the Risk of Divorce

The results of multivariate analysis of the conditional probability of marital breakup by duration of marriage are summarized in table 4.1 (see Ermisch, 1986, for details). It shows the *relative risk* of marital dissolution associated with different ages at marriage. Table 4.2 shows the effects of different timing of motherhood and table 4.3 those of different amounts of experience in paid employment. In each table other factors are held constant. The risk of

Table 4.1 Relative risks of divorce by age at marriage: estimated impact of age at marriage on risk of marital breakdown during specified duration relative to someone who married at 23

| | | Duration of marriage (years) | | |
Age at marriage	1–5	6–10	11–15	16–20
17	3.21	6.05	2.11	4.19
19	2.05	3.06	1.55	2.35
21	1.39	1.68	1.21	1.46
23	1.00	1.00	1.00	1.00
25	0.76	0.64	0.88	0.76
27	0.62	0.45	0.82	0.64
29	0.53	0.34	0.81	0.60
31	0.48	0.28	0.85	0.62
33	0.47	0.25	0.95	0.71
35	0.48	0.24	1.12	0.90

Source: Parameter estimates of a multivariate logit model using data from the *Women and Employment Survey*, Ermisch, 1986.

divorce for woman A relative to woman B, or her *relative risk*, is the ratio of the odds of divorce for woman A to those of woman B. The economic view of marriage (developed by Becker, 1981) suggested that these characteristics are likely to influence the risk of divorce (Ermisch, 1986, explains the links more fully).

The analysis comfirms, at all marriage durations, the well-known tendency for the risk of breakup to decline with *age at marriage* (see table 4.1). This may reflect less search for a marital partner among women marrying younger, resulting in their making a poorer match.

The *pattern of childbearing* also affects the risk of marital dissolution. At all durations, women who became mothers through a pre-marital pregnancy experience a higher risk, probably because pregnancy discourages further search for a partner, making a poorer match likely. Beyond the fifth wedding anniversary, childlessness is also associated with a higher risk of marital breakup. This may be because the presence of children discourages divorce, or because childlessness is associated with an unanticipated fertility impairment, or perhaps because it makes search for another partner easier.

Table 4.2   Relative risk of divorce by timing of motherhood: estimated impact of the timing of motherhood on risk of marital breakdown during the specified duration relative to women in the reference category(*)

| | Duration of marriage (years) | | | |
	1–5	*6–10*	*11–15*	*16–20*
Pre-marital pregnancy	1.65	2.73	1.39	1.51
Time of first birth after marriage:				
9 months to 17 months		2.73	1.39	1.00
18 months to 26 months		1.75	1.00	1.00
27 months or more		1.00*	1.00*	1.00*
Childless at start of interval	1.00*	2.34	1.39	1.51

All relative risks different from 1.00 are statistically significant at the 0.05 level or lower.

Source: As table 4.1.

Table 4.3   Effect of work experience on marital breakdown: estimated impact of one additional year's work experience up to start of a given interval, on the risk of marital breakdown during that marriage duration interval relative to a woman with average work experience at the start of the interval

| | | Work experience | |
Duration of marriage	Total	Before 1st birth	After 1st birth
1–5 years	1.04		
6–10 years	1.06		
11–15 years		1.00	1.06
16–20 years		1.02	1.04

All relative risks different from 1.00 are statistically significant at the 0.05 level or lower.

Source: As table 4.1.

Early childbearing within marriage has a similar effect on the risk of marital breakup at marriage durations of 6–10 years to that of childlessness or a pre-marital pregnancy. This may reflect financial strains produced by starting a family early, or the unsettling effects on the process of learning about one's spouse. There was no evidence that early childbearing makes marriages more stable, nor that larger families are less likely to split up.

While these findings confirm some earlier research (e.g. Murphy, 1985; Kiernan, 1986b; Haskey, 1984), the WES permits, for the first time, analysis of the impact of women's participation in paid employment on the risk of marital dissolution. The focus is on the impact of the amount of *experience in paid employment*, or, for short, 'work experience'. More work experience increases a woman's earning capacity (see, for example, Joshi and Newell, 1988 and Joshi, 1984). There is also evidence that more recent work experience has a bigger impact on women's earnings than early experience (Main, 1985). Thus, at marriage durations beyond 10 years, the analysis distinguished between work experience before and after a woman's first birth.

Women with higher earning capacity tend to have higher incomes if unmarried, making them better able to cope financially with divorce – what might be called an 'independence effect' when severe marital strains arise. Also, women with higher earning capacity tend to gain less from any given marriage because the traditional marital division of labour is practised less when a woman's earning capacity is closer to her husband's. A smaller expected gain from marriage makes it more likely that the gain may disappear over time for one of the partners. Thus, the divorce risk tends to be higher for women with higher earning power.

More work experience during marriage is also likely to be associated with better opportunities for meeting another spouse (i.e. a better marriage offer being received). In this way work experience may directly affect the risk of divorce.

The multivariate analysis indeed shows that, during the first 10 years of marriage, women with more work experience at a given duration of marriage are more likely to dissolve their marriage subsequently. The analysis also shows that work experience after the first birth has a larger positive effect on the risk of marital breakup at marriage durations beyond 10 years, thereby supporting the hypothesis that the impact of work experience on the risk of divorce operates through its effect on earning capacity.

Nevertheless, another interpretation of these associations of divorce risk with work experience puts the causation elsewhere. A poor financial situation may produce marital strains that raise a couple's risk of divorce while at the same time increasing the wife's participation in paid employment. The extent of her work experience may be merely an indicator of the couple's financial strains, which affect the divorce risk. Studies indeed show an inverse relationship between couple's income and wife's labour force participation, although this association became weaker after 1970 (Fry, 1984; and Joshi, 1985), but the link between a couple's income and their divorce risk is less well established.

There may also be aspects of 'reverse causation'. Women who perceive a high risk of divorce may participate in paid employment more in order to 'insure' themselves financially if divorced. These other interpretations appear unlikely to be the whole story, however.

As a consequence of the combination of these influences, newly divorced mothers tend to be younger, to have started childbearing earlier and to have higher earning capacity. All of these characteristics affect their economic circumstances if divorced. But the composition of the divorced population also depends on who remarries, and how quickly they do so.

Factors Affecting Remarriage

Focusing on the probability of remarriage within 3 years of the end of the first marriage (during which 27 per cent remarry), multivariate analysis found that the probability increased with a *woman's work experience* at the end of the first marriage. An additional year of work experience increases the odds of remarriage in the first 3 years by 6 per cent. Women with more work experience during the first marriage may have better opportunities for receiving an offer which improves on their current marriage, thereby precipitating divorce and early remarriage. In addition, work experience in the first marriage is strongly related to participation in paid employment after the end of the first marriage, and employment is likely to provide better opportunities for finding a new mate. Also, the higher earning capacity of women with more work experience may make them more attractive to prospective second husbands.

Women with *'high' educational attainments* (3 or more years of post-compulsory education) are also more likely to remarry quickly. The odds of their remarriage within 3 years is 2.5 times higher than other women.

In comparing the importance of experience and education for the likelihood of early remarriage, account should be taken of the variation of these among women. The standard deviation of work experience at the end of the first marriage is about 6.5 years, around a mean of 10 years. A woman with one standard deviation more work experience than the average woman faces odds of remarriage in the first 3 years that are 1.2 times higher, while the odds for a woman with one standard deviation less work experience than the average are only 60 per cent of the average woman's. Although having higher work experience appears to have a smaller impact than having a high level of education, only 10 per cent of women have post-compulsory education of 3 years or more while the odds of remarriage of all women are affected by the amount of their work experience.

The multivariate analysis did not suggest that *children* are a large impediment to remarriage. Women with 1–3 children appear as likely as childless women to remarry within 3 years, holding education, age, work experience and period of divorce constant. Mothers of 4 or more children are, however, less likely to remarry quickly. Their odds of remarriage in the first 3 years are 65 per cent lower. Bivariate analysis of the pattern of remarriage according to the number of children (shown in figure 4.3) suggests that larger differences may emerge beyond the first 3 years after the first marriage. But when other factors are controlled for in multivariate analysis, the impact of the number of children among women with less than 4 children remains small. The bivariate association between the number of children and remarriage in figure 4.3 may operate through the effect of children on their mother's work experience.

The *age of a woman* has a strong impact on the probability that she remarries. Figure 4.2 showed the bivariate relationship between the age of a woman at the end of her first marriage and her remarriage probabilities, and

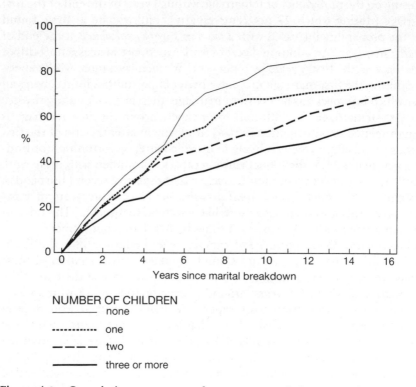

NUMBER OF CHILDREN
——————   none
·············   one
— — — —   two
——————   three or more

Figure 4.3   Cumulative percentage of women remarried at successive years since marital breakdown: by number of children at marital breakdown
·*Source*: Ermisch (1986)

the multivariate analysis confirms this picture. Older women are less likely to remarry, and this probably reflects the poorer marriage market for older women because of the steep decline with age in the ratio of unmarried men to women. Being an additional year older at the end of her first marriage lowers the odds of remarrying in the first 3 years by 10 per cent.

The probability of remarriage in the first 3 years was found to be higher *after 1971*, and more recent research (Ermisch, Jenkins and Wright, 1987) confirms a significantly higher likelihood of remarriage after 1971. The Divorce Reform Act, which made divorce easier, came into effect in 1971. When more people are divorcing, there is a better marriage market for divorced women, which may explain the better odds of remarriage after 1971.

Remarriage is the primary source of flows out of lone parenthood (the other is through a woman's youngest child reaching adulthood). Characteristics of a woman that raise the likelihood of her remarriage reduce the expected duration of her period as a lone parent. Thus, the expected duration for a particular woman depends on her age, the size of her family, her educational attainments and her work experience. The analysis suggests that the average duration of lone parenthood became shorter after 1971. The tendency for older women, women with less experience in paid employment and women with large families to remain unpartnered also clearly affects the economic circumstances of the population of divorced women.

Economic Circumstances of One Parent Families Headed by Mothers

Divorce and remarriage represent the flows into and out of lone parenthood by mothers married at least once. By affecting these flows, the influences of a woman's economic characteristics on divorce and remarriage discussed in the preceding two sections interact in a complex way in determining the distribution of economic circumstances among lone mothers. It is particularly complex because the impacts of these factors vary with marriage duration and the length of time a woman remains unmarried after divorce. Some rough assessment of how these factors which 'select' women into and out of lone parenthood affect the economic circumstances of one parent families can, however, be made.

There is evidence (Kiernan, 1986b) that, in Britain, Women who marry younger, particularly as teenagers, tend to come from the least advantaged family backgrounds and educational and occupational careers. Thus, if their marriage dissolves, they would tend to be in poorer economic circumstances. The high risk of marital dissolution among women marrying young tends, therefore, to produce one-parent families in poor economic circumstances. A tendency for selection factors to produce poor lone mothers is reinforced if higher rates of participation in paid employment, which raise the risk of dissolution, are indicative of a couple's poor financial situation. On the other hand, a woman who has had more work experience would tend, *ceteris paribus*, to have higher earning power on her own account.

It is not possible, therefore, to say conclusively whether the woman's characteristics that affect her risk of marital dissolution select women for lone parenthood who are better or worse off than average. There is, however, some suggestion that it may select those in poorer economic circumstances, which would reinforce the economic plight of lone mothers.

Women with more experience in paid employment and high educational attainments, who are more likely to remarry quickly, tend to have higher earning power, making them better able to support their families. Women with smaller families are also more likely to remarry. Many of the factors influencing the likelihood of remarriage tend, therefore, to select out of lone parenthood those likely to be in better economic circumstances, leaving those in poorer circumstances as lone parents. All else equal, older women are also more likely to remain lone parents. The incidence of receipt of Supplementary Benefit (SB) by age among previously married lone mothers suggests that older lone mothers may be better off economically, thereby working in the opposite direction to the other selection factors in its influence on the circumstances of one-parent families. But this simple relationship between age and receipt of SB may reflect other variables, like work experience and family size that are correlated with age.

The Duration of Lone Parenthood

Little has been known about how long women remain lone parents. Figure 4.4 displays the distribution of the duration of lone parenthood for all women (in the WES) who had been lone parents at some time in their lives. Figure 4.4 distinguishes between whether a woman became a lone parent because of birth while single or because of the end of her marriage. The latter group, who make up the vast majority of lone parents, have been the group upon which we have concentrated.

While quite a large proportion of lone mothers are in that state for a relatively short period, particularly single mothers, substantial numbers remain lone parents for a long time. For those becoming a lone parent through marital dissolution, the median duration of lone parenthood is about 5 years, in contrast to 3 years for single mothers. The different durations of these two groups of lone parents are also illustrated by their respective *survival curves* in figure 4.5. These show the proportion remaining a lone parent according to the number of years since they became one. The faster exit from lone parenthood by single mothers is readily apparent. It is clear that one of the reasons

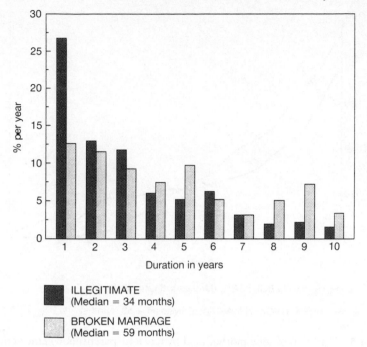

Figure 4.4 Probability distribution for exit from lone motherhood by way lone parenthood came about (durations over 10 years omitted)
Source: Ermisch (1986)

that single mothers represent a relatively small proportion of lone mothers is their much shorter average durations as lone parents.

While divorced mothers' median duration of lone parenthood is 5 years, their mean, or expected duration is longer because of the skewness of the distribution of exits shown in figure 4.4. The mean duration among all divorced mothers is about 7.5 years, but the analysis above has shown that the expected duration for a particular woman depends on her age, educational attainments, her experience in paid employment and the size of her family. Some calculations based on research by Ermisch, Jenkins and Wright (1987) suggest that a woman dissolving her marriage at the age of 26 could expect to be a lone parent for about 3 years less than a woman aged 33 (the average) at the end of her first marriage, and 5 years additional work experience reduces the expected duration by a year. Having 4 or more children rather than 2 raises a woman's expected duration of lone parenthood by about 3 years. Finally, the expected duration of lone parenthood may have fallen by as much as 4 years after the Divorce Reform Act took effect in 1971.

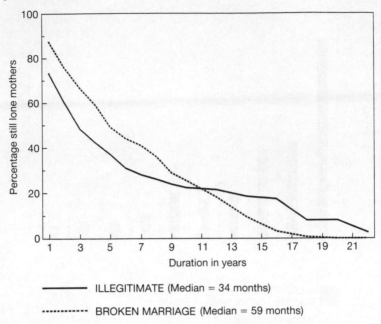

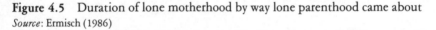

ILLEGITIMATE (Median = 34 months)

BROKEN MARRIAGE (Median = 59 months)

Figure 4.5 Duration of lone motherhood by way lone parenthood came about
Source: Ermisch (1986)

Conclusion

The analysis has shown the importance of taking remarriage into account in assessing the economic consequences of divorce for women. It has also shown that characteristics of a woman that contribute to a higher risk of divorce also affect its consequences in terms of the economic circumstances of divorced women. They do so by, in effect, 'selecting' particular types of women into divorce and lone parenthood.

The analysis has also examined the durations of lone parenthood experienced by divorced mothers. While the median duration of all women who had ever been a lone parent is about 5 years, it varies systematically with the characteristics of a woman, because these affect the likehood and speed of her remarriage. There is also evidence that the expected duration of lone parenthood may have become shorter since the Divorce Reform Act increased the number of people divorcing, thereby improving the marriage market for divorced women. In this respect, lone parenthood lasted longer when it was less common.

The poor economic circumstances experienced by a substantial proportion of lone mothers was noted at the outset. Although, because of remarriage, such experiences are short for many mothers, many also remain lone parents for a long time. In Britain, lone mothers are assisted primarily through means-tested social security benefits, although there is also a higher rate of Child Benefit for lone parents. There are, however, other policy measures which may reduce reliance on means-tested benefits. These would include child support assurance schemes, which would assure mothers of child support payments from the father and enforce the father's obligations. More and cheaper day care for both one and two parent families could be encouraged, either by direct state provision or subsidies that could be used in the private care market, and equal opportunities policies could be enforced more vigorously. While these last policies (also advocated in chapter 10 below) have more general effects, they particularly help lone mothers by improving their economic prospects, and the empirical analysis here suggests that, by encouraging stronger labour force attachment, they may also shorten the duration of lone parenthood. Variants of these policies are in operation in a number of European countries. Future research should consider the contribution that different policy packages can make to mitigating the economic consequences of divorce in Britain.

Acknowledgement

The research reported in this chapter has been supported by grants from the Joseph Rowntree Memorial Trust and the ESRC grant no. G00222005 to the London School of Hygiene.

Selected Key Reading

Duncan, Greg J. and Hoffman, Saul D. 1985: Economic consequences of marital instability. In T. Smeeding and M. David (eds), *Horizontal Equity, Uncertainty and Well-being*. National Bureau of Economic Research, Income and Wealth Conference. Chicago: University of Chicago Press, 429–70.

Haskey, John 1986: One parent families in Great Britain. *Population Trends*, 45. 5–13.

Millar, Jane 1987: Lone mothers. In Caroline Glendinning and Jane Millar (eds), *Women and Poverty in Britain*. Brighton: Wheatsheaf Books, 159–77.

5 Old Age: Burden or Benefit?

Pat Thane

Introduction

Between 1911 and the 1980s the proportion of the UK population over the age of 65 had tripled from 5 per cent to 15 per cent. In addition many more now survive into their eighties and nineties. This phenomenon, often referred to as the 'ageing' of the population, is widely viewed as a serious problem or 'burden'. Over the coming decades, it has been argued, a shrinking working population will be obliged to finance the pensions, health care and other services required by a burgeoning elderly population. This chapter argues for a less pessimistic approach.

The 1980s have seen a public debate about the effects upon the economy of the growing proportion of old people in Britain; and the stress has been on the increasing burden of costs that will result (Department of Health and Social Security (DHSS), 1985). Yet for many years gerontologists, in the many disciplines that make up gerontology, have been arguing that the gloom is overstressed, that future prospects need not be so bad as is often suggested. This chapter is a brief review of some of the large body of evidence for this more positive view, intended as a contribution to placing the debate about cost in a more balanced framework. It is not a comprehensive overview of all aspects of a complex set of issues. This is a field in which speculation and clearly attested fact are not always kept in distinct compartments. It is important to try to distinguish between fact and speculation and amid the speculation – since contemplating the future is inevitably to a high degree speculative – between the speculation that makes sense and that which does not.

The proportion of the population over 65 will remain more or less constant until after the turn of the century, giving a respite in which to acquire knowledge and formulate policies. Not until the twenty-first century is the proportion of the elderly expected to grow again. If fertility remains low and life expectancy continues to improve, it could reach 20 per cent by the year 2025.

The Changing Age Structure

The facts about the shift in British age structure since the mid nineteenth century are set out in table 5.1 and figure 5.1. These show that by the 1980s a higher proportion of the population is above the age of 65 than at any time in statistically retrievable history. As was shown in chapter 2, this is primarily due to the falling trend in fertility over this century which has reduced the proportion in younger age cohorts. However, as table 5.2 and figure 5.2 show, the other very important component of the trend is that more people than before are living to be *very* old, into the high eighties and nineties, and this is to some degree due to changing mortality trends at later ages. In the United Kingdom and the United States the over-eighties are the most rapidly growing age group (Grundy, 1986).

Table 5.1   Percentage of population aged 65 and over, Great Britain 1851–1981

Census year	%
1851	4.6
1881	4.6
1911	5.2
1931	7.4
1951	10.9
1971	13.2
1981	15.1

Source: Censuses of Population

Table 5.2   The very old as a percentage of the elderly in the UK (1901–2001)

	All elderly people[a] (millions)	Elderly, 75 and under[a] (millions)	All over 75 (millions)	% of all elderly[a] people who are over 75
1901	2.4	1.9	0.5	21
1951	6.9	5.1	1.8	26
1977	9.6	6.7	2.9	30
1999[b]	9.9	6.3	3.6	36
2001[b]	9.5	5.9	3.6	38

[a] males over 65, females over 60
[b] projected

Source: Tinker, 1981, p. 12.

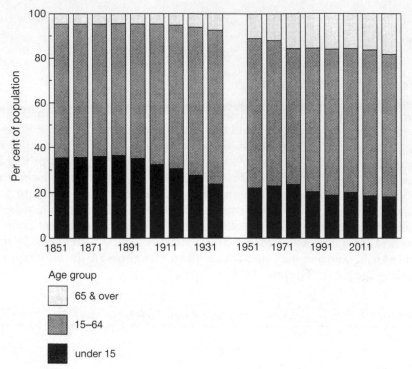

Figure 5.1   The age structure of the population of England and Wales, 1851–2021
Source: Censuses of England and Wales and OPCS *Population Projections*, (1985-based)

It should be noted that although the *total* population over 65 is not expected to increase for the remainder of the twentieth century, this is due to a projected fall in the numbers aged 60/65–74 (by 5 per cent between 1981 and 1991) combined with a rise in the numbers at older ages. At present 38.2 per cent of the elderly population are aged over 75 and 6.5 per cent are aged 85 years or more. Projections by the Government Actuary suggest that by 2001 these proportions will have increased to 47.2 per cent and 12.1 per cent respectively (Falkingham, 1987). However, still in 2001 those aged over 85 will still constitute only 17 in each thousand of total population. As regards the cost implications of these shifts, although the over-85s are heavier users of costly services than younger age groups, the heaviest financial cost of the elderly arises from pensions not from services and, to repeat, the total pensionable age group will remain stable for the next two decades.

Another important point is that about 60 per cent of the over-65 population is female and the numerical superiority of females rises with each succeeding age cohort. This is an important reason why the old have a high

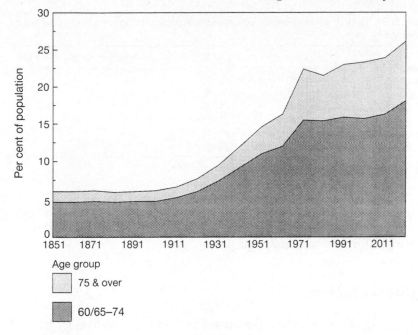

Figure 5.2 The population over pension age and its age composition, England and Wales, 1881–2021
Source: As table 5.1

propensity to be poor. Women in the past (and still) have had more limited access than men to financial resources, for example, to occupational pensions, which will be discussed below (Groves, 1986, 1987).

This long-run shift to an older population is not peculiar to Britain. It is occurring in almost all economically developed countries including those of Eastern Europe and the Far East, though with some different effects in different countries due to different patterns of mortality. It is occurring at especial speed in those countries in which development has been recent and fast. It is projected, for example, to take Japan only 26 years to move from having 7 per cent of her population aged over 65 (in 1970) to 14 per cent (in 1996), a process which took France (with her deviant demographic history) the 115 years from 1865 to 1980, Sweden 85 years and the UK 45 years from 1930 to 1975 (see table 5.3). Japan has experienced a recent and rapid fall in fertility combined with more gradually lengthening life expectancy. China, if the one-child policy continues to be pursued successfully at the same time that life expectancy is being extended, looks set for an extraordinarily rapid transition to being the oldest society ever known – an apparently unforeseen

Table 5.3   Dates of reaching certain percentages of population above age 65 in selected countries

	7%	14%	*Period of transition in years*
Japan	1970	1996	26
France	1865	1980	115
W. Germany	1930	1975	45
Sweden	1890	1975	85
UK	1930	1975	45
USA	1945	2020	75

Source: Japanese Ministry of Health and Welfare.

conseqeunce of her birth-rate policy, according to work being carried out by James Smith and Peter Laslett at the Rank Xerox Unit for the Study of Ageing, University of Cambridge.

Ageing as a Problem

The ageing of society is being discussed as a problem worldwide. In the US the Carnegie Foundation has established a Centre for the Study of Societal Ageing at the University of Michigan. The real problem is, as the Carnegie Foundation has realized since establishing the Ageing Society Project of the Carnegie Corporation of New York in 1982 (Pifer and Bronte, 1986), that we know surprisingly little about what happens to a society and its economy when its age structue changes significantly. Ageing is a fundamental feature of social structure and social change. It is reasonable to assume that such changes have significant social and economic effects, yet they have been conspicuously neglected by social scientists. There has been interest in these questions from time to time in the past, in particular in Britain between the end of World War Two and the early 1960s. At this time the low fertility of the inter-war years caused serious fears about the high proportion of elderly people in the population in relation to those of normal working age, especially since it was a period of labour shortage and acute need to restructure the economy. A certain amount of research into the effects of ageing went on in that period (and not only in Britain) but much of it was forgotten when the crisis of ageing and labour shortage seemed less acute in the 1960s – the 'age of automation' (Bagrit, 1965), of greater availablity of female and immigrant labour and of youth. Much relevant research has gone on since then, but it seems to have made very little impact upon the public debate about the ageing of British society. The work of gerontologists seems often not to have reached the policymakers, the economists and the public.

The chief issues that are singled out in this debate are: that the growing proportion of retired people will impose a burden of increasing cost upon a shrinking population of working age in terms of pensions and services; and the fact that a growing proportion of these will be very old and therefore more in need of medical and other care will make this burden more onerous still. Other associated policy problems are pinpointed – for example, an increasing proportion of old people is assumed to imply a changing pattern of demand for housing, in the direction of smaller units.

It is in examining these questions that we need to separate out fact from speculation. There will be more people in future above current pensionable ages than in the past, barring some fairly improbable changes in fertility and mortality trends (DHSS, 1984; Ermisch and Joshi, 1987). This is clear from table 5.4 and figures 5.1 and 5.2. Whether all of these older people will be *retired* is a separate point, not to be taken for granted, to be discussed below. There will also be, as certainly we can tell, more very old people in the future than in the past, something also clear from table 5.4. But, as will also be discussed later, the problems they will pose and their cost cannot be predicted with such certainty.

Table 5.4   Age composition of the population of Great Britain

| | *Percentage aged* | | |
	0–14	*15–64*	*65+*
1951	22.4	66.7	10.9
1961	23.2	65.0	11.8
1971	24.0	62.8	13.2
1978	21.8	63.5	14.7
Projected			
1986	18.4–19.5	66.4–65.4	15.2–15.0
1991	18.3–20.5	66.3–64.5	15.5–15.0
1996	19.2–21.9	65.6–63.4	15.2–14.7
2001	18.8–21.9	66.4–64.0	14.9–14.2
2001[b]	17.5–21.5	66.9–63.6	15.6–14.9
2025[b]	16.2–21.4	63.8–61.8	20.0–16.8

[a] The projections illustrate the range between, respectively, a low and a high fertility assumption.

Source: O'Higgins, 1986; and for [b], *World Population Prospects as Assessed in 1984*, UN, New York, 1986.

A Stable Elderly Population for Twenty Years

It is important at this point to repeat another reasonably clear fact already referred to: the rise in the total elderly population will not be immediate. The proportion of the population over pensionable age is projected to remain more or less level between now and the end of the century, indeed to decline somewhat around the turn of the century and then to rise again in the early years of the twenty-first century when the larger birth cohorts of the war and post-war years move into their sixties (see figure 5.1). The levelling-off will be due to the coincidence of the smaller birth cohorts of the pre-war years entering old age whilst the larger war and post-war cohorts are of working age. This, of course, depends again upon no sudden upturn in fertility in the next couple of decades (see table 5.4). If no such upturn does occur we actually face about 20 years of demographic stability in respect of overall age structure, indeed probably the most stable 20 years of the entire twentieth century (O'Higgins, 1986). This at least ought to quieten panic about ageing because, if no more, it gives us a breathing space in which to research and to plan for future policy.

Dependency Ratios

Table 5.4 also suggests another reason not to panic: that over the longer run the rise in the elderly population in the next century and the rise in the numbers of very elderly in this century is to some degree offset by a projected fall in the number of very young non-workers, i.e., that the relationship between total so-called 'dependency' and the size of the population of working age may not change significantly. Though what will happen in the next century up to 2025, as table 5.4 suggests, we can only calculate with a large margin of error. In that period the overall 'dependency ratio' may or may not rise significantly. If we aggregate together everyone in that 'dependent' age group, i.e., those below the age of 16 and above pensionable ages, remembering the heaviest demands on services are made at each end of the age range, the percentage of dependants to total UK population has indeed remained remarkably stable throughout this century – 30 per cent in 1901, 36 per cent in 1951, 41 per cent in 1977 – and it is likely to remain so for the remainder of the century; it is projected to be 40 per cent in 2001 (Grundy, 1986, p. 21; table 5.4). The fact remains, however, that within this stable total age dependency ratio, the proportion of very old will continue to increase to the end of the century and the age structure of the population of normal working age will increasingly be weighted towards higher age cohorts (Falkingham, 1987, pp. 5–7).

There are major problems about defining dependency in these simple, age related terms, to be discussed below. But staying with this definition for the time being, there is a general assumption in much writing in this field that althoguh *total* age related dependency may not be about to rise very much, the shift to larger numbers of elderly and the fall in the numbers of the very young will increase the costs of dependency because the elderly are more costly; they make more demands on expensive services than the young. Also the services to old and young are not easily substitutable for one another. But it is surprisingly difficult to find precise quantification of these comparisons. A still incomplete, unpublished calculation for 1953–1979 by David Thomson of the Rank Xerox Unit at Cambridge is suggestive. Using a variety of official statistics he calculates that the total cost of the elderly in terms of publicly funded services and benefits was at most 103 per cent of the cost of a child in 1979. More, that is, but only narrowly. It can be argued of course that the disparity will increase due to the coming growth in the numbers and demands of the very elderly. This is likely, but *how great* these demands will be is another difficult question. It is actually the key question in the whole debate, but one in which it is especially difficult to make convincing, informed predictions.

The Health of the Aged

It seems natural to assume that as in the twenty-first century more people live to be very old, more of them will *necessarily* make heavier demands on health and social services; that people who die in their nineties experience a longer period of dependency and illness before death than those who die in their seventies. At present this is so. According to 1986 Treasury figures, in 1985 per capita health and personal social service expenditure for those age 75 and over was £1,340 compared with £530 for those aged 65–74 and £305 for the population as a whole (HM Treasury, 1986). They occupy about 50 per cent of all hospital beds. But as Nicholas Bosanquet (1975, 1978) points out this is partly because younger people are now dependent, ill and hospitalized much *less* than in the past. Health standards have risen in society at large. Also Bosanquet has argued vigorously for over a decade – and has not been alone – that this suggests that younger age cohorts are growing up fitter and will not necessarily need such varied and prolonged care in the future. Alan Pifer of the Carnegie Foundation has recently made similar suggestions (Pifer, 1987): that, for example, the intense and historically novel current interest of the middle aged and young in preventive care – good diet and exercise – may significantly affect their future health (Pifer and Bronte, 1986).

Others, however, suggest, less cheeringly and no less convincingly, that the duration of disability proceeding death rises with age, so the more people who live to a longer life span, the bigger the health bills. Emily Grundy (1986) has rightly stressed how little is known about the epidemiology and aetiology, let alone prevention and treatment, of some of the major disorders affecting the very old, such as dementia. But it is equally true that there is no way of foreseeing the health status of the very elderly of 2010 or 2022; people grown up in the historically exceptionally prosperous period since World War Two may have very different health expectations than those currently aged over 75 who were born before 1911 in a very different environment from the present. Many of the elderly of the twenty-first century, however, will have experienced the effects of unemployment in the 1980s or perhaps longer, though these may not be the survivors into old age (Moser, Fox and Jones, 1984; Whitehead, 1987). It is possible that we will see a further slowing of the ageing process as time goes on so that in the next century the experience of being in one's eighties is more like the experience of being in one's seventies at the moment. What has happened over the course of this century has been an improvement in people's states of fitness at particular ages so that whereas at the beginning of the century people in their sixties were regarded as being old, it is clear that people who survive into their sixties are now mainly, as is described below, generally quite fit. The disabilities associated with old age do not seem to strike people signficantly until they reach their later seventies. It may be hard to imagine a situation in whch the onset of old age occurs at later ages than in the past, but a hundred years ago or less it was difficult to imagine the present situation in which old age does not effectively begin until people are in their seventies. We have to try to imagine a complex future in which different groups of the elderly will have different experiences from those of the present and from one another. This is already the case, but it is possible that the variety of future experiences in old age will be greater still.

Nor are states of health and states of dependency automatically related to the biological facts of ageing. An impressive body of research in psychogerontology demonstrates that a good deal of ill health and dependency even in very old age is induced by society's *expectation* that age brings infirmity and dependence. This structures personal attitudes of and towards the elderly and is the underlying premise of much policy and its administration. Such services as 'meals on wheels' assume helplessness, but are not what many old people want or need. As Malcolm Johnson (1982, p. 144) has suggested, they would prefer help with shopping so that they can prepare often more palatable meals of their choice and when they choose, thus maximizing their independence and probably their health. We should also remember that we expect many of the elderly to function under circumstances of stress which would strain people of *any* age: bereavement, repeated as contemporaries gradually die, worry about money, fear of increasing infirmity, isolation and death. Among younger people equivalent circumstances of stress are regarded as legitimate qualifications for counselling. But among the elderly the tensions and illness that may result are defined as natural accompaniments to ageing (Bosanquet, 1978). Certain biological and functional 'changes thought to be intrinsically associated with ageing may be influenced by extrinsic and possibly preventable factors' (Grundy, 1986, p. 6). Certain changes in muscular structure and performance, for example, can be reversible.

Obviously the elderly have 'real' needs also. The point is that we have a very indistinct line between the real and unavoidable problems of ageing and those which are socially and psychologically constructed and may, with care, be reducible. The serious problem is that in this key area of the debate about ageing so much is speculative. Where the future cannot usefully be predicted, it makes sense for policymakers to assume the worse and plan for heavy demands on services by the very old. But this does not mean that we can simply extrapolate from current trends in the use of services to estimate future demands and costs. Extensive work by gerontologists on service provision for old people and their responses to it suggest that cheaper alternatives to some costly services might enable more of the elderly to remain fitter and independent of institutions for longer. Over the past ten years it has been government policy to encourage this (DHSS, 1976a). New approaches to community care, using low-paid or unpaid neighbours or other local carers, as substitutes or supplements to family or friends and supported by official social services, are currently being experimented with in the Kent Community Care Scheme, the Age Concern and Guy's Hospital Home Support Project and a scheme being tried out in Bexley (Challis and Davis, 1983; Maitland, 1987). The aim of these and other schemes is to provide flexible cost-effective services responsive to the needs of the frail elderly and designed to keep them as long as possible in their own homes rather than an institutional environment. If such schemes can successfully be developed they may provide future services better suited to the needs of the elderly at lower costs than the continued use of social and health services on current levels. Even if they do not cut effective costs, they will bring about changes in patterns of demand for services. They may of course enable people to live in the community longer *before* a prolonged and expensive period of institutionalized decline until death; or they may fail to bring about any significant changes. The recent history of community care projects has not been encouraging (Grundy, 1986, p. 22) But this is precisely the sort of area to which research needs to be directed in the immediate future of relative demographic stability, because it is so crucial and because our ignorance of future patterns of demand is so great.

Economic Dependency of the Aged

It is worth adding at this point, in the context of discussion of the cost burden of the elderly, that according to further calculations by David Thomson (1987) based on Family Expenditure Survey data, the share of national resources going to the elderly has *not* risen proportionately with their numbers over the past two decades. Such calculations are difficult, due to difficulties in obtaining data on income or wealth distribution among age groups, and this aspect of distribution has received little study. However, it appears from Thomson's calculations that the shares of the elderly and the non-elderly have remained roughly stable. However, the elderly have had to spread their share among growing numbers and the non-elderly among falling numbers. In 1963 the personal spending of the elderly amounted to 9 per cent of GNP; it was still at this level by the late 1970s and was up only to 10.8 per cent by 1983. Meanwhile the non-elderly increased their expenditure from 51 per cent to 56 per cent of GNP. *This* has given the impression of a significant shift of resources in their direction. But this shift should be seen in the context of the total demands of the elderly on resources which appears not to have risen so fast; they have so far not been a dependent burden of significant dimensions despite their growing numbers, though as Thomson points out, this could change in coming years.

The Inputs of the Elderly into the Economy

Another problem, however, lies in the very assumption that all of those past retirement age *are* more or less automatically dependent 'burdens' on the economy rather than contributors to it. Paul Johnson (1987) has pointed out that there is something wonderfully absurd about assuming that a retired 66-year-old millionaire is more 'dependent' in an economic sense than a 64-year-old employed road mender. But this is precisely the type of assumption statistical calculations of age-related dependency ask us to make. This is adequate if one is simply trying to calculate who is receiving certain benefits, such as old-age pensions, from official sources, but if we are seeking a realistic conception of who is and who is not a dependant or a net contributor to the economy in a broader sense such definitions are not helpful (Grundy, 1986, p. 13). Calculations that assume that women over 60 and men over 65 are 'dependent' must indeed be diverging *increasingly* from reality. On the one hand more men are effectively retiring in their fifties due to unemployment (Walker and Walker, 1987). On the other hand *more* retired people will have greater power than before as *consumers* in coming years. Obvious indicators of this are the numbers with occupational pensions: in 1973 only 60 per cent of men over 55 in full-time employment belonged to a pension scheme run by their current employer. In 1983 the figure was 75 per cent. The equivalent figure for women was 31 per cent in 1972 and 63 per cent in 1983. And the number of house owners among the elderly is rising: in 1985 only 47 per cent of household heads over 65 were house owners. But of household heads aged 30–60 65 per cent were house owners (Thomson, 1987, p. 47). Pessimists may say that this will lead to more elderly people being burdened with the costs of deteriorating houses; optimists, that a higher proportion of future cohorts of the elderly will be accustomed to capitalizing on their assets. They will either buy down into smaller accommodation in good repair and consume the profit, or borrow or buy annuities on the security of their properties, as many are apparently doing in the United States.

Of course not all of the elderly of the future will be relatively affluent, and, to repeat, we need to be alert to inequalities among the elderly – between age cohorts and within them: the cohorts who will be bringing more occupational pensions and owner-occupied houses into old age will also bring in experience of early retirement and early run-down of resources due to unemployment.

The retired are also important to the economy as suppliers of a wide variety of services and other forms of labour. It should be remembered that the large *majority* of the elderly are fit people in their sixties and seventies. This should be stressed because it is another important fact of change in the elderly population over time. As was mentioned earlier, at the beginning of this century the consensus was that most people were in a state of physical decline by their early to mid-sixties (Williams, 1970). Now the consensus among gerontologists is that those who survive into their sixties mostly retain quite a high degree of fitness into their mid-seventies. *That* is when old age now begins. For most people ageing now takes place more slowly than in the past. The reality of life past 60 for most people has changed faster than society's expectations of it.

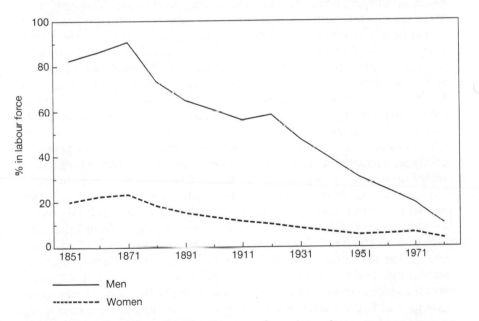

Figure 5.3 Labour force participation rates of people aged over 65, 1851–1981
Source: Censuses of England and Wales

Figure 5.3 charts the falling rate of economic activity among elderly people over a century. Of those people in their sixties and seventies in the 1980s only about 5 per cent are in full-time employment past normal retirement age; a somewhat larger number, around 10 per cent, let it be known that they work part-time (*Social Trends*, 1979, Table 11). A larger number still provide a wide range of formal and informal voluntary services. In 1981 43 per cent of over-65s give regular help to other elderly people, 25 per cent to the sick and disabled, 11 per cent to neighbours (*Social Trends*, 1985, Table 11.5). Twenty-one per cent of those aged 65–74 engaged in some formal voluntary work for a voluntary agency, and 11 per cent of those aged over 75. Fifty-two per cent of over-65s could be said to give regular practical help to other individuals (*Social Trends*, 1984, Tables 11.4 and 11.6). In 1979 22 per cent of local authority councillors were aged over 60 (*Social Trends*, 1979, Table 15.7).

It is reasonable to assume that all such figures underestimate the real activities of the elderly. In particular I know of no estimates of the numbers who continue on a part-time basis, undeclared for tax, to sell skills acquired during their working life time. Professional people do so on a consultancy basis, skilled manual workers as and when they can.

The majority of elderly people are also, as already mentioned, female and continue long past retiring age to perform the tasks almost universal among women at all ages: domestic and other unpaid services for themselves and others, some older, some younger, some the same age as themselves. They support people active in the labour force, and provide services which would otherwise fall to the health and social services. The analysis at the University of Surrey by Sara Arber and her associates (financed by the ESRC as part of their Ageing Initiative) of the 1980 General Household Survey suggests that elderly men also provide such services to a greater degree than has been assumed (Gilbert et al., 1989). But it is unusual for personal care to be given by non-related carers (Evandrou et al., 1986; Grant, 1986).

Ian Timaeus (1986) suggests that the family demands on older people's services may actually increase in future. Over the 50 years to 1981 a significantly increasing proportion of people have married and have had children. This is an important change. The age cohorts who in the 1980s constitute the very old population over 85 are characterized by high rates of childlessness. Research by Mark Abrams (1978) on those over 75 in 1977 found that one third had no children. Timaeus estimates that only 16 per cent of those reaching the age of 60 in the early 1990s will have no children at time of death. In general the never-married elderly make greater use of statutory services including institutional care than others of the same age, so change in marriage and fertility patterns pointed out by Timaeus may have important implications for future service use. Another possible implication is that into the early years of the next century fewer old people will lack kin support or would be living alone than is often assumed. And more will have spouses and children to provide services for. What we can not tell is whether the trends to increasing divorce and remarriage will be a force for increasing the solitary living or for extending the range of family contacts available to the divorced. There is not, of course, *any* serious evidence that kin support for the elderly is declining, despite the persistent myth that it is. There is a large amount of evidence (summarized by Grundy, 1986) that it continues to be the *major* source of support for the elderly. The data produced by Timaeus suggest that kin support has a potential to increase rather than to decline.

The picture which emerges from research, from that of Dorothy Wedderburn in the 1960s to that of Sara Arber and her colleagues in the 1980s, on the relationship between pensioners and younger relatives, friends and neighbours, is not one of simple dependency of the old upon the young, but of an exchange relationship to which both sides contribute which shifts only gradually over time towards the younger participants being the predominant givers (Cole and Utting, 1962; Gilbert et al., 1989; Evandrou et al., 1986) providing a significant volume of services which would otherwise be a costly burden on the state.

Now that we have learnt to take account of the unpaid domestic labour of younger women as positive inputs into the economy (Piachaud, 1985; Joshi, 1987a), it is time to extend this approach to the variety of unpaid activities of older people if we are to obtain an accurate picture of their role in the economy and of the extent to which they are a net 'burden' upon it. It is clear that the simple conception of them as a burden will not do, in view of their roles as consumers, producers and suppliers of services.

In addition there is a mass of evidence that a very high proportion of people in their sixties and seventies are physically capable of remaining longer than they do in the formal labour market. A good deal of research carried out in Britain and elsewhere between the late 1940s and the present, chiefly by industrial sociologists and psychologists, demonstrates fairly con clusively that a high proportion of people in their sixties and seventies can work effectively at their accustomed or preferred occupation, even when this is physically quite heavy or makes significant intellectual demands. The quality of work produced even by mathematicians appears to decline little over their careers, contrary to popular belief. At many tasks workers in their sixties and seventies can out-perform those in their twenties, though not those at their peak in their thirties and early forties. Losses in speed and agility are compensated by greater experience, concentration and motivation. A certain mental and physical deterioration of course occurs with age, but its speed and effects are popularly exaggerated. Practice keeps most skills at a high level. If kept in tune such facilities as memory, flexibility and capacity to make decisions do not easily decline. Furthermore most workers are under-stretched for much of their working lives and have spare capacity on which to call at later ages. Older people may take longer to retrain for new tasks than younger, but not to a degree that makes such retraining not worth while. The greatest disability of older people in the labour market is the erroneous belief of employers and the population at large that competence at most tasks declines seriously with age. It does not and very few people decline in all spheres of competence at once. The mental functioning and range of capabilities at any age is related at least as much to expectation and habit as to age and physical condition, hence the underused capacity in almost any population at any time is considerable. Problems are most likely to arise for older workers where work is at a fast continuous pace, fixed at a pace suited to younger workers and over which the worker has no control, or where there are other time pressures. Where these problems are absent there appears to be little that a reasonably fit older person cannot do with an efficiency equivalent to a high proportion of younger workers (see Stones and Kozma, 1985 for a good survey of research findings in this field). 'It is clear that as a piece of anatomical and physiological machinery, the human organism becomes progressively impaired from the late twenties onwards. The effects of the impairments are, however, substantially offset by learning and experience' (Welford, 1985, p. 360).

All of this supports the growing insistence of many gerontologists that we should conceive of the elderly as a *resource* not as a burden. However, as a resource of *what* is a question in a flagging economy which is unlikely in the near future to be in search of recruits to the labour force from marginal groups, as it was in the days of labour shortage in the 1950s (Harper and Thane, 1989). Things may perhaps be different in the next century. The evidence does indicate in a high-employment economy the proportion of workers to non-workers can be kept up by keeping more people in full-or part-time work past the current retirement age. However, apart from the question of whether the British economy will be in this condition in the future, the experience of the last attempt, in the 1940s and 1950s, to keep older workers in the labour force is not very encouraging (Hannah, 1986). It was not very successful, and reversing culturally well-established retirement practices is unlikely to be easy.

In the short run it may be more realistic to build upon the commitment of formal and informal voluntary service which already exists among the elderly. Indeed they are being mobilized in some of the innovative caring schemes mentioned above. The fit 'young elderly' are already an important resource for caring for the very old and may more become so.

Conclusions

To sum up: to some, uncertain, degree the needs of the elderly at any point in time are not fixed but are malleable in response to policy and environmental changes. At no time is it sufficient simply to extrapolate from current costs and patterns of use to the future. There is, of course, something risible about proposing that armies of 70-year-olds should come to the rescue of those older still, and by no means all of those who will be among the young elderly in the year 2010 will want to perform that role. But the central point is that we need firmly to shift out of the mode of thinking that assumes that at pensionable age most people become useless burdens; to realize that most of them have at least as much to offer as many people in their twenties, and hence actively seek ways to use their abilities positively. It is necessary to be aware that future conditions and demands may be very different from those of the present. It is quite inadequate, when assessing the relationship of the elderly to the economy, just to aggregate the costs of services; their inputs should be taken into account. It is essential to work with a more complex picture of who the elderly are and of their role in society than the simple, depressing picture of a costly burden. And research must be concentrated on the needs of the very elderly and how to meet them.

Acknowledgements

The research project 'The Social Construction of Old Age in Britain 1945–1965' on which Sarah Harper collaborated with Pat Thane was financed by the ESRC under the Ageing Initiative of the Social Affairs Committee. Other projects in this initiative are also reported in the volume edited by Margot Jeffreys cited below.

The graphs for this chapter were contributed by Susan Owen. Mr Kingo Tamai, Osaka City University, is gratefuly acknowledged for supplying table 5.3.

Selected Key Reading

Grundy, Emily 1986: Ageing: Age Related Change in Later Life. In J. Hobcraft and M. Murphy (eds) (forthcoming): *Population Research in Britain*. Oxford: Oxford University Press.

Ermisch, John F. 1983: *The Political Economy of Demographic Change*, London: Heinemann for the Policy Studies Institute.

Jeffreys, Margot (ed.) 1989: *Growing Old in Twentieth-Century Britain*. London: Routledge.

Department of Health and Social Security 1984: *Population, Pension Costs and Pensioners' Incomes*, London: HMSO.

6 Education and Changing Numbers of Young People

Ian Diamond

Introduction

The large decline in the number of births in Britain between 1964 and 1976 led, in turn, to a decline in the number of school age children. Education is one of Britain's resources which is channelled predominantly to young people and expenditure on it is thus very sensitive to changes in their numbers. Informed policymaking in education is dependent on accurate forecasts of the future demand for places. For education up to the age of 16, the minimum school leaving age, forecasts of the number of potential pupils in a particular school or area will reflect trends in births and migration. After the age of 16, there are many other factors which influence demand for educational places. As well as demographic trends these include such social and economic factors as alternative opportunities for employment and the supply of places.[1]

This chapter demonstrates the important role which demographic data and projections play in planning education provision. It focuses specifically on the contribution of demographic projections to education planning in the context of declining numbers of young people in the 1980s and 1990s. However, decisions regarding the provision of education cannot be based solely on demographic trends. For example, the decline in numbers of young people could be a chance to improve educational standards, thus making Britain better prepared to enter the next century and to manage the demands of an ageing population. This chapter will therefore also discuss the implication of alternative strategies of education planning.

The Provision of Compulsory Education

The area of education most dependent on the number of births is compulsory schooling. In Britain compulsory schooling starts at age five and continues to

[1] This chapter concentrates on state provision for education at ages 5 and above. There is no discussion of pre-school or private education.

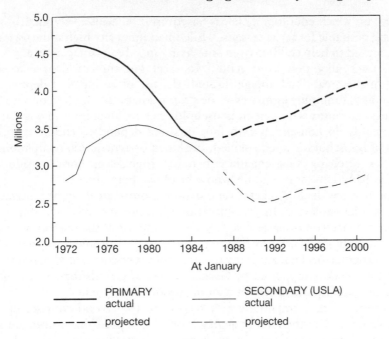

At January

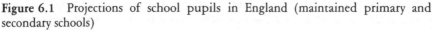

──────── PRIMARY actual	──────── SECONDARY (USLA) actual
─ ─ ─ ─ projected	─ ─ ─ ─ projected

Key: USLA - under school leaving age

Figure 6.1 Projections of school pupils in England (maintained primary and secondary schools)
Note: USLA – under school leaving age.
Source: DES (1986a)

age 16, to which it was raised from 15 in 1972. The decline of around 35 per cent in the number of births between 1964 and 1977 led rightly to a review of the provision of educational places. Figure 6.1 shows the forecasts of the numbers of pupils in primary and secondary education to the year 2000 (Department of Education and Science (DES), 1986a). This echoes the fluctuations in the number of births discussed in chapter 2. At a macro level the decisions could involve the option of a reduction in the number of teachers and the closing of some schools, which keeps the cost per child constant and reduces total expenditure; or the improvement of educational standards through reducing the number of pupils per teacher and therefore increasing unit costs.

However, compulsory education in Britain is essentially provided at a local level and the number of pupils at a particular school can be subject to rapid fluctuations as a result of factors such as changing economic circumstances or new housing developments. In addition, economic costs may not be the only criteria on which education policy is based: in rural areas a very small school may be desirable for social reasons, while in an inner city high unit costs may be accepted to help children overcome living in a disadvantaged area.

Resource allocation from central to local government does take into account the areal disadvantage through the use of an index of deprivation derived by combining estimates of the proportion of the children under 17 in the local authority who were in households lacking amenities; in one-parent households; in households with four or more dependent children; with a head of household in a semi-skilled, unskilled or agricultural occupation; in families receiving supplementary benefit; themselves born outside the United Kingdom, or in a family whose head was born abroad.

There is considerable debate over the most appropriate index of deprivation in particular situations. In the context of educational deprivation this index can be criticized on two grounds. First there is no use of the proportion of the population in local authority housing. In chapter 7 Murphy shows that net of many other factors local authority tenants still experience added deprivation. Murphy's work is supported by Garner (1988) who finds that, in Glasgow, tenancy is an important determinant of school achievement.

Garner's work is important with respect to the second criticism of this deprivation index; the level of aggregation. She reports that within areas of medium deprivation there can be pockets of extreme deprivation. In the context of educational provisions this could imply that a school in such an area should be allowed to have a very high unit cost. Sufficient funds for this may not be allocated if the allocation is based on the medium deprivation of the larger area.

The need to control for both the individual and areal characteristics is demonstrated by table 6.1 taken from Garner (1988). The probability of

Table 6.1   Probability of advantaged and disadvantaged school leavers qualifying for entry to Higher Education

Disadvantaged (home) Disadvantaged (area)	0.03	Disadvantaged (home) Advantaged (area)	0.22
Advantaged (home) Disadvantaged (area)	0.26	Advantaged (home) Advantaged (area)	0.70

Note: Advantaged school leavers   *Disadvantaged school leavers*

Advantaged school leavers	Disadvantaged school leavers
Father in social class I or II	Father in social class IV or V
Mother's education – beyond 15	Mother's education – not beyond 15
Father's education – beyond 15	Father's education – not beyond 15
Family with fewer than 4 siblings	Family with more than 4 siblings
Male	Female
Area with mean deprivation score equivalent to Bearsden, a very advantaged area.	Area with mean deprivation score equivalent to Easterhouse, a very disadvantaged area.

Source: Garner (1988)

achieving the minimum qualifications to enter higher education (three Highers)[2] varies between advantaged and disadvantaged areas after controlling for the individual's demographic and familial characteristics.

It is clear that a comprehensive review of both the variables to be included in the deprivation index and the level of disaggregation to be used is necessary and Hobcraft's call for more work in this area in chapter 9, is timely.

School Roll Forecasting

Funds allocated from central to local government are passed on to individual schools. This allocation requires information on the future demand for places in particular schools – school roll forecasts. There are five main ways in which these forecasts are used: for resource allocation in the near future; to plan longer-term capital expenditure; to assess planned admission limits for schools; to aid reorganization; and to help forecast the future budget for the local authority – both educational and corporate.

It has long been the view of central government that these forecasts are much more accurate if they are made at a local rather than at a national level (Hammond, 1984). This is because they will always be small area forecasts. There is a large literature on small area forecasting techniques (e.g. Platek et al., 1987). The best tend to require the use of ancillary information, such as, in this context, headteachers' estimates of future rolls.

The choice of data and the accuracy required of the forecasts depends on the use to be made of particular forecasts and the time scale to which they relate. Resource allocation in the near future requires accurate information not only for each school but within a school for each year. These forecasts will be based on information on the number of children in a school augmented by headteachers' estimates. In general, mistakes here are small, and can be corrected the next year.

Medium-term forecasts, say up to five years ahead, are often made for primary schools using recent birth records, together with ancillary information from health records, headteachers and on proposed housing development. Secondary school forecasts also use these sources together with information from current primary school rolls and data on the recent patterns of movement between local primary and secondary schools. The effect of housing developments is usually dismissed as being small unless the developments are very large – typical estimates are around one half a child aged 0–16 per household.

It is for longer-term forecasts that accuracy becomes harder to achieve. This

---

[2] Highers are the public examinations set by the Scottish Certificate of Education Examinations Board and sat by the majority of Scots school pupils at the age of 17.

is because they require information on future births and migration, for which accurate predictions at a local level are always difficult, and because the ancillary information available will also be less detailed. However, as Simpson (1987) observes these longer-term forecasts are required to inform policymakers of the potential costs and benefits of alternative strategies as well as for general monitoring. Therefore they need only be made at a higher level of aggregation and should highlight potential peaks and troughs. The accuracy of point estimates of pupil numbers is not paramount but it is essential to produce a range of forecasts under different assumptions.

In the main, most Local Education Authorities (LEAs) use a similar method of forecasting. In his excellent review, Simpson (1987) calls this a cohort survival method. The numbers in each year are progressively multiplied by some survival ratio to forecast the number going on to the next year, with ancillary information added in as appropriate. However, there are many variations in the data available and in the forecasts produced.

Among the most common are first, variations in the data available to obtain estimates of the population aged less than five in an LEA. Health Authority data are often used but their quality varies. For example, in the Cambridgeshire Health Authority, Jenkins and Walker (1985) found that data were around 20 per cent in error. Second, little is known about the accuracy of the estimates of the number of school pupils who will come from recent and future housing developments. Third, there is variation in the level of disaggregation, both demographic and geographic, at which school roll forecasts are made. Simpson (1984) argues that for compulsory education disaggregation by demographic characteristics is not particularly useful. However, for post-compulsory education (between ages 16 and 18) 'staying-on' rates by, say, gender and social class are essential. This subject will be dealt with fully with respect to higher education in the second part of the chapter. A clear example of the need to allow for demographic characteristics when forecasting staying-on rates is provided by Mao Qing and Mar Molinero (1986) who demonstrate that LEA forecasts of the number of school pupils aged 16–18 in Southampton are too low because they fail to take into account variations in enrolment by social class and geographic location. A good review of the major determinants of staying on is provided by Pissarides (1981). The key is that disaggregation is only necessary if there are distinct differences between the levels of the variable under question.

Fourth, it may be necessary to allow for potential policy decisions. For example, forecasts may be made for a group of schools and then the results of different patterns of parental choice can be simulated. Such forecasts will need to take into account planned admission limits for particular schools and can be of great benefit when planning school reorganization.

In summary there is a need for a unified approach to school roll forecasting based on demographic data augmented by local information. Such an approach should also build in the potential for tests for accuracy as well as the flexibility to assess different policy decisions.

Reorganization and Parental Choice

The impact of the decline in fertility between 1964 and 1977 on the numbers of children enrolled in schools in England and Wales is illustrated in figure 6.1. This decline led to a review of provision, and the DES issued its circular on The Falling Numbers and School Closures to LEAs in 1977 (DES, 1977). This stated that full consideration would be given to 'any social or other problems that may arise', but that 'the general policy would be for the Secretary of State to approve proposals to cease to maintain under-used schools.'

Pressure on LEAs to reduce provision was increased after the change of government in 1979 and the 1980 Education Act permitted LEAs to open, close or substantially alter schools without central government approval. The 1980 Act also made it possible for parents to send their children to a school of their choice provided that places are available in their chosen school. To encourage LEAs to accelerate the reduction of places the DES issued another circular in 1981 (DES, 1981) which asked the LEAs to inform the DES how they intended reducing the number of places available.[3]

The procedures for closure allow for periods of consultation and these have often led to bitter disputes within the community with the result that decisions regarding closure are delayed, or based on non-scientific data. As a result local authorities have often referred the matter to the Secretary of State (85 per cent of cases between 1980 and 1985 according to Audit Commission, 1986). This has led to further delays. Meredith (1984) had not been alone in calling for the Secretary of State to reply within a specified length of time. He argues further that from a legal point of view objectors have few opportunities to present an effective case.

These procedures are essentially intended to assess the social costs of school reorganization. For these discussions to take place in an effective manner, accurate forecasts are needed over the medium term. These will require, in addition to the factors described in the previous section, an allowance for the effect of increased parental choice. In two excellent papers Adler and Raab look at the effects of parental choice in Dundee and Edinburgh (Adler and Raab, 1987; Raab and Adler, 1988). They analysed data on requests to place pupils in particular schools together with census-based area deprivation indices and school-based characteristics. Their findings are now summarized briefly.

[3] The procedures in Scotland are rather different. A concise review is provided by Adler and Bondi (1986).

Requests to place pupils in particular schools have been increasing during the 1980s. The trends tend to be that schools either gain or lose pupils with little interchange. Most moves are of a short distance and into larger schools, away from schools in areas with a high proportion of local authority housing, towards less disadvantaged areas and to schools with high academic attainment.

These trends are perhaps not surprising but it should be noted that the result will be for schools in disadvantaged areas to lose pupils and to increase their unit costs per pupil. Mar Molinero (1988) points out that this often leads to a negative correlation between school cost and attainment. This creates grounds for closure of the less popular school and thus reduces educational provision in the more deprived area.

An allied but unresearched question is that of the extent of parents moving house within an area towards a popular school. This means that parents would not need to request the preferred school over a less favoured alternative. Anecdotal evidence such as provided by N.S. Groves (1986) exists but there is currently little systematic research in this area.

A comprehensive review of contemporary school reorganization is beyond the scope of this paper. However, it is apparent that there is a need for clear procedures which allow rational decision-making taking into account specific factors at a local level. A very sensible scenario for primary schools is suggested by Adler and Bondi (1988) who propose the following division of responsibilities:

1 *central government* – to balance the competing expenditure claims of education and other public expenditure programmes, and to provide a general framework for the education authorities, which are actually responsible for the provision of primary and secondary education
2 *local authorities* – to decide, within the broad financial constraints laid down by central government, what priority should be given to education at a local level; to formulate, within the statutory framework, general policies for local education provision, and, where appropriate, to allocate resources to local communities
3 *the local community* – to decide within the broad financial constraints laid down by the local authority and in accordance with more general policies, what pattern of schooling woud be best suited to the needs of the local community.

This approach would require improved provision of information from local government to the community and hence increased accessibility of school roll forecasts. These debates must be informed and the guidelines for forecasts outlined in the previous section would provide a sound basis for practice.

Forecasting the Demand for Higher Education

The reviews of primary and secondary provision were followed, in turn, by a review of higher education (HE) provision. Higher education is defined in the 1988 Education Reform Bill as courses leading to degrees, higher diplomas or to professional examinations where the standard is higher than that of the advanced ('A') level of the General Certificate of Education. Therefore it comprises courses which will typically require a high level of school qualifications, and when forecasting demand for HE it is necessary to consider the social and demographic characteristics of those achieving such qualifications. Higher Education in Britain is divided into two sectors. The university sector receives funds directly from government while the public sector is funded through local authorities – public sector institutions, such as polytechnics and teacher training institutions, tend to be rather smaller and offer more vocational courses than universities.

The DES (1978) outlined five possibilities for dealing with the declining number of school leavers. One extreme assumption was that demand would mirror the demographic decline, while at the other extreme there would only be a shallow decline in demand due to increases in both the proportions of school leavers wanting to advance their education and in the number of mature entrants. In Britain, 15 per cent of the 18–24-year-old population are enrolled on higher education courses. This is somewhat less than France (19 per cent), Japan (21 per cent) or the Netherlands (22 per cent) and far less than the U.S.A. (44 per cent), (DES, 1987). If the British proportion were increased in the 1990s then this would only have the effect of bringing Britain into line with her industrial competitors and, presumably, investing for the future.

The DES made explicit forecasts, DES (1983), which acknowledged that both demand for HE and the decline in fertility was not uniform across social classes. Accordingly they forecast a decline in demand in the thirteen years after 1982/83 of around 25 per cent rather than around 35 per cent as implied by the general demographic decline (see Jones, 1981).

These papers led to a number of alternative forecasts being produced (Diamond and Smith, 1982, 1984; Association of University Teachers (AUT), 1983; Committee of Vice-Chancellors and Principals (CVCP), 1983; Collins, 1983). Each projected that there would be little, if any, decline in the demand for HE relative to 1980/81 levels. The subsequent debate led the government to prepare a new set of forecasts (DES, 1984a). These were characterized by a much shallower decline in the demand for HE into the 1990s than previously. The DES (1986b) updated their forecasts in 1986 to suggest that there will be no decline in the demand for HE relative to

1985/86 entry levels. In this respect all commentators now agree. The 1987 Green Paper on Education was notable in that it forecast an increase in the number of students in HE in the 1990s.

The reasons for the conflict in the various forecasts lie in the fact that the demand for higher education depends on a multiplicity of factors including the distribution of entrants into HE by age, gender, social class, region of residence, parental qualification and family size; the effects of unemployment and comprehensive education; the national demand for graduate-level skilled labour; and last, but by no means least, the effect of the supply of places on demand.

Methodological Considerations in Forecasting the Demand for HE

Two approaches to forecasting the demand for HE have been commonly used – component forecasts, and aggregate forecasts based on national age participation rates. The choice is often dictated by the availability of appropriate data. Lack of data is not a new problem – Burnhill (1985) cites Moser and Layard (1964), who in a paper on planning the scale of HE, stated that 'on many important topics there were no data at all', and that 'we lacked comprehensive data on the school background and GCE performance of students in different sectors of higher education.'

Many of the recent forecasts (Diamond and Smith, 1982, 1984; Diamond, 1985; AUT, 1983; Collins, 1983) have been limited to the university sector because the existence of the Universities Central Council for Admissions (UCCA) means that some individual level data are available at a national level. Such data have not been available for the public sector in England and Wales until the OPCS Survey of School Leavers (Redpath and Harvey, 1987). Scotland has historically collected more comprehensive data and the Scottish Educational Data Archive at the University of Edinburgh permits comprehensive analyses over time of the characteristics of Scottish school leavers entering HE.

The aggregate approach, used by the DES, first forecasts the number of qualified school leavers and then multiplies this by the proportion entering HE. The problems with this approach lie in the fact that the influence of individual components cannot be assessed. In particular these forecasts assume implicitly that individuals demanding HE will accept the best offer they receive even if the institution is not their first choice and would require them crossing the divide between the university and public sectors.

Component forecasts are common throughout demography. For example, population projections for England and Wales are made by aggregating separately the components of fertility, mortality and migration. For HE such forecasts have been confined to the university sector as data are not available for the public sector. Specific rates of the demand for HE from individuals with particular characteristics – these typically include age, gender and social class – are calculated and then forecasts are made of the future demand from individuals with these characteristics. It is to be hoped that data become available to permit this type of forecast for the whole of HE.

Two further approaches have been proposed. The first is the use of econometric forecasts (Fildes, 1985). These have been used retrospectively by Pissarides (1982) who showed that the percentage of the 18-year-old cohort gaining two or more A-levels had responded to changes in real permanent income and the ratio of expected earnings of manual workers to university graduates. He also found that the proportion of school pupils staying on after the minimum school leaving age responded to changes in registered adult unemployment.

The second is to model the transition between compulsory schooling and finishing HE (Royal Statistical Society) (RSS), 1984). At any age an individual could enter one of a number of states such as university, work or a polytechnic. This approach would model the probability of moving between different states. Unfortunately very comprehensive data would be required as there are many possible flows through HE. It seems unlikely that adequate data will be available in the near future.

Factors influencing the demand for HE

The reason for the increasing size of forecasts of the demand for HE into the 1990s has been the recognition of the offsetting effects of a number of factors on the falling numbers of eighteen-year-olds. Table 6.2 contains a list of many of these factors. Most component forecasts have allowed explicitly for at least two out of gender, social class and age (Diamond and Smith, 1982, 1984; Diamond, 1985; AUT, 1983; CVCP, 1983; Collins, 1983) and the DES have discussed their effects thoroughly (DES, 1984b). In addition, Burnhill, Garner and McPherson (1987a,b), and Diamond (1988) have considered the effects of parental education on demand for HE in Scotland.

The first requirement of any forecast is to choose the base year from which it will start. The essential criterion is that data are available to assess actual

Table 6.2 Factors influencing the demand for higher education in Britain

Major factors	*Secondary factors*
Gender	Region of residence
Social class	Unemployment
Age at entry	Demand for skilled labour
Parental education	Comprehensive education
Supply of places	Social climate
Family size	Overseas students

demand. There are few data available which explicitly measure demand and all forecasts have used the number of entrants as a proxy. This means that the base year's entry must reflect unconstrained demand. The DES (1983, 1984a, 1986b) have used the most recent year for which data are available, arguing that although there were government-induced reductions in the entry of UK students to universities in the early 1980s these were more than offset by increases in the public sector. Demand was thus satisfied for HE as a whole, although clearly there would be unsatisfied demand for particular courses or institutions.

Diamond and Smith (1982, 1984) and Diamond (1985, 1987) have argued that there is little evidence that all students not admitted to their first-choice institution will be prepared to substitute an alternative institution particularly if this is one from a different sector. Instead they may be prepared to delay entry. This means not only that forecasts must be made for each sector separately but that the base year should be the last one for which there were no constraints on the supply of places. Diamond and Smith base their forecasts for young UK entrants to university on 1980. In another context Mao Qing and Mar Molinero (1986) argue that for school pupils staying on at school after the minimal school leaving age the mid-1970s were the last time that external factors such as high youth unemployment did not influence demand.

In summary, it seems rather unlikely that forecasts taking the mid-1980s as a base year can claim to be measuring demand accurately. At the very least the government forecasts should provide a sensitivity analysis of the effects of using different base years.

Gender

One of the most important trends of the past 20 years in HE has been the increased participation of women. At all levels of education the ratio of women to men has been increasing steadily. Figure 6.2 shows these ratios for four levels of education: first, achieving five or more O-levels; second, gaining two or more A-levels; third, applying to, and fourth, being accepted for admission to university. For example, between 1970 and 1982 the ratio of women to men achieving two or more A-levels rose steadily from 75:100 to 95:100 and the corresponding ratio for university entrants rose from 40:100 to 70:100. Given these trends it was perhaps surprising that in 1984 the DES (1984b) assumed that, despite this steady increase, the sex ratio at university entry would remain constant at its 1982 levels. Figure 6.3 is adapted from DES (1984b) to include two alternative scenarios. The first (a) is that the ratio would continue to increase and would approach even numbers during the 1990s. The second (b) suggests that the ratio may not increase as steadily in the mid-1980s as it had hitherto because the freeze on places and the shift towards science and technology would militate against women. However, as the number of 18-year-olds in the population declined, this effect would

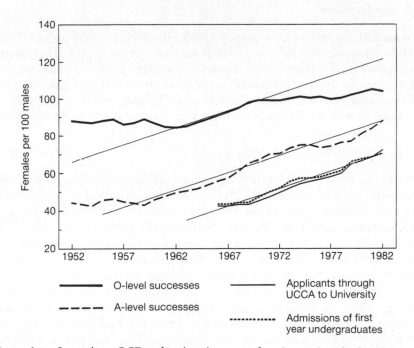

Figure 6.2 Sex ratio at GCE and university entry: females per hundred males
Note: O and A level results: England and Wales to 1976, England only after 1976. University data refer to home students only
Source: Smith (1985)

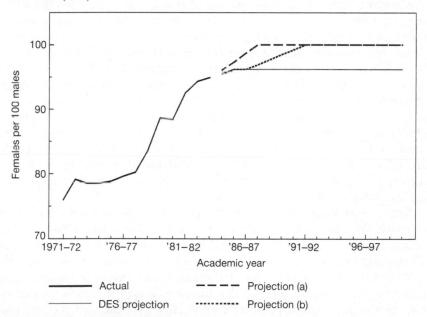

Figure 6.3 Sex ratio of qualified school leavers: actual and projected
Note: Qualified leavers are defined as those with 2 or more A-levels.
Source: DES (1984b) and author's variants

reduce and the ratio would increase again. The DES's 1986 forecasts (DES, 1986b) allow the ratio to increase a little but still not to equality. There seems little reason why the proportion of women entering HE should not equal that of men in the future, particularly as research from Scotland (Raffe, 1984; Willms and Kerr, 1986; McPherson and Willms, 1987) shows that in Scotland women are not outperforming men in all SCE school examination.

Social Class and Parental Education

One of the major factors influencing forecasts of the demand for HE has been the social class of the entrant. Since 1945 the distribution of university entrants by social class has been relatively stable with around 60 per cent coming from upper non-manual backgrounds (social classes I and II) (Robbins, 1963; UCCA, 1986), a group which until recently have comprised only around 18 per cent of the births. Although the entrants to public sector HE do have a higher proportion from lower non-manual and manual backgrounds (social classes III-V) they are still in the minority (Redpath and Harvey, 1987). If the distribution of births by social class between 1965 and 1976 and the propensity of each class to enter HE had remained constant then this would not have affected the demand for HE. However, as figure 6.4 shows there was actually a small increase in the number of births to parents from social classes I and II over this period while births to parents in social classes III–V declined.

A major reason for this contradiction of trends was a change in the structure of British employment away from manufacturing towards service industries in which there are a higher proportion of non-manual occupations. Associated with this trend is intra-generational social mobility of parents between the birth of a child and its reaching the age of 18. The DES (1984b) argue that the effect of such mobility is small compared to that of the change in occupational structure. They assume that any movement is upward and of no more than one (numeric) social class. Burnhill, Garner and McPherson (1987) have demonstrated that, in Scotland at least, there is much more mobility. Using data on Scottish school leavers in 1981/82 they find that only around one half had not experienced social mobility between birth and leaving school. Around two thirds of the mobile increased their social class while around one third moved downward.

Intra-generational mobility raises the question of assimilation – the extent to which the educational performance of the children whose fathers have changed classes resembles that of the children of the established members of a particular social class. In the absence of any data on assimilation the DES (1984b) fitted two models – No Assimilation and Full Assimilation – and prefer the former on the grounds that for males it appeared to fit the experience of the past ten years rather better. However, Burnhill, Garner and

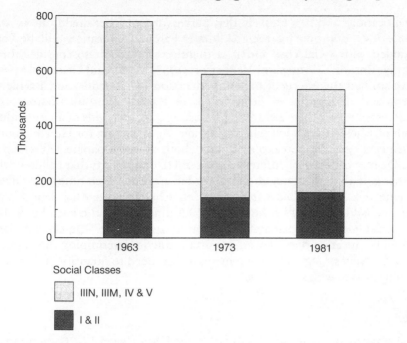

Figure 6.4 Legitimate births by social class, England and Wales
Source: DES (1984b)

McPherson (1987) disagree with the DES (1984b) finding. They report that the odds of qualifying for HE for the upwardly mobile are doubled relative to those who have stayed in the same social class. Furthermore, they do not find a 'downward assimilation' among the downwardly mobile and propose the existence of a 'ratchet effect' which could lead to increased demands for HE during periods of high gross social mobility.

The effects of the net changes in social class have been modelled explicitly for the university sector in a number of forecasts (Diamond and Smith, 1982, 1984; Diamond, 1985; AUT, 1983; Collins, 1983) as well as implicitly by the DES (1984a,b, 1986b).[4] These effects have been the most important single factor for which data have been available at a national level albeit only for the university sector.

There are now more parents either one or both of whom will have higher

---

[4] It has been suggested (Nichol, 1985) that while this may permit comparisons between UCCA data this may not be adequate for true comparisons with other sources. Subsequently Rudd (1988) has compared the measure of social class gained by UCCA with a full OPCS definition and found that in around 75 per cent of cases the two codings were identical while in the remaining 25 per cent there was typically not more than one class difference.

qualifications and it is unlikely that parents with higher qualifications will desire less education for their children. Parental education will be confounded with social class and it is therefore important to consider them jointly. Burnhill, Garner and McPherson (1987, 1988), and Diamond (1988) have studied the effects of parental education on the educational achievement and destination of Scottish school leavers. Burnhill, Garner and McPherson report that, controlling for social class, the odds of an individual both of whose parents left school after age 17 qualifying for HE are around seven times greater than a contemporary both of whose parents left school at 15. Diamond considers different sectors of HE and reports that children who do not gain the formal qualifications for HE are around ten times more likely to enter HE if both their parents had left school after age 17 than if both parents had left school by the age of 15. A drawback of these studies is that the variable defining parental education is rather crude. The evidence that parental education does play an important role in determining the demand for HE is very strong and there remains a clear need to quantify these effects in conjunction with social class.

Age

The majority of home entrants to HE in the UK are aged 17–20 – around 80 per cent of home entrants throughout the 1970s and early 1980s. It was this that first prompted the forecasts that there would be a dramatic decline in demand for HE as a result of the decline in the number of births between 1965 and 1976. However the early forecasts by the DES (1983) were flawed for two reasons. First they were based on an 'Age Participation Rate' (APR) defined as 'the number of young home initial full time and sandwich entrants to HE in a given year expressed as a percentage of the 18 year old population'. This approach has subsequently been adapted by the DES (1984a, 1986b) in what is termed an 'Age Participation Index', a weighted average of age-specification participation rates suggested by Diamond and Smith (1982, 1984) and by the CVCP (1983).

The second area of contention was the treatment of mature entrants. The DES (1983) assumed implicity that all mature entrants would come from a pool of qualified individuals who had deferred their entry into HE. They argued contentiously that high unemployment might cause mature entry rates to fall, 'perhaps because potential entrants would prefer to retain their existing employment rather than risk unemployment following a spell of full time higher education.' As a result the DES (1983) forecasts assumed that mature entry rates would fall at the same speed as the fall in 21–25 years olds – who constitute the majority of entrants to HE aged over 20.

These forecasts were criticized because both current practice and future intentions with regard to increased access to HE meant that many mature entrants to HE particularly in the public sector – who admit between 70 per cent and 80 per cent of mature entrants – do not possess the formal qualifications for HE. As a result the later DES (1984a, 1986b) forecasts considered the population of 21–25 year olds with only one A-level. The effect of this improved treatment of the mature entrants was the major component of the increase in the DES forecasts.

Other Factors Affecting the Demand for HE

In the main there has been little work to evaluate the effects of the other demographic and economic facators listed in table 6.2. However, the evidence suggests that the net effect of each factor will be to increase rather than decrease the demand for HE. First, it is unlikely that the decrease in family size will lead to a reduction in the demand for HE. In other societies parental expectations for the children have increased as the number of children decrease. In China, for example, the 'one-child' is known as the 'Little Emperor' and is the subject of very high parental expectations.

The effects of unemployment and of the economic situation on the demand for HE have been the subject of little study. The work by Pissarides (1982) described above is a notable exception. Also, Dolphin (1981) showed that demand for HE falls when the value of the student award is cut. In this paper separate equations were constructed for the university and public sectors with the effect of the value of student support being higher in the public sector. The DES (1984b) reports some work to identify a link between the proportion entering higher education of those qualified (QPI) and unemployment, and conclude from some aggregate level analyses that if these results are valid they imply that much of 2.1 per cent rise in QPI in 1981/82 could be attributed to the total increase in unemployment – from 1.8 million to 2.7 million between July, 1980 and July, 1981.

The RSS (1984) noted that comprehensive education (non-selective secondary education introduced over the 1960s and 1970s) may encourage demand, particularly from female students. McPherson and Willms (1987) have produced evidence for this. The region in which a child is brought up may also have an effect on the propensity to demand HE although this effect will be confounded with many of the factors listed above (see Rees, 1986).

Summary

The second part of this chapter has demonstrated the importance of considering demographic trends and other factors when making forecasts of the demand for HE. The choice between the two main approaches to forecasting demand for HE – aggregate and component – is often dictated by the availability of data which also affects whether the university and other sectors should be treated separately. It remains to consider whether the routine collection of data to permit component forecasts of HE could be justified.

There are many reasons in favour of component forecasts for each sector. The non-university institutions have more mature entrants, more without formal qualifications, more from social classes III–V, their effective length of course is shorter, and they will be less affected by a switch to longer science and engineering courses than will the university sector.

In addition, there is little evidence that qualified entrants who demand university education but who are not admitted will be prepared to substitute a public sector place. Between 1980/81 and 1982/83 the freezing of university places at a time when the cohort of 18-year-olds was increasing led to an increase in entry standards as measured by average A-level performance. The DES (1984b) estimate of those candidates qualified for university in 1980/81 but not in 1982/83 and who did not gain a university place in 1982/83 only 47 per cent went into public sector HE. Others presumably went into employment thus joining the pool of potential young mature age entrants.

The argument against component forecasts are those of cost. However, the main costs would be those of constructing a central data base comprising data already collected in most institutions. As the DES have agreed to update HE forecasts regularly such a development would be timely.

Conclusions

Most commentators would agree that Britain is likely to become a more technological society in future years and so it is likely that there will be an increased demand for a skilled workforce. Furthermore, the changing age structure of Britain's population described in the previous chapters will lead to increasing demands on the workforce of the twenty-first century to support an ageing population. It is essential, then, that Britain's young people – likely to be a decreasing proportion of its population – should be educated effectively. While few would disagree with such a statement it is probable that to achieve this goal education spending per pupil should be increased in real terms during the period of a decline cohort of young people.

This chapter has demonstrated the need to take account of demographic projections when planning education provision and has identified the main areas which should be considered when calculating such projections. However, it is also clear that such projections can only inform policymaking rather than dictate it and there remains a need for clear national guidelines on the provision of places at all levels of education.

There have been many statements arguing that access to education must be increased especially in higher education. It is clear that in the 1990s the demand will exist, particularly when demographic considerations such as changing family size are considered along with those already taken explicitly into account such as age and social class. The question of access is thus one of improving provision in the areas where demand is great.

Selected Key Reading

RSS 1985: Symposium on projections of student numbers in higher education. *J. Royal Statistical Society Series A*, 148, 175–213.
Simpson, Stephen N. 1987: School roll forecasting methods: A review. *Research Papers in Education*, 2, 63–77.

7 Housing the People: From Shortage to Surplus?

Michael J. Murphy

Introduction

Housing is clearly and directly associated with population trends: for example, a larger population will usually require a larger number of homes. However, the relationship is more complex than simply that between overall numbers of people and of dwellings (i.e. structurally distinct physical living areas). An increased number of children may not lead to more dwellings being required, but rather to the same number of larger homes; or may affect the types of homes needed, such as those with amentities like gardens: conversely, an ageing population, which tends to consist of smaller household sizes, may need a larger number of dwellings, perhaps smaller and with special requirements such as ease of access. Thus population numbers and age distribution affect housing needs directly: other demographic trends such as those in marriage, cohabitation and marital breakdown are also important.

Among policy areas, housing must clearly be responsive to demographic factors and therefore those concerned with housing should be aware of current demographic trends. However, it is less appreciated that in many cases the causality also appears to work in the opposite direction; that is, the nature of the British housing system tends to form and perpetuate major demographic differentials in terms of fertility, nuptiality and marital breakdown, and mortality.

The nature of the relationship is complex since it will be shown to interact closely with employment patterns as well, leading to a web of interacting 'careers'. The rest of this chapter is concerned with the description and policy implications of some of these aspects.

The household, the group of people who live together in a separate living space, is the main link between population and housing. Analysis of the structure of households can provide indicators of shortage such as the number of families doubling up, and show changing patterns of housing needs. I will discuss past and likely future trends in households and housing, and give particular attention to the experience of young people setting up home for the first time. The definition of a household varies between different statistical sources and, in particular, the definition of a household changed between the 1971 and 1981 Censuses of Great Britain. In the former one, a household was required to share meals as well as a living space, but the 'common cooking pot' concept was dropped from the 1981 Census. One result of this change was that the number of households enumerated was about 300 thousands more under the new definition or about $1\frac{2}{3}$ per cent (Todd and Griffiths, 1986). Analysis based on historical changes should take account of this fact. However, definitional factors pale into insignificance when compared with recent changes in household size.

Trends in Households: Past, Present and Future

In order to set the scene, figure 7.1 shows that average household size has fallen over the past century. It had been relatively constant for at least the

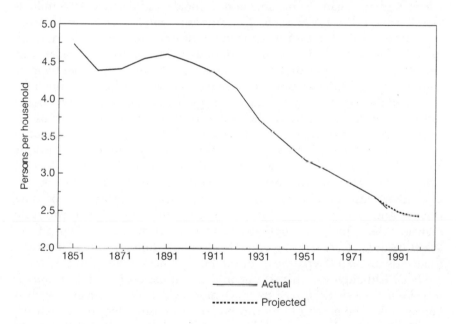

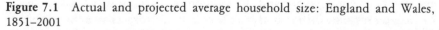

Figure 7.1 Actual and projected average household size: England and Wales, 1851–2001

Sources: Laslett (1972, p. 130); General Household Survey and Department of the Environment Official Projections (various years)

previous three centuries as shown by the work of the Cambridge Group for the History of Population and Social Structure (Laslett and Wall, 1972). However, since that time, there has been considerable change. Between 1951 and 1985, the population of Great Britain increased by 12 per cent, but the number of households increased far more – by about 40 per cent. This means that average household size in Great Britain fell from about 3.21 to about 2.56 persons over this period and this decline is expected to continue at least until to the end of the century (*Social Trends* 10, 1979, Table 2.3; *General Household Survey* 1985, 1987, Table 3.11; Department of the Environment, 1986a). Recent changes in large household sizes have been even more spectacular – in 1971 6 per cent of households contained six or more persons: by 1985, this figure had fallen to 2 per cent (*General Household Survey* 1985, 1987, Table 3.11). These falls have been due in part to straightforward changes in age structure: fewer children – who tend to increase average household size – and more elderly people – who tend to live in smaller households – will both lower the overall average household size. However, as will now be discussed, age structure is insufficient to account for observed changes.

The number of dwellings in Great Britain in 1981 was 21.2 million, considerably greater than the number of households, estimated as 19.5 million (*Social Trends* 17, 1987, Table 2.2; *Housing and Construction Statistics* 1976–1986, 1987, Table 9). Even if the number of households were to be suddenly increased, if, for example, all households consisting of more than one family were to split into single-family households, there would apparently still be a crude surplus of dwellings. However, this does not take account of the fact that some of the housing stock will be vacant for frictional reasons, or because of government policy, or its unattractiveness, or use as second homes: furthermore, some dwellings may be unfit, lacking amenities or requiring substantial repairs – in England alone two million had at least one of these physical problems in 1981 (*English House Condition Survey*, 1982, p. 3). Nevertheless, these data might suggest that a golden age of housing had arrived, but there is also clear evidence of substantial housing stress in Britain in the mid-1980s. House prices and house price inflation are high, and the number of people accepted by local authorities in England and Wales because of homelessness doubled from 53 thousands in 1978 to 103 thousands in 1986 (Department of the Environment 1980, Table 1: 1987, Table 1). Although this chapter can only look at national-level data, indicators of acute housing shortage are much more evident in certain areas such as London since the geographical distribution of housing does not match the availability of employment and the location of places in which people want to live, and regional differential price rises in houses exacerbate this problem. See chapter 8 for further discussion of the regional distribution of population.

These pressures are much greater among the young who are attempting to find their own accommodation for the first time. Before looking at this group, I will first consider some general trends. Between 1961 and 1971, the number of households in England and Wales increased by 2 million, and by a further 1.1 million in the decade up to 1981. Over this 20-year period, there were substantial changes in the types of households. Although care must be taken in interpreting data because of changes in definitions of households, and imprecision in terminology such as 'married couple', some trends are nevertheless clearcut.

The presentation of data on households is frequently based on the concept of the 'head of household', particularly by use of 'headship rates'. (The 'headship rate' for a particular group, such as single men aged 15 to 29, is the proportion of such men who are designated as 'head of household'.) While the concept of headship has been criticized on empirical and political grounds, see for example Murphy (forthcoming), it is necessary to use it here because it is the familiar way of presenting data and also because many data from earlier years are available only in this form.

Changes in the number of households may be broken down into those which can be attributed to the changing numbers in each age group and those attributable to changes in headship rates. The method is to show the number of households which would be found if the headship rate were to be kept constant at the values in each age-group in 1971, but allowing for actual changes in number of persons within these age groups. An alternative way is to undertake a similar exercise allowing for sex and marital status as well as age. The results of this exercise are shown in figure 7.2. Within each of these age groups, the difference between the 'observed' and 'age standardized' bars gives that change which is not attributable to changing numbers in the age group, and the difference between the 'observed' and 'age/sex/marital status standardized' bars gives the change attributable to changes in the headship rates for each marital status of each sex, at each age, i.e. to factors other than the change in the numbers in each age, sex and marital status group. The main feature is the increase of nearly two million in the number of elderly households in the period 1961 to 1981. This is largely due to the increase in the numbers of those over pension age during this period, rather than to changes in the propensity to live separate lives. As the figure shows, about three-quarters of the change in the number of elderly households would have occurred even if their household structure had remained unaltered. This increase has clear policy implications since these elderly people tend to live in the worst accommodation, and owners often have difficulties in undertaking their own, or paying for, maintenance.

However, there was also an increased tendency for the elderly to live independent lives. The proportions of elderly people living in households who were neither living alone nor as a couple on their own fell by about half in the period 1961 to 1981, so there is reduced scope for similar falls to occur

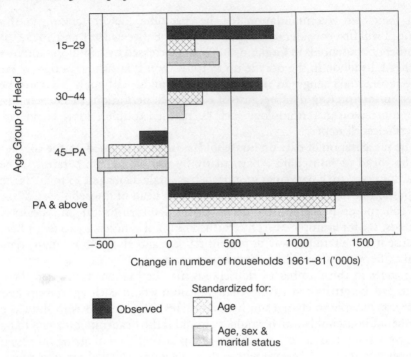

Figure 7.2   Change in number of households: observed and standardized, England and Wales, 1961–81

Notes: Standardized on 1971 age and age/sex/marital status specific headship rates
PA is conventional pensionable age of 65 for males and 60 for females.
Source: Census of Population England and Wales, 1961, 1971 and 1981

in the future. This greater propensity for elderly married and widowed people to live on their own was found in many developed countries as work by Richard Wall (1984, 1988) has clearly demonstrated. The reasons for this are diverse: the elderly are better off than formerly, but this is not a sufficient explanation. We do not have relevant data to investigate such topics as do countries such as Australia and the USA. From studies of these countries, there appears to be an unwillingness of the elderly to seek assistance from their younger kin, although paradoxically the young report that they are more willing to give help than the elderly are willing to seek it. While kin are a major source of support, especially when elderly people become unable to live on their own, a considerable number of the elderly have no kin to turn to for assistance: it has been estimated that about one quarter of elderly women aged 60 in the early 1970s had no surviving children (but the proportion will drop in years to come) (Timaeus, 1986).

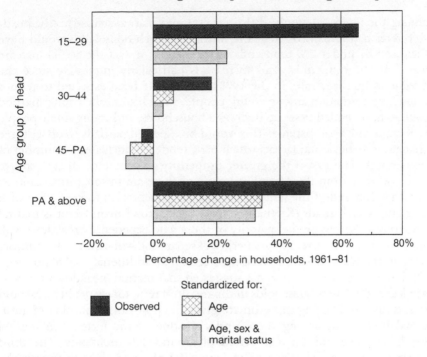

Figure 7.3 Percentage change in number of households: observed and stand-ardized, England and Wales, 1961–81
Note: See notes accompanying figure 7.2.
Source: see figure 7.2

The increased number of elderly households, coupled with increased life expectancy, is leading to a greater number of frail elderly widows living alone. Since they are increasingly owner-occupiers, they may find substantial financial as well as emotional costs in moving to a more suitable home. One result is considerable under-occupation among the elderly. The overall number of those above pension age in Great Britain is expected to remain very close to 10 million for the next 20 years. However, the numbers of the very elderly will increase substantially: there are likely to be 1.2 million people aged 85 and over in 2006 (*Population Projections* 1985–2025, 1987, Appendix II), an increase of 75 per cent over the 1986 figure. Present evidence suggests that the numbers of the elderly who will find difficulties in looking after themselves will therefore increase: for example, about 20 per cent of the 80-and-over group are likely to suffer from dementia (Grundy, 1986). The housing needs of the elderly, in particular, must be a prominent policy issue in years to come.

Figure 7.3 shows the values of figure 7.2 expressed as percentage change over the period 1961–81. The sharpest behavioural change has been found among the under-30 group: if the age, sex and marital status-specific head-ship rates had remained fixed, the number of such households would have increased by under 200 thousands in the period; in fact the actual increase was over 800 thousands. This increase is particularly impressive since the decline in marriage rates in the 1970s would have been expected to reduce household formation among young people, since historically young married couples have tended to set up their own households, and young single people to remain with their parents. This would be expected partially to offset three changes in behavioural factors which have tended to increase the number of households. The first is the greater propensity of people of all ages to live alone or away from their families; many of these are in cohabiting unions, and therefore reflect the failure of statistical presentation to keep pace with changing social trends (Kiernan, 1986a). The second main factor is marital breakdown. Although the majority of those who experience breakdown will find a new partner, a temporary period of separation will increase the number of households and it will also feed the need for an additional pool of housing. David Eversely (1983, p. 89) has suggested that marital breakdown on aver-age leads to 1.5 new households in the medium term for every old household that is dissolved. Using this estimate gives an approximate number of addi-tional households among those under 45 due to the increase in marital breakdown over this 20-year period of around 200 thousands. The third factor which is mainly relevant to young couples and their parents is the reduction in the proportion of young people who start off married life sharing with their parents (Murphy and Sullivan, 1985). The numbers of such couples living in someone else's household fell by three-quarters between 1961 and 1981.

Among those in the middle age band, that is between 30 and pension age, the main reasons for the rise in the number of households are the increase in marital breakdown and the tendency for non-married people to live on their own (Haskey, 1987a). These two emerging types of household have tradi-tionally sought their housing in the rented sector, both public and private. In this respect they are going against the trend of owner-occupation accounting for a larger and larger proportion of the housing stock – in 1986 about 63 per cent in Great Britain, up from 26 per cent in 1947 (*Social Trends* 18, 1988, Table 7; Donnison 1967, Table 10). [Estimates based on the proportion of owned dwellings give a figure about 3 percentage points higher than esti-mates based on the number of owner households from sources such as the *General Household Survey*.]

Since only adults set up households, all those who will do so in the next 15 years are alive now, and we can estimate accurately how many will actually be alive in each age group – except perhaps for the oldest age groups – for at least that period ahead. Other demographic factors which have a considerable influence on household formation are less easy to predict – one is marriage: for example, the 1978-based official population projections expected two-thirds more married men in the 20–24 age band than were actually found in 1985 (*Population Projections* 1978–2018. 1980; Sparks, 1986, p. 24). Another is marital breakdown which leads to additional housing requirements, even if remarriage ultimately takes place. While any set of projections will be subject to some error for these sorts of reasons, the official household projections produced by the Department of Environment have provided a generally satisfactory framework for consideration of likely future trends in household composition.

In the 1960s and 1970s, the growth in households has been concentrated largely among non-married couple households: the number of those headed by a married couple has remained relatively constant and it is only expected to grow by one million in the period 1961 to 2001. Therefore the proportion of households headed by a married couple has been decreasing through time – it was 74 per cent in 1971, 70 per cent in 1981, and is expected to be only about 55 per cent in 2001 in England and Wales (Department of the Environment, 1986a). Married and non-married couple households differ in their housing types: in 1981, 65 per cent of married couple households were owner-occupiers, but only 45 per cent of the others (1981 Census: *Housing and Households*, Table 15). If these proportions were to continue to apply to the projected household population, the proportion of owner-occupier households would fall from 58 per cent in 1981 to 55 per cent in 2001 (including allowance for difference in concepts of married male heads and married couple households). However, present government statements are envisaging up to 80 per cent of households being owner-occupiers. To achieve this target, something like 9 out of 10 married couples and two-thirds of the others – lone parent families, single people and flat sharers – would also have to be owners at the turn of the century. Demographic and economic trends make higher rates of owner-occupation increasingly difficult to achieve without further selective measures in favour of owing at the expense of renting. At present, subsidies to owner-occupiers in terms of mortgage interest tax relief and capital gains tax forgone on owner-occupied dwellings amount to £5 billion per annum: a sum about four times the total spent on National Health Service hospital buildings – i.e. capital spending (*Social Trends* 18, 1988, Table 7.33). Increasing further the proportion of owner-occupiers could be achieved by giving substantial inducements to potential owners, or by making the public rented sector less attractive, as is being done in a variety of ways in the late 1980s by the Conservative administration.

The changing demographic composition also has implications for the physical housing stock – trends towards non-family, smaller households suggest that the traditional three-bedroom house is becoming less appropriate for present needs. Although there has been a substantial move away from the building of three or more bedroom houses in recent years, they still accounted for 60 per cent of the total housing stock in 1986 compared with nearly three-quarters a decade earlier (*Housing and Construction Statistics* 1976–1986, Table 6.8, 1987). However, since new additions comprise under one per cent of the total stock each year, they will have only a trivial effect on the distribution of housing types in the near future (it should be noted that conversions of dwellings are not included in the figures given above).

Housing, Demographic and Employment Careers

So far, this chapter has been concerned mainly with the stock of dwellings and the stock of households. For most people, change of type or tenure of housing has been relatively infrequent once they have obtained a home of their own in either the owner-occupied or local authority sectors. However, some of the sharpest effects are seen at the point where household formation takes place since that usually means obtaining a home of one's own. Demographic circumstances around that time tend to have substantial effects on the type and quality of housing which many people will live in for the rest of their lifetimes.

The time of leaving home usually marks the point where accommodation must be found in the housing 'market' (using the term 'market' loosely). Patterns of leaving home are affected by housing availability – indeed the relatively late age at which British children leave home compared to many other countries is probably tied up with the lack of suitable type and tenure of housing for young single people (Kiernan, 1986a; Sullivan, 1984; Jones, 1987). However, at this time when there is an increasing desire among young people to move away, the traditional tenure of first resort, the privately rented sector, has been declining rapidly from 61 per cent of the total in 1947 to 10 per cent in the mid-1980s (Donnison 1967, Table 10; *Social Trends* 18, 1988, p. 132). As many commentators, including the Building Societies Association, have noted, owner-occupation is not an ideal tenure for young people who are often mobile and may neither want nor be able to afford owner-occupation. One consequence of the British housing system is that although young Britons leave home relatively late by European standards, they have some of the highest rates of owner-occupation in the world. This problem of the lack of suitable housing for young people is exacerbated by the large number of 20–24-year-olds in the 1980s due to the baby boom of the early 1960s. This is another area where it appears difficult to reconcile demographic and housing trends.

Even if young people do obtain a home in the privately rented sector, it is nearly always a transient tenure whether they are married or not. Over 90 per cent will subsequently obtain a home of their own in either the owner-occupied or local authority sectors (Murphy and Sullivan, 1985). Higher and higher proportions of young couples are in one of these sectors at or soon after marriage (Murphy, 1984; Holmans, 1981). It is between these two sectors that some of the sharpest demographic differentials are found, and I will argue that the unique nature of the British housing market tends to perpetuate and reinforce these differentials in terms of patterns of early marriage, high fertility and marital breakdown.

It is, of course, the case that those from relatively advantaged groups are more likely to obtain the socially preferred type of housing, namely owner-occupation, those whose parents are in higher social classes and/or owner-occupiers being more likely to do so. In 1983, the General Household Survey, which is the major source of data in this area, showed that among professional worker heads of household, 90 per cent were owner-occupiers, but only 28 per cent of unskilled workers were owner-occupiers (*General Household Survey* 1983, 1985, Table 6.13). The National Child Development Study, a longitudinal study of a group of children born in 1958, showed that the children of owner-occupiers had four times the chance of being in their own owned home rather than in a local authority rented home at age 23 in 1981, compared with those children who were in the local authority sector at age 7 (*Social Trends* 15, Table 8.11; see also Jones, 1987).

However, apart from their own and their parents' socio-economic characteristics, demographic factors such as early marriage and childbearing experience also have a substantial effect. Young single women with children are overwhelmingly likely to be living in local authority housing, and those who married early and/or had a pre-marital conception are more likely to do so as well. Figure 7.4 shows that women under age 50 who were still married to their first husband were more than three times as likely to be owner-occupiers than local authority tenants. Conversely, the reverse pattern was found for single women who had given birth who were five times more likely to be local authority tenants rather than owner-occupiers. In the mid-1980s, about one-third of first births are illegitimate as was discussed in chapter 3. Although the context of illegitimacy may be changing, in that relatively permanent cohabitation is essentially equivalent to formal marriage, if similar proportions of these women were to look towards the local authority sector in future, it would indicate a substantially increased need for public housing. It should be stressed that similar conclusions to those of figure 7.4 hold when comparisons are made within a particular social class to control for the fact that higher social classes are both more likely to marry late and to be owner-occupiers. Indeed when social class and housing tenure variables were included in a multivariate statistical analysis, the effect was to reduce the magnitude of social class effects, but to leave the housing ones largely intact (Murphy and Sullivan, 1986, Table 9). The more detailed and precise analyses on which

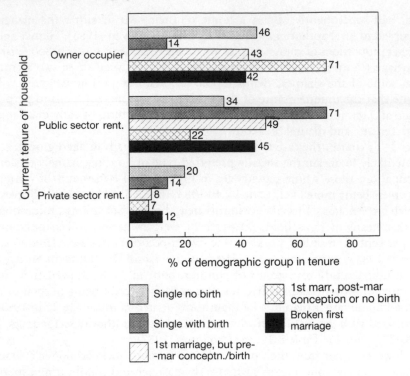

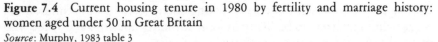

Figure 7.4   Current housing tenure in 1980 by fertility and marriage history: women aged under 50 in Great Britain
Source: Murphy, 1983 table 3

these conclusions are based are taken from the Office of Population Censuses and Surveys' 1976 Family Formation Survey (Dunnell, 1979), the latest available major national survey on this topic which includes detailed housing and fertility histories, but we simply don't have more up-to-date evidence on which to make judgements.

To return to the main topic itself, that of the nature of the relationship between housing and fertility, it can be argued that for those who choose a local authority tenancy, early childbearing, with or without marriage, is a rational strategy because it facilitates access to such a dwelling. There are a number of small-scale studies by researchers, such as Beatrix Campbell (1984) and Paul Willis (1984), that suggest that at least some young unemployed teenage girls see childbearing both as a method of obtaining fulfilment and a purpose to life since the usual source, that of paid work, is not available to them, and also as the only means of obtaining a home of their own. For owner-occupiers, on the other hand, the need to save for a deposit and other expenses, together with the relatively large mortgage payments in the early years means that two incomes are necessary for an extended period and therefore childbearing will be delayed. This may be illustrated by considering the position of a man on average wages whose wife doesn't earn, who has two children under 11, and who takes out a mortgage of three times annual income. With earnings of £188 per week (Nov. 1984 figures), the family would have a disposable income (after tax, national insurance and mortgage and typical rate payments, but including child benefit) of £89 per week: this is not much more than the Supplementary Benefit Long-term Scale Rate for that family of £76 per week at that time. Of course, mortgage payments will tend to be eroded by inflation, and eventually be paid completely. In contrast, rental payments are likely to form a more constant proportion of current pay over the life cycle. This 'front-loading' of mortgage payments in the early years of the mortgage (which very frequently coincides with the early years of marriage) will tend to require two earners at that time. On average, owner-occupiers have tended to marry about one year later and have their first birth about two years later than local authority tenants (Murphy and Sullivan, 1985).

A rational choice model is clearly oversimplified: the idea that couples have a free choice between sectors is – in both senses of the word – untenable: access to different types of housing is determined by 'constraint' as well as 'choice' (Rex and Moore, 1967). In Duesenberry's words if 'economics is all about how people made choices, sociology is all about why they don't have any choices to make' (1960, p. 233). For many, the idea of a free choice in housing is a sick joke, especially among the unemployed, those in insecure jobs, and for many in high house-price areas. Moreover, demographic factors such as unplanned pregnancy may also foreclose options. If a pregnancy is pre-marital, it trebles the relative risk of a couple ending up in the local authority sector rather than the owner-occupied one (Murphy, 1983). Nevertheless there is clear evidence that some couples have modified their childbearing patterns in order to obtain a particular type of housing (Busfield and Paddon, 1977; Madge and Brown, 1981). One consequence of this is that the sharp rise in the proportion of young couples in the owner-occupied sector over the post-war period (and the even greater number who aspire to this sector) must have had some effect in reinforcing fertility decline in Britain in recent decades although, of course, many developed countries have also experienced declines over this period, so it would be naive to emphasize this (or indeed any single cause) as the sole or primary explanation.

A consequence of these differences in the early years of marriage and childbearing is that fertility levels are much higher among those who live in the local authority rather than the owner-occupied sector – and fertility differentials by housing tenure are much greater than other conventionally used socio-economic variables such as social class, female employment, education, or income (see figure 7.5). This has the result that, in particular, large

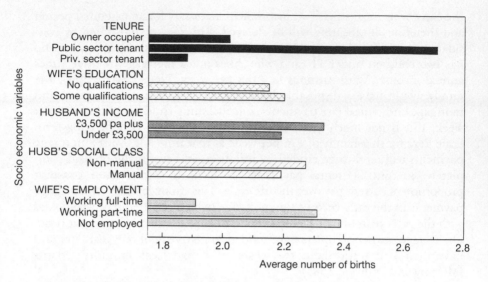

Figure 7.5   Births in current marriage to women aged 40–44 by selected socio-economic variables, Great Britain, 1977
Source: Murphy and Sullivan, 1985, table 1

families are very disproportionately concentrated in the local authority sector. We found roughly equal numbers of women in their forties with manual worker husbands in the local authority and owner-occupied sectors in the mid-1970s – but 29 per cent of the former group, and only 17 per cent of the latter, had had four or more children (Murphy and Sullivan, 1986, Table 8). This means that a higher proportion of children will be brought up in the local authority sector than figures for the distribution of tenure in their parents' age-band would suggest. Figure 7.6 shows that the average number of dependent children in the household is generally higher in the local authority sector, especially for young heads of household, but by the late forties, the younger ages of childbearing (and the earlier leaving-home patterns of those brought up in the local authority sector) mean that the values are very similar. (The privately rented sector has low values for a number of reasons: it contains a larger non-married proportion, and the form of stock is often considered to be less suitable for childrearing.)

As in the case of young people and privately rented accommodation, housing for families is another area where there is a clear mismatch between trends in housing policy and the demographic realities. Since 1979 nearly a million local authority homes have been sold to tenants, out of an initial stock of 7 million homes (*Social Trends* 15, Chapter 8, p. 123). The stock which has been sold has been disproportionately in the form of family

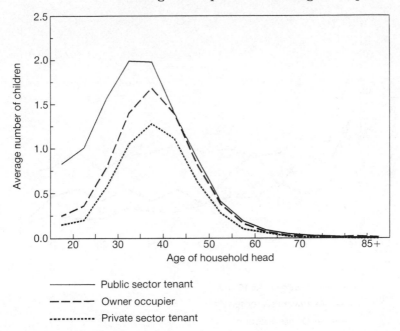

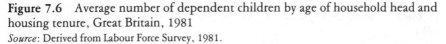

Figure 7.6 Average number of dependent children by age of household head and housing tenure, Great Britain, 1981
Source: Derived from Labour Force Survey, 1981.

houses. In 1982, a study found that only 2 per cent of sales in the previous six years had been flats (*General Household Survey* 1982, 1984, Table 5.44). Moreover, this ravaging of that part of the publicly owned stock which is most desirable and most in demand is not being made up by new building. In contrast to the private sector, the very small number of new public sector dwellings now being allowed to be built consists mainly of flats, under one-fifth being three or more bedroom houses (*Housing and Construction Statistics* 1976–1986, 1987), even though there are larger numbers of four or more child families living in local authority accommodation than the owner-occupier sector.

The first type of housing achieved is likely to have long-lasting implications – like childbearing. Rates of movement between tenure types have been very low (Murphy and Sullivan, 1983, Table 3.9). Childbearing acts as a powerful filter for channelling couples into one or other of the tenures and therefore it tends to reinforce the differences between groups. Each additional child makes it more likely that a couple who are not already local authority tenants will become so.

Since early influences are so important, early adult unemployment is

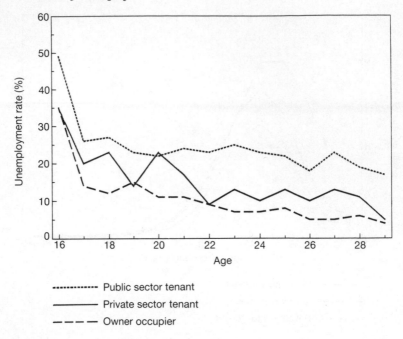

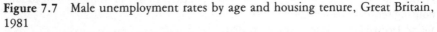

Figure 7.7   Male unemployment rates by age and housing tenure, Great Britain, 1981
Source: Murphy and Sullivan, 1987, table 1

clearly associated with life chances in many areas especially housing. It is also one where things have got much worse in the 1980s: in 1984, only 18 per cent of 16-year-olds were working compared to 61 per cent a decade earlier (Department of Education and Science, 1985). For the unemployed, rented accommodation is the only feasible type of housing, and, as figure 7.7 shows, they are disproportionately being found in the local authority sector. The overall differential is about two and a half to one. A subsequent government report repeated some of these analyses for England in 1984, and concluded that these differences had become drastically widened (*Labour Force Survey 1983 and 1984*, 1986, p. 45). They found that for married men who were household heads under age 45, the proportions 'out of work' (a wider concept than we used which included those who had given up looking for work because they didn't think any was available) was about nine times as high in the local authority as in the occupied sector. All these findings on the relationship between housing and unemployment are not substantially altered by allowing for the generally lower social status – and therefore higher risk of unemployment – among local authority tenants as both this study and the work of a number of other researchers has shown (McCormick, 1983;

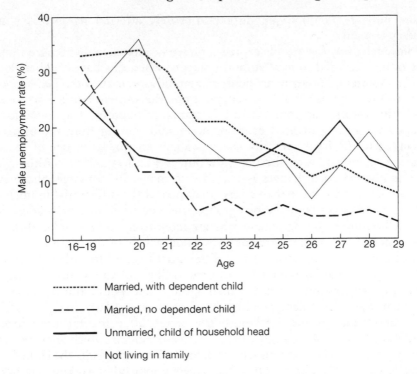

Figure 7.8   Male unemployment rates by age and family status, Great Britain, 1981
Source: Murphy and Sullivan, 1986, table 5

Hughes and McCormick, 1987; Murphy and Sullivan, 1986; an extended bibliography of the general topic of housing and labour market interactions is given in Munro, 1986; *Labour Force Survey 1983 and 1984*, 1986, Table 6.6; Sullivan and Falkingham, forthcoming, Tables 1, 2). At a time when over one third of the economically active population aged under 25 have been unemployed at some time in the last 12 months, the prospects of reaching 80 per cent owner-occupation without drastic policy changes seem dim (*Social Trends* 15, Table 4.26).

Given the link between fertility and tenure, and tenure and unemployment, a relationship between family status and unemployment would be expected: figure 7.8 shows that this is indeed the case – the unemployed are much more likely to have children (and – perhaps more surprisingly – to be living away from home). Unemployment among other household members is also associated with a higher probability of unemployment among young people (Payne, 1987). One effect is that children, especially those in large families, are disproportionately affected by increases in unemployment.

Since relatively few people express a preference for changing tenure from the owner-occupied to local authority sectors, when this happens there are often important employment and demographic aspects at work. Two factors are mainly responsible for movement from the owner-occupied to local authority sectors – unemployment and marital breakdown. The unemployment rates among married heads of household moving from the owner-occupied to the local authority sector is about six times the rate of those moving in the opposite direction (Murphy and Sullivan, 1986). Although the numbers of such changes associated with moves are not large, and they cannot account for more than a very small part of the differential in unemployment rates between the two groups, the sale of a large proportion of public housing to sitting tenants who are more likely to be employed than the general local authority sector population will have contributed to the increase in the unemployment rate differential referred to earlier. In 1985 160 thousand marriages ended in divorce in England and Wales – if these rates were to continue, over one marriage in three would end in divorce. Women with dependent children have been particularly likely to seek accommodation in the local authority sector after marital breakdown (Sullivan, 1986, p. 41; Grundy, 1985). Such movements, which often receive priority because of a legal requirement of local authorities under the Homeless Persons Act (1977), also tend to reduce access among other working families. Once more, general policies which are leading to the residualization of local authority housing are being reinforced by demographic trends.

It is clear that housing tenure is associated with major differentials in patterns of marriage and childbearing. That tenure is an even more powerful variable for population analysis is shown by looking at its relationship to the factors associated with household dissolution, mortality and marital breakdown. The long-lasting substantial differentials between social classes is well known and well established due to the excellent analyses produced in the past in the Registrar General's Decennial Supplements. What is more surprising is that differentials by housing tenure are even more substantial. For example, John Fox and Peter Goldblatt (1982) have shown that after controlling for age, mortality in the 5 years following the 1971 Census for men aged 15 to 64 was greater for the highest social class, professional workers, who were living in the local authority sector, than for the lowest social class, unskilled manual workers, in the owner-occupied sector (see figure 7.9). This strongly suggests that housing tenure is associated with more substantial and fundamental aspects than simply housing matters.

The tenure of a person's housing has been shown to be a consequence of marital breakdown in many cases. However, it is also associated with excess risk as a cause of marital breakdown. Those who start off their married life in

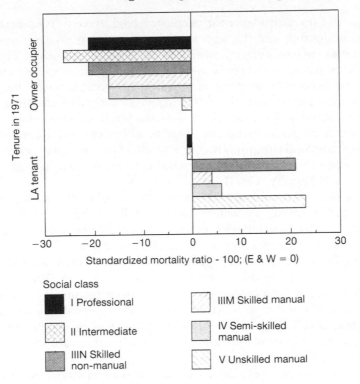

Figure 7.9 Standardized mortality ratios by housing tenure and social class in 1971: men aged 15–64, England and Wales
Source: Fox and Goldblatt, 1982, table 13.5

shared accommodation or in the local authority sector were more likely to experience marital breakdown later, even if other factors known to be associated with marital breakdown, such as age at marriage and childbearing patterns, are controlled for; this excess risk for tenants being of the order of 30 per cent greater than for owner-occupiers (Thornes and Collard, 1979; Murphy, 1985, Table 7).

The process of 'residualization' of the local authority sector has been discussed by a number of authors such as Forrest and Murie (1983). As more and more owner-occupiers come from relatively badly paid and insecure jobs, the growth of a group of *disadvantaged owner-occupiers* becomes likely. There is some evidence for the emergence of such a group in Britain recently. However, space precludes discussion of this topic. The reasons for these wide-ranging and very substantial housing tenure effects on demographic behaviour are not well understood; indeed, they have received far less attention than other less-striking ones. They include the characteristics, background and attitudes of the people involved, the effects of socialization in the tenure type and the ways in which successive post-war governments and parties have encouraged owning at the expense of renting. The result, however, is not in doubt; the British housing system is becoming increasingly polarized between a majority of secure owner-occupiers who have made substantial capital gains and are receiving large continuing subsidies, and the rest (this includes the group which space has precluded discussing: the marginal group of owner-occupiers, many of whom are in a more precarious position than local authority tenants, and whose problems will become much more prominent in years to come (Karn, Kemeny, and Williams, 1985; Sullivan and Murphy, 1987)).

These housing trends are largely politically determined directly by housing policy and indirectly by wider economic policies, but some features are caused by, exacerbated by and, in turn, influence demographic trends, with consequent implications for many areas of housing policy.

The relationship between population and a topic such as housing is complex because causality does not act in only one direction. The numbers of people who form (and dissolve) households affects the provision of housing, but availability and type of accommodation affects fertility, nuptiality and mortality, as well as household formation. Other variables including political decisions and labour market and economic conditions are also important. The full ramifications are well beyond the scope of this chapter.

It is not even possible to determine how far these observed patterns can be 'explained' in sociological, economic or political terms (no doubt there are people who would also see a genetic component here as well). Simple explanations are likely to come from ill-founded prejudice rather than from detailed analysis of the admittedly poor data which exist on this topic. An explicit decision should be taken as to whether the decision-making process should attempt to collect new and relevant data: the Rayner Report on Official Statistics (Rayner, 1981) stated that official statistics should only be collected when they are relevant to central government decision-making. A refusal to collect data shows a distinct unwillingness to start to tackle the sorts of issues which have been raised above.

Acknowledgements

The data used in this chapter have been derived by a number of researchers and the author acknowledges their contribution. They include: Richard Wall, David Eversley, John Ermisch, Alan Holmans and Oriel Sullivan, who collaborated on much of the work discussed here. He also thanks the Office of Population Censuses and Surveys for access to a number of surveys, including the General Household Survey, the Family Formation Survey, and the Labour Force Survey.

Selected Key Reading

Holmans, A. 1981: Housing careers of recently married couples. *Population Trends*, 24, London: HMSO.

Munro, M. 1986: Housing and labour market interactions: A review. Discussion Paper 12. Glasgow: University of Glasgow Centre for Housing Research.

Murphy, M. and Sullivan, O. 1985: Housing tenure and family formation in contemporary Britain. *European Sociological Review*, 1, 230–43.

Murphy, M. and Sullivan, O. 1986: Unemployment, housing and household structure among young adults. *Journal of Social Policy*, 15, 205–22.

Thornes, B. and Collard, J. 1979: *Who Divorces?* London: Routledge and Kegan Paul.

8 Internal Migration and the Spatial Distribution of Population

Tony Champion

Major shifts in population distribution have taken place over the two decades since the 1960s, despite the fact that the national population size is, by the 1980s, almost static. Just as with many of the aspects of population composition covered in this book, so also the patterning of people across national space is highly dynamic. This may seem surprising in view of the fact that the British tend to move house less frequently than people in some other countries like the USA and, more particularly, in view of the wide range of government measures that aim to support the existing patterns and restrict the scale of new urban expansion, such as regional policy, green belts and the urban programme. There are at work, however, powerful forces for change, including the redistribution of employment opportunities at both regional and more local scales, changes in the preferences of individuals about the types of place where they would like to live, and also the considerable changes in demographic and social structure described elsewhere in this book. The fall in birth rate, the growth of the elderly population, the rise in the divorce rate, the increase in the number of one-parent families and other factors leading to lower average household size, along with such developments as the increase in the number of working wives, cannot have taken place without having measurable effects on the geographical distribution of population, especially since, as argued in the previous chapter, these changes have tended to occur much more rapidly than the housing stock can adjust to their new requirements.

This chapter outlines the main changes which are taking place in the spatial distribution of the British population and examines the migration patterns which form the principal mechanism behind these trends. Particular attention is given to the accentuation of the drift from North to South since the late 1970s, the current scale of population deconcentration from the major metropolitan centres to smaller towns and more rural areas, and the emerging population patterns in the so-called 'inner city areas'. Each of these constitutes a traditional area of policy concern, but with the exception of the New and Expanded Towns programme and half-hearted attempts at assisting labour mobility, successive governments have tended to fight shy of the direct management of migration and population distribution, preferring to use indirect measures affecting the location of jobs and housing. Because this approach appears to generate some undesirable side-effects, this chapter concludes by arguing that closer attention should be given to more direct ways of influencing migration patterns. These should be aimed at reducing tendencies towards social polarization and at achieving a better matching of people with appropriate jobs and local facilities, thereby increasing not only individuals' quality of life but also the efficiency of public and private investment. The first stage of this argument, however, is to demonstrate the importance of regional and local perspectives on population and to indicate, by reference of the lack of official statistics on local populations and migration, how little attention is currently paid by central government to these questions.

The Importance of Sub-national Perspectives

Sub-national perspectives on population change are essential for at least two very basic reasons (Lawton, 1986). Firstly, in a society which is consumer-orientated and largely sympathetic to the provision of welfare services, a considerable proportion of both private and public investment is geared to providing goods and services to people within fairly easy reach of their homes. A single national centre is appropriate only for the few services which involve delivery to all addresses in Britain (e.g. mail order), very occasional visits (e.g. specialized medical advice) or a particular type of service or activity with a client group that lives close to it and is not represented elsewhere in the country (e.g. certain elements of central government, the national media and business services).

Secondly, regional and local populations do not by any means constitute faithful microcosms of the national population, either in terms of the rates of change in their size or in terms of their composition by age, sex, household type and socio-economic characteristics (Lawton, 1982). Not only does migration continue to produce considerable variations between places in rates of population change (Ogilvy, 1982; Stillwell, 1985), but mortality patterns also differ between places (Townsend and Davidson 1982) and so too do fertility rates, though to a diminishing extent (Newell, 1986). Even if there existed a uniform nationwide trend in the birth and death rates of each population sub-group identified on the basis of sex, age, occupation, ethnic status and so on, local populations would still develop differently from one another, and from the 'national' trend, because these rates would be operating on the distinctive demographic structures which each locality has inherited from its past histories of fertility, mortality and migration. For instance, a nationwide rise in fertility rate would produce a much larger increase in the number of births in a recently developed new town with an above-average proportion of young couples than in a retirement area with a population of similar size. Such imbalances can create major problems for the provision of basic local services such as health care and education (Briault, 1986; Whitelegg, 1986) and for the maintenance of a consistent labour supply (Salt, 1986).

These two factors have always applied, but the significance of regional and local perspectives on population changes seems greater in the last quarter of the twentieth century than previously. This is partly because of the increasing importance of employment in the service sector, much of it geared to regional and local markets and client groups, but it also has much to do with the particular circumstances of the 1980s. With the national rate of population growth running at under 0.2 per cent a year, population redistribution has virtually become a 'zero-sum game', whereby any increase in one place can take place only at the expense of population levels in another place. Gone are the more dynamic days of the early 1960s when even substantial rates of net migration loss from the larger cities to other parts of Britain were largely or completely offset by relatively high rates of natural increase and by immigration from overseas. As a result, according to the 1985-based projections (OPCS, 1988), while population increase of 15 per cent or more are expected by the year 2001 in some counties (e.g. Buckinghamshire, Wiltshire, Cornwall, Shropshire), Merseyside stands to lose over 9 per cent and Cleveland and Tyne and Wear both over 5 per cent of their 1985 numbers. At the more local scale of the metropolitan districts, the changes expected for Knowsley and Liverpool are as big as - 18.2 and - 16.1 per cent respectively, while Gateshead and Salford are also projected to lose over 10 per cent of their population in this 16-year period. With the switch in emphasis from accommodating national growth to the redistribution of an essentially fixed number of people come the problems of spare capacity and loss of investment confidence in the adversely affected areas.

These developments also come at a time when drives for greater efficiency are features of both public and private sectors. Under pressure from diminishing resources and central government exhortations, much greater emphasis is being placed on the careful targeting of policy measures to the places where people suffer from the most severe problems, as evidenced by the successive reviews of regional policy and by the initiatives of the 1970s and 1980s aimed at rejuvenating inner city areas. Similarly, the private sector, spurred on by advances in computer technology and by availability of detailed local statistics from the Population Census, has developed sophisticated targeting procedures for advertising, marketing and product monitoring. These steps recognize the existence of major differences in the composition of population both between and within regions and urban areas – differences which recent trends towards the increasing selectivity of migration streams seem to be magnifying, as will be shown further on.

The Inadequacy of Data on Local Area Populations

The success of population targeting depends on access to accurate up-to-date information, but in fact the increasing attention being given to sub-national, and particularly local, populations is running far ahead of the availability of data suitable for monitoring trends at these scales. The annual population estimates constitute the principal source of official statistics on sub-national populations. As such, they are extremely valuable and their accuracy is known to have improved considerably as a result of methodological improvements made over the last few years (OPCS, 1980; Craig and Broad, 1982). Even so, considerable errors can build up over the period of ten or more years that elapses between one Census date and the time when the finalized results of the next Census can be used. While births and deaths are required by law to be notified to the Registrar General, migration – which is generally the most significant component of population change at regional and local levels and has increased its importance as rates of natural increase have declined – is much more poorly documented (Willis, 1974; Rees, 1977; Ogilvy, 1980; Stillwell, 1986). Heavy reliance is placed on sources set up for purposes other than monitoring population change, including the International Passenger Survey (designed to estimate travellers' spending patterns), the National Health Service Central Register and the electoral roll. Furthermore, the information which the 'midyear population estimates' provide is limited to sex and age group and is not normally available for a finer grain of spatial unit than the local authority district and health authority area.

Some information on other characteristics of the population such as household structure, employment status, ethnic composition and housing situation can be gleaned from the annual *General Household* and *Labour Force* surveys, but the problem of small sample size virtually rules out their use at scales below the Standard Region. As a result, the Population Census is not just the best, but in practice the only, source of reliable data on a reasonably wide range of demographic and socio-economic characteristics at sub-regional scale. Moreover, it has the advantage of providing data down to the level of the individual enumeration district covering roughly 500 inhabitants, which, even if too small for certain purposes, can be treated as a building block for areas specially defined by the user (Rhind, 1983). Unfortunately, given the failure to repeat the practice of a mid-decade Census as first carried out in 1966, this source can provide only snapshots of the population at ten-year intervals, the most recent being 1981. Its value for indicating the population composition of local areas towards the end of any decade is strictly limited, while by definition its value for monitoring change during the inter-censal period is nil. The closing stages of the decade are not the most satisfactory time for a description and analysis of the latest trends in the spatial distribution of population!

The North–South Divide

Data deficiencies pose least problems at the broad regional scale because the various sources provide relatively firm ground for examining the latest developments in the balance between North and South. The more rapid growth of southern Britain is the longest established and apparently most intractable of the geographical shifts taking place in the 1980s, seemingly being treated as inevitable or indeed even desirable by the contemporary Conservative Government. Since the onset in the late 1920s of severe economic difficulties in areas of coal-mining and heavy industry, there has been a progressive shift of employment opportunities towards the South, albeit not always at the same rate. There were times – notably in the immediate postwar years and during the early 1970s – when it seemed that the gap between the two halves of the country was beginning to narrow (Damesick and Wood, 1987), but with the benefit of hindsight it is seen that these were periods when special factors were operating (McCrone, 1969; Massey, 1979). According to later studies (Martin, 1986, 1987; TCPA, 1987; Green, 1988) the gap in the 1980s is now wider than ever; and the latest developments in information and communications technology threaten to reinforce these contrasts (Goddard and Gillespie, 1987).

The hiatus between North and South is most directly shown in terms of trends in employment over the first half of the 1980s. As table 8.1 indicates, the economic recession of the late 1970s and early 1980s had a much more severe impact on the North, because of the concentration there of the types of economic sectors – principally manufacturing – which were most badly affected. Moreover, at this time, the boundary between the two parts of Britain was drawn southwards so that formerly prosperous parts of the Midlands, particularly the West Midlands conurbation, found themselves on the wrong side of the line for the first time (Townsend, 1983; Green, 1986).

The geographical patterning of the subsequent 'national' economic recovery has largely served to reinforce this dichotomy. Whereas the four regions of the South together gained 449 000 extra jobs between 1983 and 1986, the six other regions combined managed a net increase of only 83 000

Table 8.1   Change in employees in employment, 1979–86, and total employment, 1986, by region

| Region | 1979–83 | | 1983–86 | | 1979–86 | | Total employment 1986 |
	000s	%	000s	%	000s	%	000s
Northern	−184	−14.8	29	2.7	−155	−12.5	1,086
Wales	−145	−14.0	−27	−3.0	−172	−16.7	861
North West	−374	−14.0	39	1.7	−413	−15.4	2,263
West Midlands	−299	−13.3	90	4.6	−209	− 9.3	2,032
Yorks/Humber	−239	−11.9	37	2.1	−202	−10.0	1,809
Scotland	−203	− 9.7	− 7	−0.4	−210	−10.0	1,892
North: total	−1449	−12.8	83	0.8	−1366	−12.1	9,943
East Midlands	−129	− 8.3	99	6.9	− 30	− 1.9	1,525
South East	−391	− 5.2	233	3.3	−158	− 2.1	7,315
South West	− 83	− 5.2	73	4.8	− 10	− 0.6	1,588
East Anglia	− 14	− 2.0	44	6.4	30	4.3	732
South: total	−617	− 5.4	449	4.2	−168	− 1.5	11,160
Great Britain: total	−2066	− 9.1	532	2.6	−1534	− 6.8	21,103

Regions are listed in order of percentage rate of employment decline 1979–83 (second column). Columns may not sum, due to rounding.

Source: calculated from Central Statistical Office 1987: *Regional Trends* 22, table 8.1.

jobs and in 1986 contained 1.37 million, or 12 per cent, fewer jobs than in 1979 (table 8.1). Moreover, the latest available data on more local patterns of employment growth in the 1980s indicate the sharpness of the boundary between the two parts of the country, because they show that, though more rural parts of the North performed well at this time, the greatest concentration of rapid job growth occurred south of a line running from the Severn estuary to Lincolnshire (figure 8.1). There is a particularly marked contrast between the experience of the more urbanized areas of the Midlands and northern England and that of the broad zone to the north and west of London stretching from Hampshire and Wiltshire through to Cambridgeshire and Norfolk. Here are located a disproportionately large slice of the nation's 'sunrise industries'. The London area, too, has participated strongly in this recovery, led by the growth of jobs in financial and other business services in central London and other office centres in the Home Counties (Breheny, Hart and Hall, 1986; Champion and Green, 1987, 1988; Hall et al., 1987).

The impact of these recent employment trends is reflected clearly in the shifts in population distribution which have taken place since the early 1970s (table 8.2). In brief, the four regions of the South have been absorbing all the

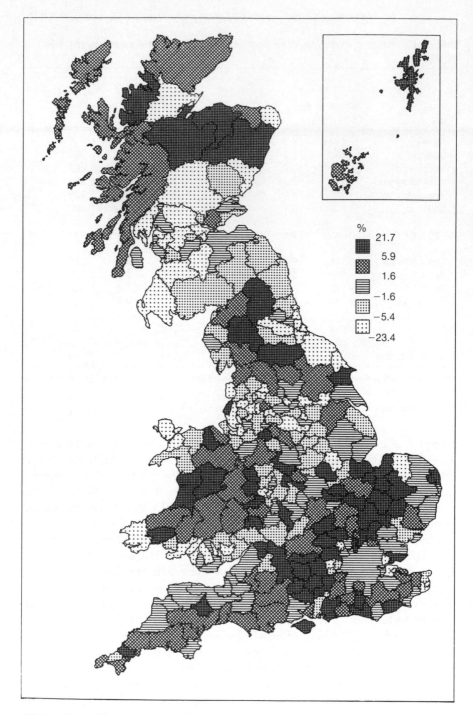

%
21.7
5.9
1.6
−1.6
−5.4
−23.4

Figure 8.1   Change in total employment, 1981–84, by local labour market area.
Source: Champion and Green 1988; calculated from data supplied by Department of Employment via NOMIS

Table 8.2   Population change, 1971–86, and total population, 1986, by region

Region	1971–76 000s	%	1976–81 000s	%	1981–86 000s	%	Total population 1986 000s
Northern	2	0.1	− 36	−1.2	− 37	−1.2	3,080
Wales	59	2.2	14	0.5	8	0.3	2,821
North West	−74	−1.1	−101	−1.6	− 85	−1.3	6,374
West Midlands	32	0.6	9	0.2	− 5	−0.1	5,181
Yorks/Humber	22	0.5	− 6	−0.1	− 19	−0.4	4,899
Scotland	− 2	−0.1	− 53	−1.0	− 59	−1.2	5,121
North: total	37	0.1	−172	−0.6	−198	−0.7	27,477
East Midlands	122	3.4	79	2.1	67	1.7	3,920
South East	−149	−0.9	34	0.2	254	1.5	17,265
South West	168	4.1	101	2.4	162	3.7	4,543
East Anglia	126	7.5	81	4.5	97	6.4	1,992
South: total	267	1.0	295	1.1	580	2.2	27,719
Great Britain: total	304	0.6	123	0.2	382	0.7	55,196

Regions are listed in same order as for table 8.1. Columns may not sum due to rounding. The percentages apply to the change over five years; they are not annual growth rates.

Source: calculated from revised mid-year estimates supplied by OPCS and the Registrar General for Scotland.

(admittedly rather limited) national increase in population and have been pulling in people from the rest of Britain. In 1971–76 their overall growth rate was already considerably in excess of that for the rest of Britain, but subsequently the gap has widened, particularly since 1981. Thus in 1981–86 the South gained 580 000 people, twice the increase recorded in 1976–81, while the rest of Britain saw its population fall by almost 200 000, an increase in the rate of loss compared to 1976–81 and moving against the national trend (table 8.2). Internal migration within Britain has been largely responsible for these trends, with the level of net in-migration to the South rising from 24 000 a year in 1971/73 to 45–50 000 a year by the end of the 1970s and rising steadily since 1981 to reach 69 000 in 1985/6 (figure 8.2). This has been reinforced by recent changes in international migration, in particular involving a major surge in net inward movement to the South East in the first half of the 1980s.

At the same time, however, these population shifts have been far less than those required to match the scale of interregional differences in employment change shown in table 8.1. Indeed, while there is concern over the long-term effects of population losses from northern regions of Britain, in some circles there appears to be even more anxiety about the failure of migration to

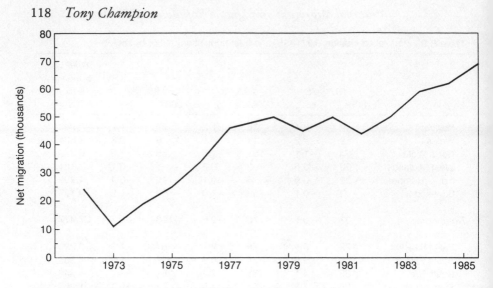

Figure 8.2   Net migration from North to South, 1971–86
Note: South refers to the South East, South West, East Anglia and East Midlands.
Source: data, 1971–78 comprise two-year running averages estimated from Ogilvy (1982); the data from 1978/79 onwards are taken from OPCS Monitors Reference MN.

produce a speedier matching of workers to jobs (Department of Employment, 1986; Minford, 1985). Neo-classical models of the labour market contend that equilibriating mechanisms such as migration should work to eradicate spatial variations in unemployment (Gleave and Palmer, 1980), but the continuation of wide regional variations in rates of joblessness through the 1980s suggests that these mechanisms are not working very efficiently (Gleave and Sellens, 1984; Green et al., 1986). According to Hughes and McCormick (1985, 1987), the key to the problem lies with the limited mobility of manual workers. Using data from the 1983 Labour Force Survey, they show that whereas unemployment rates for non-manual workers are low, with little variation between regions, those for manual workers are much higher and exhibit a much wider degree of regional variation (see columns 1 and 2 of table 8.3). In fact, comparing columns 6 and 8 of table 8.3 there is seen to be no net flow of manual workers from the six most depressed regions of the country to the four most prosperous ones. This suggests that migration's role in swelling the South's labour force is restricted to non-manual workers, for whom the South provided 61 per cent of the movers' destinations, while it accounted for only 52 per cent of points of departure. Even in relation to non-manual workers, however, serious manpower shortages and problems of relocating staff were being reported in the mid-1980s in many parts of southern England (Parsons, 1987; IMS, 1987).

Table 8.3 Unemployment and migration, by region

| | Unemployment rate | | Regional shares of all heads of households who are | | | | | |
| | | | In labour force | | In-migrants | | Out-migrants | |
Region	Non-manual (1)	Manual (2)	Non-manual (3)	Manual (4)	Non-manual (5)	Manual (6)	Non-manual (7)	Manual (8)
North West	5.5	17.7	10.6	11.7	9.0	6.6	10.5	8.9
North	4.7	17.5	4.7	6.5	6.0	4.8	4.5	6.0
West Midlands	5.5	17.3	8.4	10.9	6.9	7.7	11.1	9.5
Wales	3.8	17.1	4.0	5.3	2.4	5.4	6.0	4.8
Scotland	4.1	15.1	9.1	9.6	4.5	6.6	5.4	4.2
Yorks/Humber	5.0	14.6	8.4	10.1	10.2	9.5	9.9	7.1
North: total	–	–	45.2	54.2	39.0	40.6	47.6	40.5
London	4.8	2.8	13.8	10.1	8.4	7.7 ⎫	27.4	32.7
South East	3.2	9.2	22.7	15.7	17.5	12.5 ⎭	10.8	10.7
South West	3.8	9.6	8.3	8.0	16.6	17.3	8.1	11.3
East Midlands	3.2	9.6	6.7	8.0	12.4	11.9	6.0	4.8
East Anglia	4.2	9.2	3.3	3.9	6.0	10.1		
South: total	–	–	54.8	45.8	61.0	59.4	52.4	59.5
(Total sample)	–	–	(21,633)	(25,856)	(332)	(168)	(332)	(168)

The last six columns each give percentages of the total national sample; they may not sum, due to rounding.

Source: 1983 Labour Force Survey, based on Hughes and McCormick, 1987, Table 1.

Previous studies (see the review in Green et al., 1986) have put forward a wide range of factors to account for this relatively low level of labour mobility, particularly amongst the lower paid. They include the limited availability of jobs in the recession years, poor access to information about vacancies, lack of the requisite skills and personal attributes, uncertainty about the security of a potential job, the employment situation of other workers in the same household, the stage of children's schooling and reluctance to break family and social ties. By far the most frequently cited reasons, however, relate to housing considerations (Johnson, Salt and Wood, 1974). The small size of the private-rented sector and the difficulties which council house tenants face in moving between local authority areas have for a long time constituted major barriers to long distance migration by lower-income workers (Robertson, 1979; Hughes and McCormick, 1981; OPCS, 1983; Hamnett, 1984). The various government schemes designed to assist labour transfers (Johnson and Salt, 1980) have traditionally made an extremely limited contribution to migration and were cut back further in the first half of the 1980s. In the last few years these problems have also been intensified by the housing changes described in chapter 7, namely the accelerated contraction of the private-rented sector, the winding up of New Town Development Corporations and other official overspill schemes, the cutback in Treasury funds for new public-sector house-building in general, and the sale of council houses to tenants with 'Right To Buy' discounts (Brittan, 1986). Meanwhile, since the early 1980s the movements of home-owners to the South has become increasingly difficult as the pressures for net in-migration from the rest of Britain and overseas has outstripped the rate of new house building and led to massive inflation in the price of houses and land with planning permission (Champion, Green and Owen, 1987).

The recent changes in the distribution of people and jobs described above are indicative of a fundamental reshaping of Britain's regional structure which has major implications for private investment decisions and raises important issues for central government policymakers. Forecasts of the South's predominant share of the future growth in employment (Tyler and Rhodes, 1986; Cambridge Econometrics, 1987) indicate to the private sector the broad locations where the greatest returns on capital investment are likely to be won. Meanwhile, the many parts of the North which are anticipated to experience depopulation for the foreseeable future (OPCS, 1988) will tend to find more defensive strategies being adopted by the private sector and local authorities alike, as their revenue base contracts and as the use of their facilities falls below its optimum level. The most immediate problem facing central government appears to be the intense pressure building up in southern England. The progressive dismantling of regional development policy since 1979 has moved more swiftly than steps aimed at deregulating the housing sector. Minford, Ashton and Peel (1987) have pointed to the massive distortions caused to the housing system by government intervention, including the effects of the Rent Acts, the subsidization of council house rents, the subsidy to owner-occupiers through mortgage tax reliefs, and planning restrictions on housing land. The Conservative Government's attempts at reviving the private-rented sector have met with very little success, though in due course more substantial results are expected from the 1988 Housing Act. At the same time, the Tory-voting lobby in the country areas of southern England has so far been very effective in resisting the relaxation of planning controls. All in all, in Britain at the moment there is a major disjunction between government policies towards the economy and those relating to housing. This has reinforced the problems of regional imbalance inherited from the years of deep recession and the more distant past and looks to be heading to a showdown on the green fields of southern England.

The Exodus from Cities

The single most impressive finding of the 1981 Census in relation to population distribution was the massive decline in population sustained by Britain's larger cities over the previous decade. The population of Greater London alone fell by almost three-quarters of a million between 1971 and 1981, a drop of almost 1 in 10 (OPCS, 1984). Even bigger relative rates of decline were recorded by some of the provincial centres, notably Glasgow (– 22.0 per cent), Liverpool (– 16.4) and Manchester (– 17.5). To some extent, the latter are related to the North–South drift described in the previous section, but they are also partly the outcome of a general shift of population from more urban to more rural areas. Evidence for the importance of this 'rural–urban shift' can be found in the fact that London sustained such heavy population loss in the 1970s despite being located at the heart of the most dynamic region in the UK. Its influence can also be seen at work within the North, where sub-regional studies have shown that many medium-sized places and more rural areas fared relatively well between 1971 and 1981 despite the general appearance of economic malaise conveyed by the regional-level statistics (Breheny, Hall and Hart, 1987; Champion, Green, Owen, Ellin and Coombes, 1987; Townsend, 1986). In fact, this phenomenon is common to the majority of advanced Western countries and poses some major challenges which need to be addressed alongside the issues raised by the North–South divide.

In one sense, the shift of population away from the original urban cores is by no means a new development; suburban expansion was already underway before the end of the nineteenth century and accelerated dramatically in the interwar period. Since the early 1950s, however, urban decentralization has taken on completely new dimensions. With new forms of planning restriction limiting the amount of suburban extension that could be tacked on to existing built-up areas, housing developers increasingly looked to the surrounding rings of smaller settlements lying within commuting distance of city centres. By the early 1960s the largest metropolitan areas in Britain had moved into 'absolute decentralization', whereby the principal settlements of each began to lose population, and by 1971 several of these areas were facing overall population decline, with residential decentralization taking place across their boundaries and spilling over into adjacent city-regions or further afield (Hall et al., 1973; Spence el al., 1982). Over the subsequent decade this process intensified so much in both numbers of people and geographical scale that an inverse relationship between urban size and population change rate was generally evident and many of the more remote areas in the west and north of Britain experienced a switch into growth after decades of depopulation (Champion, 1981a; Jones et al., 1986; Champion, Green, Owen, Ellin and Coombes, 1987). These developments appear very similar to those experienced in the USA and a number of other countries where they have been variously termed 'counterurbanization', 'the rural population turnaround' and 'the rural renaissance' (see Fielding, 1986, for a review).

For a while during the 1970s these counterurban tendencies were operating so powerfully that they replaced the North–South drift as a primary dimension of regional population change in Britain (Champion, 1983). Particularly impressive was the way in which the South East's population began to decline in the late 1960s, following its rapid growth in the 1950s and the early 1960s. Indeed, by the mid-1970s all three of Britain's most heavily urbanized regions (the South East, West Midlands and North West) were recording rates of population decline similar to or greater than the traditionally depressed regions like the North and Scotland (Champion, 1983, table 8.2, p. 200). A number of different factors seem to have contributed to this extensive scale of decentralization from the major metropolitan areas, including changes in residential preferences and the search by companies for less cramped factory sites and for cheaper and less organized labour such as married women. The programme of motorway building played an important facilitating role, while direct government intervention made a substantial contribution in the form of the Location of Offices Bureau, large-scale slum clearance and the official overspill programme, the latter being expanded in the light of the mid-1960s projections of strong national population growth. Actual demographic trends also contributed to the outward movement, as the rearing of the 1960s baby boom children increased the demand for houses with gardens and as falling average household size reduced the population capacity of cities that had only limited sites available for new housing construction (Champion, 1987b). At the same time, there was an increase in the number of elderly people seeking retirement homes in the cheaper and more attractive areas away from the more urbanized regions (Law and Warnes, 1976).

On the other hand, the pace of counterurbanization has slowed considerably in the past decade. Indeed, contrary to the impression of steady acceleration conveyed by the decennial Census statistics, the urban–rural shift in population seems to have peaked in the early 1970s. According to the mid-year estimates the 'remoter, largely rural districts' experienced their highest rates of net immigration between 1971 and 1974, while at the other end of the national urban hierarchy London's rate of net migration loss peaked as early as 1970/71 (Champion, 1981b; Britton, 1986). All Britain's major cities recorded some diminution in their rates of population decline between the 1970s and the 1980s, but the recovery in London's change rate was particularly remarkable (Champion, 1987a). Whereas Greater London had been losing 90 000 people a year at the beginning of the 1970s (figure 8.3), its population is estimated actually to have grown between 1983 and 1986, reaching a level of 6.78 million in 1986.

To a large extent, this 'downwave' in the pace of urban deconcentration can be associated with a significant general fall in levels of residential mobility during the 1970s, as observed both from the NHS records (Ogilvy,

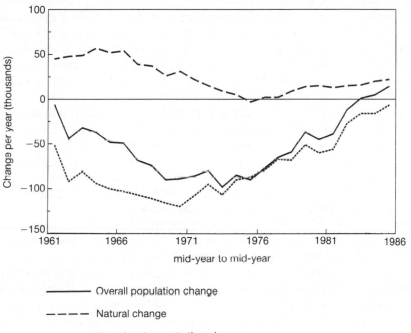

Figure 8.3   Population change for Greater London, 1961–86
Source: calculated from OPCS mid-year estimates

1982; Devis, 1984) and from Census comparisons (Devis, 1983; Brant, 1984; Stillwell, 1985). As with the rise in counterurbanization a decade earlier, however, a number of specific reasons can be suggested. Some of these are mirror images of those previously cited; for instance, the recession meant less need for businessmen to seek out large industrial sites, central government began running down the overspill programmes and giving greater attention to the rejuvenation of inner city areas, and 'baby boom' was replaced by 'baby bust'. Many of the most popular retirement areas appear to have become saturated (Warnes and Law, 1984), while the shake-out of the private-rented sector had passed its peak by the end of the 1970s (Hamnett and Randolph, 1982, 1983a). There was also a major increase in the number of small households, as a result of the growth of the elderly population, the rise in the divorce rate and the financial advantages of 'double-income, no-kids' life styles – a trend to which the building industry was relatively quick to respond in the absence of more lucrative opportunities and as part of subsidized inner city renewal projects (Champion, 1987b).

In international academic circles the counterurbanization phenomenon continues to be the subject of lively debate (Fielding, 1986). The most fundamental issue at stake is whether it represents merely a continuation of the earlier process of suburbanization and metropolitan deconcentration, albeit on a much larger geographical scale, or instead constitutes a fundamental switch away from the urban concentration process associated with industrialization towards a new 'post-industrial' settlement pattern based on medium-sized and small centres (Hamnett and Randolph, 1983a; Robert and Randolph, 1983). The apparently cyclic pattern of the past two decades raises the further possibility that the large-scale urban–rural shift of the early 1970s was a short-term event resulting from the chance combination of particular circumstances. If, however, it is the 1980s that constitutes the aberration and if the underlying tendency is instead towards a more dispersed settlement pattern and the growth of smaller cities and towns, then it is important to recognize that the British population remains highly concentrated. Despite the massive exodus from the major cities in the 1970s, in 1981 more than three-fifths (62.6 per cent) of Britain's 54.3 million people were still living in twenty 'metropolitan regions' which occupy little more than one-fifth of the country's land area. Indeed, fully a quarter of the country's population is accounted for by just the six largest cities (defined on a functional rather than administrative basis). Most remarkable of all is the degree of concentration in London, which on the same functional basis is as large as the eight next largest cities in Britain put together (Champion et al., 1984, Champion, Green, Owen, Ellin and Coombes, 1987).

While there may be some uncertainty about what the future holds for Britain's larger provincial cities, there can be little doubt about the massive strength of decentralization forces in the case of London. Even during the recession years of the early 1980s, the rate of net outward migration from Greater London to the rest of the South East never fell below 40 000 a year and with the subsequent economic recovery it had risen to 65 000 by 1986–87 (Champion and Congdon, 1988). The massive surge in house prices in London between 1984 and 1987 provides some indication of the scale of pent-up demand for new housing, only a relatively small fraction of which can be met within London itself. According to Tyler and Rhodes (1986), between 1985 and 1995 there will be a demand for 605 000 new houses in the South East outside London, almost twice the provision then anticipated by the planning authorities. The future pattern of urban development and resultant population growth therefore depends very much on the outcome of political battles between the various interest groups, including central and local government, the developers and the different types of conservation lobby (HBF, 1985). Considerations in favour of a more flexible approach towards new building in the South East include the need to continue the momentum of the national economic recovery and the search for alternative uses of surplus farmland, but if no firm guidance on this matter is forth-coming in the near future, decentralization is likely to occur more slowly but take place over longer distances. This would aggravate the problems of urban penetration into essentially rural areas described by Herington (1984) and would also reduce the options available for dealing with the difficulties faced by lower-income groups in the London area (Eversley, 1972; Buck et al., 1986).

The Inner City Problem

As with the other two scales of population redistribution surveyed above, the distinction between the inner and outer parts of individual cities and towns in terms of their inhabitants' relative prosperity is not new, nor is it unique in Britain (Herbert, 1972). Though some prestige residential areas survive in the 'west ends' of many cities, Britain's inner areas have in general followed the American model in their physical and social characteristics (Hall, 1981). Here is found the cities' oldest remaining housing stock built to accommo-date low-paid workers in adjacent factories and menial city-centre jobs and generally receiving very little maintenance as the owners await the transition of the land to a higher-value use like shops or offices or the threat of compul-sory purchase for the construction of new relief roads or other types of public-sector development. These areas continue to constitute the best option for lower-paid workers, not just because of the relatively low cost of the housing but also because they provide access to a large pool of appropriate jobs both in the central area and in the suburbs thanks to the essentially radial pattern of public transport facilities. At the same time, the inner city forms the 'sink' to which gravitates a range of marginal and minority groups, including non-white immigrants, young single people, one-parent families and various types of social deviants who prefer the anonymity of big-city life or who have been ostracized by their community of origin (Knox, 1982; Peach, 1982).

As also has been found for the other two scales, however, the inner city problem has become much more evident over the past decade since the deteriorating situation prompted central government to introduce more comprehensive powers in the 1978 Inner Urban Areas Act, to the extent that it was identified by the Prime Minister as the single most important challenge for the new Parliament after the 1987 General Election. Such has been the rate of change in the last few years that the 1981 Census has become woefully outdated. For instance, in January 1986 the male unemployment rate for Inner London stood at 21.9 per cent, compared with 14.4 per cent at the 1981 census – a much steeper rise than for Outer London, where the rates were 9.9 and 8.0 per cent respectively. Even so, the 1981 Census still performs useful functions in showing how these recent trends relate to the pre-existing socio-economic gulf between inner and outer areas and in highlighting the strong association between different types of deprivation. In London, for instance, the most severely affected boroughs like Hackney and Tower Hamlets, with male unemployment rates of over 28 per cent in 1986, had already seen sharp rises in joblessness between 1971 and 1981, which had driven more people to work outside the boroughs of residence and brought a marked fall in the numbers of women in paid work (Townsend el al., 1987). Such areas of high unemployment also tend to have below-average numbers of households with two or more wage-earners and disproportionately large numbers with low earnings, while they also score highly on 'multiple deprivation' indices based on measures such as educational attainment, life expectancy, ethnic composition and household structure (Donnison and Soto, 1980; Begg and Eversley, 1986). Table 8.4 gives an indication of the degree of social differentiation across London according to the characteristics available from the Population Census.

It might have been thought that the massive level of population decline experienced by Britain's cities since the 1960s, principally affecting their inner areas as it did, would have helped to reduce these problems. After all, the planning policies of the earlier postwar period were explicitly designed to reduce congestion and overcrowding in these areas by decanting lower-paid people to the New Towns and redeveloping the inner areas at lower density. As described in great detail by Hall et al. (1973), however, the success of these efforts was undermined by various factors including the inadequate scale of the original overspill programme, the influx of immigrants from the New Commonwealth and Pakistan, the 1960s baby boom, and a reluctance among both Tory-controlled shires and Labour-held city authorities to countenance the transfer of large numbers of low-income people from town to

Table 8.4 Inner and outer London contrasts

Characteristics	Inner Boroughs		Outer Boroughs		Inner London	Outer London
	Hackney	Tower	Bromley	Sutton		
Population change 1961–71	−14.5	−19.4	4.1	0.2	−13.2	−1.8
Population change 1971–81	−18.1	−13.8	−2.9	−0.1	−17.6	−4.6
Number of households						
1971–81	−13.9	−7.5	4.6	7.4	−13.2	0.9
Born in NCWP	16.5	13.7	2.5	2.7	12.3	8.0
Social Class I and II	14.5	8.5	37.8	32.5	19.8	27.5
Males with higher education qualifications	9.9	5.2	21.0	16.9	15.1	15.6
Males 16–64 unemployed	18.2	19.2	6.3	5.5	14.4	8.0
Males 16–19 unemployed	29.2	23.2	13.5	11.0	25.2	15.5
Households with no car	65.6	67.4	29.2	31.0	58.7	36.0
Households with 2+ cars	5.0	4.3	22.0	20.2	7.4	17.4
1 person households	30.0	28.9	21.4	23.0	31.8	22.4
6+ person households	6.0	5.5	2.8	2.7	4.3	3.8
Households with 1 parent family	4.9	3.6	1.8	1.8	3.6	2.1
1 parent families with mother working	35.5	29.7	46.8	52.8	38.9	45.8
Owner occupied households	16.6	4.6	69.9	68.1	27.3	61.9
Renting from local authority	57.5	82.0	17.2	20.1	42.8	23.2
Households with 1+ person/room	29.6	27.8	10.8	11.4	25.7	15.1
Persons per hectare (numbers)	92.6	72.4	19.5	39.0	77.9	33.5

NCWP – New Commonwealth and Pakistan. All figures are percentages, except bottom row. Data relate to 1981 except where stated otherwise.

Source: 1981 Census extracted from OPCS (1984). See there for full details of the variables.

country. As a result, even during the peak years of labour mobility in the early 1970s, the outflows from the cities were dominated in both net and gross terms by people who were home-owners and had higher-paid jobs (Kennett, 1983). Since then, as has previously been noted for interregional migration, the composition of migration streams from the cities has become even more highly skewed towards the better-off. Data for Greater London's outflows to the rest of Britain, for instance, reveal the even more important role of the owner-occupied sector in 1981 compared to 1971 and also show that in 1981 there was virtually no net migration loss of people in the lower-paid occupations in both manual and non-manual groups (table 8.5).

Various factors thus appear to be at the root of the inner city problem, many of them similar in nature to those behind the problems underlying the North–South divide. In the first place, even though the population of inner

Table 8.5   Migration between London and the rest of Great Britain, 1970–71 and 1980–81, by socio-economic grouping and housing tenure (thousands)

Characteristic at time of census	Outmigration 70–71	Outmigration 80–81	In-migration 70–71	In-migration 80–81	Net outmigration 70–71	Net outmigration 80–81	Change
Socio-economic groupings							
Prof./managerial	37.1	24.3	19.3	18.1	17.8	6.2	−11.6
Other non-manual	71.4	38.6	44.3	37.2	27.1	1.4	−25.7
Skilled manual	28.0	12.4	9.8	6.9	18.2	5.6	−12.6
Other manual	21.7	11.7	12.6	11.6	9.1	0.1	−9.0
Armed Forces & ID	7.0	12.1	6.4	8.3	0.6	3.8	+3.2
All econ. active	165.2	99.1	92.4	82.1	72.8	17.0	−55.8
Housing tenure							
Owner-occupiers	142.9	94.3	41.3	37.6	101.6	56.7	−44.9
Renting from LA/NT	38.2	17.2	8.9	12.0	29.3	5.2	−24.1
Other renters	48.8	25.6	68.3	42.5	−19.5	−16.9	−2.6
All in private households	229.9	137.0	118.5	92.1	111.4	44.9	−66.5

ID = inadequately described; LA/NT = Local Authorities and New Towns. A negative sign for net outmigration denotes net immigration to London; a positive sign in the final column indicates greater net outmigration.

Source: Migration Regional Reports of the 1971 and 1981 Censuses.

city areas has declined markedly since the early 1970s, the job opportunities available to inner city residents have contracted even more rapidly. Secondly, migration from the cities has in net terms been removing the types of people that are least affected by increasing unemployment. Despite the fact that numerous vacancies for less-skilled work are reported to exist in outer city areas, particularly in South East England, a combination of a badly structured welfare system, high transport costs, and difficulties of moving house appears to constitute a major barrier to taking advantage of these opportunities. In particular, the virtual absence of the private-rented sector in the suburbs and new growth areas, together with the rundown of public-sector housing construction, have made almost impossible a net transfer of lower-paid people out of the inner city areas in the 1980s. Indeed, pre-existing opportunities have contracted as a result of the sale of council houses, which has proceeded at faster rates in more attractive suburban-type locations (Forrest and Murie, 1983; Kleinman and Whitehead, 1987), while the prices in the owner-occupied sector have risen so far that first-time buyers appear increasingly to be excluded from the housing market (NBS, 1986).

In these circumstances, it is not surprising to find that population loss from inner areas has been running at a lower rate in the 1980s and that the government's efforts at introducing more private investment have met with some measure of success. As mentioned in the previous section, there are sound reasons for the slowdown in big-city population decline. They include the effect of rising divorce rates on the number of one-person households and single-parent families, which disproportionately seek accommodation in the rented sectors because of relatively low average incomes, but are also able to take advantage of the low-cost home ownership schemes introduced by the 1980 Housing Act and largely confined to the urban stress areas. Further sources of inner city rejuvenation are derived from the bulge of school leavers and young adults who are traditionally drawn towards metropolitan centres and from the changing structure of the labour market. In particular, the growth of financial and related services, and of the information economy in general, has encouraged young upwardly mobile professionals to buy into renovated inner city districts, particularly in London. Indeed, according to Hamnett and Williams (1980), gentrification or 'Chelseafication' was already proceeding rapidly in London during the 1970s – to the extent that the proportion of professional, managerial and intermediate non-manual workers in Inner London's population increased by the same amount as for Greater London as a whole (Hamnett, 1986).

These developments do not, however, mean that the end of the inner city problem is in sight, but instead tend to mask its growing severity. It is all too easy to make the mistake of treating it as a purely physical problem that can be overcome by renewal, as was discovered by costly experience in the USA during the 1960s and in Britain a decade later. In reality, it is a social and economic problem which is not fixed to a particular geographical space but which can transfer itself from place to place if it is not tackled at its source. One line of evidence is the fact that severe 'inner city' deprivation is no longer to be found just in older urban areas but also in the outer council-housing estates on the edges of cities which were built to house inner city residents displaced by renewal programmes (CES Ltd, 1985). To the extent that the new private initiatives in inner city areas are geared to 'outsiders', they do nothing to ease the shortage of accommodation for the less wealthy indigenous residents who are increasingly trapped by the contraction of alternative options. The plight of the latter is thrown into even sharper relief by the juxtaposition of considerable wealth and severe deprivation which result from these developments. In common with the number of other world cities, London is characterized by a shift towards a bipolar social structure with a marked under-representation of the middle-income groups which dominate the suburban and outer city locales (Hall, 1986). Unless firm steps are taken, the traditional residents of inner city areas are likely to become even more peripheral to mainstream national life and act as a drain on national economic growth rather than a resource contributing to it.

Conclusion: The Challenges of Population Redistribution and Associated Social Polarization

This chapter has argued that it is not only national population size, composition and behaviour that matter but also their changing patterns across regional and urban systems. The reason for this is that few localities contain populations which closely replicate the national profile and even fewer record rates of change similar to the nation as a whole. The long-term trends in population redistribution during the latter half of the twentieth century have broadly been serving to undo the principal features of population change in the nineteenth century when the North's share of national population increased and people concentrated into the major urban and industrial agglomerations. The so-called 'North–South drift' and 'urban–rural shift' have become particularly important issues over the past two decades, because with the slower rate of national population growth these forms of redistribution lead not only to relative decline but to an absolute fall in population numbers for many of the less dynamic areas. These issues have been intensified by the fact that, because of the very restrictive conditions operating in the Britain of today, most notably those relating to the labour market and housing, the migration processes which are largely responsible for these shifts have proved more than normally selective in terms of the types of people involved.

Several implications arise from these developments. In the first place, population decline means less than optimum use of the urban infrastructure built up during the major redevelopment phase of the later 1960s and 1970s. Secondly, the increasing selectivity of longer-distance migration brings greater spatial polarization of socio-demographic groups. There is, of course, nothing new about social segregation, whether by life-cycle stage, wealth or ethnic status; the geographical literature on this topic is extensive (see Herbert, 1972; Knox, 1982, for reviews). Most attention in the past, however, has been given to residential differentiation *within* urban areas, whereas the current trends are operating on a much broader canvas, such that young school leavers are drawn to London from all over Britain, older people retire to remoter rural areas where they previously enjoyed holidays, and young married couples move not just to the suburbs but to smaller cities and towns situated at considerable distance from the major urban centres. Because the British planning system reinforces a natural tendency towards 'lumpy' growth, individual places tend to grow rapidly for a relatively short time and then consolidate more gradually, with the result that a place takes on a particular profile which then becomes relatively 'fossilized'. The settlements developed under the 1946 New Towns Act provide an extreme example of this process because of rapid initial growth and often sharp cessation of planned in-migration, leading to major age-structure imbalances which will continue to work themselves out well into the next century (Champion, Clegg and Davies, 1977). In the short term, it may be very efficient to have an unbalanced socio-demographic structure since a full range of urban facilities may be unnecessary, but the serious longer term implications outweigh these temporary advantages.

Finally, it is important not to neglect the more insidious effects likely to arise from increased spatial polarization. One is the way in which selective migration tends to lead to cumulative effects on the origin and destination areas, respectively the vicious circle of decline for those places being denuded of their younger and better qualified people and the virtuous circle of growth resulting from the acquisition of young couples and the upgrading of the labour force. Another is the way in which the less mobile, whether living in declining regions or inner city areas, have tended to become trapped by their lack of resources, skills and housing options within labour markets which offer relatively few jobs and even poorer chances of career development. Such concentrations of multiple deprivation contain their own built-in momentum that has been characterized as a 'cycle of poverty' (Raynor et al., 1974). If through such processes these populations become even more distinctive and 'one-class', there is a real danger of their becoming progressively more isolated. Meanwhile, the existence of labour shortages in the most favoured parts of late 1980s Britain is evidence that opportunities remain, but lie beyond the grasp of the potentially available workforce. A more effective matching of workers and jobs constitutes one of the major challenges facing central government in the final years of the twentieth century. It was not faced squarely even in the heyday of regional policy, when measures placed much more emphasis on the mobility of industrial investment than on the movement of workers, and it has been almost completely ignored since the dismantling of regional planning in 1979. The London area plays a pivotal role in national migration patterns (Flowerdew and Salt, 1979; Salt and Flowerdew, 1980), so policy developments relating to south-east England over the next few years will be crucial to the way in which urban and regional patterns of population distribution evolve in the foreseeable future. If the housing market in southern England remains as tight as it stands in 1988, then the problems created by recent trends in social polarization are unlikely to diminish at any of the three scales treated in this chapter. There is a clear need for a population-orientated strategy to complement and reinforce policies aimed at local and national economic restructuring, but, as is argued further in the next chapter, if such an approach is to stand a good chance of success much more attention must be given to the improvement of data sets suitable for monitoring population change at regional and urban scales and to the study of the causes and consequences of internal migration.

Acknowledgements

The author is grateful to the University of Newcastle upon Tyne for allowing study leave and to the ESRC and British Academy for grants towards research expenses during the period when some of the results included in this chapter were obtained. The data for figure 8.1 were derived from the 1981 and 1984 Censuses of Employemnt, using the Manpower Services Commission's National Online Manpower Information System, programmed by Robert Nelson and Peter Dodds of the Durham University Geography Department. These data are Crown Copyright and are reproduced by the permission of the Department of Employment. Figure 8.1 was produced using GIMMS. Particular thanks go to Marilyn Champion for typing the manuscript.

Selected Key Reading

Richard, Lawton 1982: People and work. In John W. House (ed.), *The UK space*. London: Weidenfeld and Nicolson, 103–203.

Champion, Tony, Green, Anne, Owen, David, Ellin, David and Mike Coombes, 1987: *Changing Places: Britain's demographic, economic and social complexion*. London: Edward Arnold.

Goddard, John and Champion, Tony (eds) 1983: *The Urban and Regional Transformation of Britain*. London: Methuen.

Buck, Nick, Gordon, Ian and Young, Ken (eds) 1986: *The London Employment Problem*. Oxford: Clarendon Press.

Gould, Bill and Lawton, Richard (eds) 1986: *Planning for Population Change*. London: Croom Helm.

9 People and Services: Central Assessment of Local Needs

John Hobcraft

One of the most important uses of demographic data, particularly the Decennial Census, is in allocating funds from Central Government to Local Government and to the National Health Service. The purpose of this chapter is to review how demographic and other information are used in determining expenditure needs, as assessed by Central Government. As will become clear, the approaches used for Local Government and for the Health Service differ radically. We present several criteria by which such allocation systems should be judged and indicate many failings, for which remedies can often be suggested. The allocation procedures, especially for Local Government, are very complex and we cannot provide full details here (a more detailed account of the current system is given by Hobcraft, forthcoming; for a broader, historical sweep see Bennett, 1982; see also Department of the Environment, 1985, and Association of County Councils, 1985). Instead, we concentrate upon some key components and examples, which serve to illustrate the issues and problems involved.

Local Government accounts for about one-quarter of all public expenditure in the United Kingdom. Since 1981/2, Central Government has assessed the basic expenditure needs of Local Authorities through a complex formula for determining Grant Related Expenditure (GRE). This central assessment of local needs totalled £21.2 milliards (i.e. £21 200 million) for England alone in 1985/6. GRE forms a major component in the formula for determining the actual resource allocation, or the Block Grant (£8.5 milliards in England for 1985/6), which consists of the transfer from Central Government to augment the income that is derived from property rates.

When introduced, the new system was intended 'to be more comprehensible, stable and equitable as between authorities' (Heseltine, 1980, as quoted in Bennett 1982). Yet, by 1986, in the Green Paper *Paying for Local Government* we were told that 'The Government is concerned, however, that GREs have been subject to frequent changes' (Department of the Environment, 1986b). What went wrong so quickly? I shall later argue that the instability arose mainly from frequent policy changes by Central Government and from the imposition of cash limits on an inherently bottom-up system. The broad philosophy underlying the system is not at fault, although the somewhat inevitable complexity may have led to a failure to grasp implications of changes in time to prevent the odder features of instability.

The National Health Service relies almost entirely upon Central Government assessment of its budgetary needs. Since 1977/8, funding for hospital and community health services (about £9 milliards for England alone in 1985/6) has been determined according to a formula named after the acronym of the Resource Allocation Working Party (RAWP), which had the avowed aim of eventually achieving 'equal opportunity of access to health care for people at equal risk' (DHSS, 1976b). Since its inception, this procedure has been fiercely attacked on many occasions, including *The Black Report* (Townsend and Davidson, 1982) and *The Health Divide* (Whitehead, 1987) for failing to take account of morbidity and of social deprivation (see Mays and Bevan, 1987, for a review of the vast literature generated by the debate

Table 9.1   The main components of Grant Related Expenditure for England and Wales, 1985/6

Major heading	Sub-heading	Milliards of pounds	Per cent of total
People			
	Totals	1.9	9.0
	Age Groups	0.7	3.1
	Pupils	7.7	36.5
	Total (all items)	10.3	48.6
Physical features			
	Roads	1.4	6.6
	Density of population	0.7	3.3
	Domestic properties	0.5	2.2
	Total (all items)	3.0	14.2
Environmental and social			
	Assessment of Educational Needs (AEN)	0.9	4.3
	Other social	0.4	1.8
	Transport	0.2	1.0
	Recreation	0.4	2.0
	Total (all items)	1.9	9.1
Special requirements			
	Actual expenditures	2.5	11.8
	Personal Social Services	2.3	10.8
	Total (all items)	5.1	24.9
Total		21.2	100.0

Source: Association of County Councils, 1985.

on the use of the RAWP formula). The formula is being subjected to a review by the NHS Management Committee.

Grant Related Expenditure

The key principle underlying the assessment of Grant Related Expenditure is to combine estimates of the basic unit cost of providing a service, as judged by Central Government, with estimates of the basic need for the service, which might be the population requiring the service or the physical requirements, such as road mileages or numbers of dwellings. Thus the expenditure needs are built up from a whole series of estimates, referring to the many components of Local Government expenditure. Basic expenditure needs for each Local Authority are assessed using over 60 major indicators of needs and associated unit costs, with some 200 indicators being used overall. Table 9.1 provides a breakdown of the expenditure assessment for England in 1985/6 by very broad headings. Demographic and social indicators are crucial components of most of these estimates. Our treatment here focuses on examples where such inputs are important and pays less attention items such as actual expenditure and roads and transport, where demographic inputs matter less.

Central Government assessments of total basic expenditure needs for Local Authorities in England for 1985/6 ranged from £359 per head of population for Surrey to approximately £717 per head for Islington. Some examples of the sources of major differences between authorities are given in table 9.2, which shows the contributions per head of total population from each of the main expenditure headings. Figures are presented for Surrey, with the lowest GRE per head of any Authority, for three Authorities with fairly high assessed expenditure needs of around £500 per head (Cleveland, Knowsley and Waltham Forest), and for two Authorties with among the highest of all assessed needs, at about £675 (Hackney and Westminster). The final column of table 9.2 presents the range of assessed needs per head across all authorities for each expenditure heading. The figures for the London Boroughs present several problems of comparison: the estimates for both education and socio-economic deprivation refer to the entire Inner London Education Authority (ILEA), rather than to the individual Boroughs; the estimates based on population density and for transport and recreation redistribution should be the larger of the two figures presented for comparative purposes, in order to include the provisions for the Metropolitan Police; finally, where relevant, we have added average expenditure assessments for the Greater London Council (GLC) to each London Borough, in order to obtain total figures. The choice of 1985/6, rather than a more recent period, is deliberate, since the comparisons over time made later in this chapter would be precluded by

Table 9.2 Components of Grant Related Expenditure assessment, 1985/6 (£ per head of population)

Expenditure heading	Surrey	Cleveland	Knowsley	Waltham Forest	Hackney	Westminster	Maximum range
Education (pupils)	146	187	189	163	(130)	(130)	74
Total population	40	41	41	34	45	84	51
Age-groups	14	14	14	14	14	13	2
Density	10	20	19	17(39)	27(64)	30(70)	21(62)
Roads	30	29	25	19	17	20	19
Property & Development	15	15	12	16	17	41	29
Socio-economic deprivation	12	38	52	50	(60)	(61)	62
Transport & recreation redistribution	6	21	24	17(34)	31(74)	45(92)	39(86)
Personal social services	31	54	66	71	124	90	92
Housing Revenue Account deficit	0	1	0	20	84	31	148
Actual expenditure	44	60	51	61	97	93	54
London costs	11	–	–	36	56	60	60
Residuals (mainly interest adjustments)	–	15	25	–3	–23	–29	
Total (per head)	359	495	518	515	679	669	358
Million (pounds)	320	243	68	93	67	64	

Surrey is a Shire County near London; Cleveland is a Shire County in North East England; Knowsley is a Metropolitan District in the Merseyside Conurbation; Waltham Forest is an Outer London Borough; Hackney and Westminster are Inner London Boroughs.

Source: Derived from Association of County Councils, 1985.

the discontinuity introduced for 1986/7, through the dismantling of the major Metropolitan Authorities, such as the GLC.

The estimated needs for education differ simply as a result of differing proportions of the total population being pupils. Allocations under this heading are based upon estimates of actual numbers of pupils, with the result that discretionary expenditure on children above the minimum school leaving age is compensated, rather than adhering to a principle of assessing basic needs equitably. A further adjustment (the 'Assessment of Educational Needs' component of the socio-economic deprivation figures, considered below) is intended to allow for varying requirements for special schooling and remedial teaching for deprived groups.

On the whole, there is very little variation between Authorities in the amounts per head allocated on the basis of total population figures, although Westminster provides a striking exception; the very large amount for Westminster derives from the large daytime population, since *all* provision for library expenditure for commuters is transferred to their place of work! The quite complicated allowances for provision of expenditure based on different age groups result in almost no differentiation between authorities, suggesting that considerable simplification would be in order.

The London Boroughs derive considerable extra assessed needs from their higher population densities, particularly when the figures are made more nearly comparable (those in parentheses); moreover, density is used in several of the other expenditure needs assessments and is probably one of the major factors in providing the higher assessed needs for London, especially Inner London, in comparison with other major Metropolitan Districts. Rural Shires get slightly larger allocations for roads and there is generally small variation in the allocations for property and development, with Westminster again being unusual because of the large number of shops and restaurants requiring attention.

The next major expenditure heading refers to measures reflecting supposed socio-economic deprivation. We shall return to this issue later, but it surprised me to discover that the population of Waltham Forest needed more expenditure per head for such deprivation than that of Cleveland and about the same amount as Knowsley; similar observations stem from the comparison of Hackney and Westminster, although this is hampered by including components referring to ILEA.

The London Boroughs again do rather well in terms of provision for transport and recreation (again using the figures in parentheses for comparative purposes), with these allocations being quite dependent upon population density.

The allocations for personal social services differ very substantially between authorities. It is again perhaps surprising that needs in Waltham Forest are greater than in Knowsley and striking how much higher the estimated needs are for Hackney than for Knowsley; part of the reason for the lowish assessment for Knowsley is due to the very low proportion of elderly, although this might easily be offset in principle by the atypically high proportions of children there. We shall discuss these apparent anomalies more fully later.

The next two items refer to actual expenditures incurred, rather than estimated nominal needs. Housing Revenue Account deficits are zero for most Authorities, but can be quite large; Camden had the highest figure per head in 1985/6, but the subsequent transfer of GLC deficits to individual Boroughs in the following year led to Tower Hamlets showing by far the largest deficit per head, at £286. Several items appear under the 'actual expenditure' heading, including contributions to educational pools and debt servicing. The final major item covers all allowances for greater costs incurred in London, including differences in salaries.

The notional expenditure level assessed by the GRE plays a vital role in the process of allocation for the Block Grant element of the Rate Support Grant, so that it is of considerable importance for the assessment procedure to be equitable. A similar though perhaps simpler procedure is expected to be used in assessing expenditure needs for the allocation of central funds to Local Government under the proposed 'community charge'.

The RAWP Procedure

The complexity of the client group/unit cost approach which is the basis for the GRE contrasts with the formula used to allocate the great majority of current expenditure to the National Health Service. The main elements of the approach are fairly straightforward, although many subsidiary complexities exist.

Information is available from the Hospital In-Patient Enquiry (HIPE) on national bed-use rates by sex, age group and medical condition for non-psychiatric patients, where conditions are grouped according to the seventeen major Chapter headings of the International Classification of Diseases. Similar, but more limited, national estimates are available for bed-use rates by psychiatric (mental illness) in-patients by age, sex and marital status. Day and out-patient visit rates and psychiatric (mental handicap) in-patient bed-use rates are obtainable by age and sex. Community health service use-rates are available by broad age groups.

These various rates are used in conjunction with the estimated age–sex (and marital status) distributions for Regional Health Authorities in order to derive expected bed-occupancy days (or visits) for each condition in each region. These estimates thus assume a nationally undifferentiated level of disease prevalence or bed-occupancy.

The second key component in the RAWP procedure consists of an adjust-

Table 9.3 Differentials in health indicators for Standard Statistical Regions

	Standardized Mortality Ratios (persons), 1972	1972 Male certified incapacity (stand, for age)	GHS, 1972 Self-reported chronic illness, (stand for age and sex)	GHS, 1972 Self-reported acute illness, (stand for age and sex)
North	110	128	112	105
North-West	110	120	100	98
Wales	107	151	113	112
Yorks & Humb.	106	129	116	118
West Mids	103	86	102	95
East Mids	99	107	103	101
GLC	97	(74)	96	102
South West	93	86	89	81
Outer Metrop.	92	(74)	87	105
East Anglia	89	72	101	85
Outer South-East	89	(74)	88	93
Higest/lowest	1.24	2.10	1.33	1.46

Source: DHSS (1976b) Sharing Resources for Health in England (Report of the Resource Allocation Working Party). HMSO.

ment which is intended to represent regional differentials in need for each service. This adjustment depends solely on the age–sex (and marital status) Standardized Mortality Ratios (SMRs) for each of the 17 major Chapters of disease. Table 9.3 shows the overall SMRs for 1972; these indicate, for example, that there was a 10 per cent relative excess mortality in the Northern Region and an 11 per cent relative advantage in East Anglia. It is then *assumed* that these mortality measures *correctly reflect* more general health (or morbidity) differentials and, furthermore, that *10 per cent extra resources* are needed to compensate for a *10 per cent excess risk*. There seems to be absolutely no evidence in favour of this second, crucial assumption (nor is there evidence against; the issue is remarkably unresearched and rarely even regarded as worth discussing; see Mays and Bevan, 1987).

The use of the SMRs as the sole measure of regional disparities in health needs has, not surprisingly, been the source of much criticism: put bluntly and unfairly, why reward incompetence, since health services are meant to save lives? The Working Party did consider the possibility of using other measures of health (or morbidity), but gave them short shrift. Thus 'factors such as occupation, poverty, social class and pollution are likely to interact in ways which are not fully understood' (DHSS, 1976b, p. 15). But the Working Party did not need to dally with morbidity indicators, since 'the reasons for the pattern of differential Regional mortality are not wholly understood but it is believed that Regional differences in morbidity explain the greater part of it and that statistics of relative differences in Regional morbidity, if they existed, would exhibit the same pattern as those for mortality' (DHSS, 1976b, p. 16). If we examine the three morbidity indicators shown in table 9.3, which do exist in the RAWP report, we see cases where the differences are consistently larger than for the SMRs. Wales, Yorkshire and Humberside, and East Midlands always fare worse on the morbidity indicators than on the SMRs; and West Midlands and the South-West always appear even more advantaged on these morbidity indicators. Although the broad patterns of Regional differences may be smiliar (and even fairly highly correlated) they are manifestly not absolutely the same. Indeed, other things being equal and accepting the other aspects of the RAWP formula, the SMRs suggest that the worst region requires 24 per cent more resources than the best; each of the three morbidity indicators would suggest that much greater disparities in health and therefore funding needs existed, with the worst region requiring respectively, 110, 33 or 46 per cent more resources than the best. It is remarkable that the Working Party could be so cavalier in ignoring its own evidence; it is perhaps even more surprising that no crash research programme was advocated in order to provide a solid base for the allocation of such a vast sum of money. It is little short of a national disgrace that allocations are still being made using such a crude approach.

However, many of the severest critics of the RAWP formula seem to have adopted fallacious lines of argument. There are very large and probably widening socio-economic differentials in mortality in Britain. Most of the studies which show this are based on SMRs. Clearly, the SMRs (as used in the RAWP formula) capture these differences rather well, so that a case cannot *thus* be made for inclusion of measure of socio-economic deprivation in the RAWP formula, as for example *The Black Report* (Townsend and Davidson, 1982) appears to argue. However, there are a number of studies which do suggest that socio-economic characteristics are related to morbidity and to access to health services. There is an urgent need for research to clarify whether socio-economic differentials in ill-health persist at the level of Health Authorities, once the SMRs have been controlled. Without such research we shall never have a conclusive demonstration of the need (or lack thereof) to include other indicators in resource allocation to the NHS. A serious extension of the simple analysis presented in the previous paragraph would be of more help than a thousand more studies documenting that socio-economic differentials in mortality exist.

Because the RAWP formula is only used to determine shares of the nationally allocated budget for the NHS, it has not suffered from the same instability of allocations for individual Regional Health Authorities that has occurred for Local Authorities. It is less susceptible to tinkering with individual unit costs in order to make the total budget for a particular service conform to externally imposed cash limits. However, this is also a major limitation of the approach, which fails to capture explicit changes in unit costs and thus makes it far harder to discover what criteria are being used in order to reach the total budget. The use of the RAWP formula also tends to rigidify the allocation of resources between different specialisms, and thus reflects past expenditure patterns rather than an explicit assessment of needs. The principles under-lying the formula for GRE seem preferable in this respect.

The previous paragraph is not intended to suggest that there have been no problems with the allocation of funds through RAWP. At the time of writing (in early 1988), there is a commonly recognized 'crisis' in the funding of the National Health Service. Much of the debate properly focuses upon the total amount allocated for the NHS, rather than the RAWP procedure which is used to share most of this money out. But some of the problems, particularly those of provision of hospital services in inner-city areas, do arise from the progressive reallocation of funds since the introduction of RAWP. Table 9.4 shows the percentage difference of allocations for Regional Health Authorities from their 'RAWP Targets' for four funding years, each three years apart. The goal of achieving equal provision for equal need would be met (on RAWP criteria) when allocations actually equal the targets.

In the early period of the application of the formula, Oxford RHA was rapidly brought down to to RAWP target levels and Merseyside RHA brought up. It seems that these two RHAs were singled out as examples, since elsewhere the pace of change was slow.

Table 9.4 Percentage distance of Regional Health Authority allocations from RAWP revenue targets

		Year		
Regional Health Authority	*1977/8*	*1980/1*	*1983/4*	*1986/7*
North-West Thames	14.7	12.7	10.7	7.6
North-East Thames	13.4	10.0	8.7	5.9
South-East Thames	12.1	10.6	6.0	3.9
Oxford	6.3	−0.3	0.0	−2.0
South-West Thames	5.8	5.2	6.4	1.9
Mersey	−4.9	−0.9	−1.5	0.1
Yorkshire	−5.7	−3.5	−4.3	−2.2
South-Western	−6.5	−4.4	−4.3	−2.4
East Anglia	−7.2	−5.9	−6.4	−3.8
West Midlands	−8.0	−4.9	−3.8	−3.9
Wessex	−8.3	−4.1	−4.8	−1.4
Northern	−13.2	−6.0	−3.7	−1.9
Trent	−13.3	−7.5	−5.0	−3.7
North-Western	−14.5	−7.5	−4.0	−0.8
Range (percentage points)	29.2	20.2	17.1	11.5

Source: DHSS (1983), and personal communication from Brian Benson.

In the three years from 1983/4 to 1986/7, this situation changed and the Conservative government began to make the RAWP targets 'bite'. This has led to particularly large reductions in the 'over-allocations' to the four Thames RHAs, at a time when London was undergoing further population loss. The combination of population loss and greater implementation of the RAWP criteria for achieving equity has led to substantial relative losses of resources for the District Health Authorities covering Inner London. These Districts contain the most prestigious teaching hospitals, which are staffed by the medical establishment. Serious issues of equity of provision arise in this context, since major cut-backs in relative resources are likely to be destructive of excellence, which serves in part as a national resource. Yet it is hardly convenient for patients in areas with growing population to have to travel to Inner London for routine treatment. And it is surely time that the relatively under-resourced areas of England had a fairer allocation of resources to help fight their manifestly worse health and survival chances. Perhaps the only viable solution to these problems is to remove one or more major teaching hospitals from London and establish regional centres of excellence.

The Quality of Indicators

We now turn to a discussion of a series of issues associated with the quality of indicators used. As already shown, these issues are important for the RAWP formula, but the examples considered will be drawn mainly from the procedures used in assessing Grant Related Expenditure. Estimation of unit costs is always extremely difficult, particularly when the aim is, quite properly, to assess the basic cost of providing a necessary service, rather than the average discretionary expenditure on all service provision. Such a goal usually makes it almost impossible to use past expenditure levels in estimating unit costs and considerable ingenuity is often required, which sometimes regrettably leads to estimates which are almost pure fabrication.

Although we shall return to unit costs briefly, the main focus of this chapter is on the use (and abuse) of demographic and related data, which feature in population estimates and in the derivation of specific deprivation indicators and of estimates of risk groups or client populations. There are several criteria by which the specific quality of indicators should be judged, including *timeliness, accuracy, reliability, consistency, specificity,* and *the choice and construction of the components involved.* Elements of the formulae used in assessing Grant Related Expenditure needs can be shown to fail by all these criteria. Such failure should, wherever possible, be rectified and a number of suggestions are made. The failings may also justify some simplification, if only to allow greater resources to be devoted to the most important indicators. But the failings are not a reason for abandoning a system which is based upon very reasonable principles, although not always working in practice.

Timeliness of inputs is a major problem in the GRE formulae. Basic population estimates are updated annually, but heavy reliance is placed upon very dated sources, most notably the 1981 Census, which is already nearly seven years out of date and will be eleven or twelve years old before the 1991 Census results become available. Sudden and infrequent changes of many inputs clearly undermine stability.

Several inputs used in assessing the population over age 65 'at risk' of requiring personal social services are derived from the 1977/9 National Dwelling and Housing Survey (NDHS). For example, each person aged 65 and over who lives alone and has mobility problems attracts £729 for personal social service provision, which is by far the largest component in the relevant formula. Yet the proportion of the total population aged 65 and over in this category is estimated from the NDHS for each Authority and is now ten years out of date, during which period there has been a significant increase in the numbers of elderly, including the very old.

Accuracy of inputs is also crucial. The 1981 Census was estimated to have been under-counted by about half a per cent (around two hundred thousand people) in England and Wales as a whole and by about two and a half per cent in Inner London (about fifty five thousand people). The population estimates used in the GRE formulae include a rough and ready adjustment for this under-count, but other Census-based indicators are not adjusted (e.g. single parent families and privately renting households, both of which are differentially under-counted; see Britton and Birch, 1985).

Mid-year population estimates are derived through a continued and complicated updating procedure, with the most recent (adjusted) Census estimates of population as a base. Comparisons of the 1981 estimates (derived using the 1971 Census as a starting point) with the results from the 1981 Census showed some moderately large discrepancies. The total population estimates for Districts in 1981, based on updates from the 1971 Census, were generally accurate to within two per cent, but the error was in excess of five per cent in some cases (Thatcher, 1985). For sub-divisions into broad age-groups within Districts the *average* error was about five per cent.

The numbers of elderly people were considerably overestimated in London during the late 1970s: this led to an understatement of the SMRs, with consequent loss of health resources; it also resulted in a relative over-allocation for personal social services. Given that retroactive adjustment (especially downwards) is politically infeasible it is important to achieve higher quality estimates.

A third, closely related issue is *reliability* of indicators. An example is provided in assessing the needs for Personal Social Services for children under the age of five, which primarily consist of residential care and foster care. A notional £75 million per year is shared out on the basis of a regression formula derived from a 1974 survey, which included only 75 children identified as being in need of personal social services, the dependent variable (see Derbyshire, 1987, for a fuller discussion). A very limited range of deprivation indicators were used and at least one of the regression coefficients included in the final model is not statistically significant. Standard errors are large on all the coefficients used in the regression equations for estimating both the population at risk and the unit costs and this could lead to considerable potential error in the estimated expenditure needs for individual Authorities. Larger samples and a better choice of indicators are required.

Indicators should also be *specific*. To continue with the example of assessing expenditure needs for Personal Social Services for the under fives, lone-parent families are the main source of the population at risk, but there is no attempt to target the risk group more specifically. For example, the DHSS maintain records of lone-parent families in receipt of Supplementary Benefit, who are probably at higher risk of requiring support from the Social Services. It would be possible for these records to be analysed in order to produce statistics at the Local Authority level, which could then be used to improve the specificity of the estimates. As was shown in chapter 4, some 55 per cent of lone-parent families are in receipt of Supplementary Benefits, suggesting that such specificity could be important in this instance, especially since these poorer families will not be proportionately distributed among all Local Authorities. Many further examples of this need for greater specificity could be given. Formulae are often heavily constrained by lack of available data at the Local Authority level, which could be remedied at some cost through the 'Resource Allocation Survey' which is later advocated.

In addition to being *consistent* over time, it is clearly desirable that indicators used within a single year be consistent. Yet the estimates of the incidence of lone-parent families as used in various formulae for the 1985/6 GRE assessment are mutually inconsistent and also inconsistent with the estimates used in 1983/4. In 1983/4, estimates of the numbers of lone-parent families seem consistently and wrongly to have been based upon early tabulations from the 1981 Census, which identified 414 298 *households* in Great Britain containing one or more children aged under 16 living with only one adult. But the best official estimates for the number of lone-parent families in 1981 suggest that there were in fact some 900 000 such families in Great Britain (see Haskey, 1986, who indicates that an estimate of 825 000 lone-parent families for 1978 was given to Parliament in 1981). Thus the estimates used in the GRE for 1983/4 were less than 50 per cent of the likely true figures. For the assessment year 1985/6, the Department of the Environment continued to use these raw Census figures, which show just over a million *people* in one-parent families (very poorly defined), in their index of an area's social conditions. In assessing additional needs for educational expenditure (AEN) and the needs for Personal Social Services for children aged less than 17, both the Department of Education and Science and the Department of Health and Social Security use better estimates, which give a total of nearly 1.5 million *children* in lone-parent families.

Issues of *reliability* also arise here, since the adjusted national figures are based upon a grossing up of estimates from the General Household. Haskey (1986) provides estimates of the confidence interval around the adjusted estimate for 1984 of 940 000 families of plus or minus 60 000 families. It is not clear whether these are true sampling errors, which take account of the clustering of lone-parent families; if not, then the confidence interval would be considerably larger. The sums of money allocated on the basis of these unreliable estimates are large: each additional child aged 5–17 in a lone-parent family attracts just over a thousand pounds in GRE. Use of the same proportionate sampling error would suggest a 95 per cent confidence interval of plus or minus 74 000 children in this age-group, leading to a possible error in the GRE under this heading of about £75 million.

Issues of *consistency* of approach also arise in the *choice and construction of indicators*, especially those relating to deprivation. The Department of Education and Science use the most transparent and crude approach to the assessment of deprivation. For each primary pupil estimated as being in a household where the child, or the head of household, was born outside the United Kingdom, Eire, the United States or the Old Commonwealth, the Authority receives an extra £274; if the pupil is estimated to be in a household which is lacking amenities or overcrowded, is in a one-parent household, has four or more dependent children under the age of 16, where the head is semiskilled, unskilled or a farm worker, or whose family is in receipt of Supplementary Benefit, the authority accrues an additional £137 on each count. Multiple deprivation is therefore treated as being strictly additive, which is questionable. The certain selection-out of advantaged families into private education is ignored, since proportions of disadvantaged pupils are derived from Census figures covering all children aged under 17. A child qualifying on every indicator would attract an extra £958 to its Local Authority, compared with the basic £825 for each primary pupil. Similar but slightly larger amounts are allocated in the same way for secondary pupils. The eventual impact of this redistribution is to alter the amount allocated per primary school pupil from the national average of £950 by fairly small amounts. ILEA gets £1041, or an extra 9.6 per cent per pupil. Outer London gets an extra 1.4 per cent, the Metropolitan Districts an extra 0.6 per cent, and the Shires lose 0.9 per cent (or £9) per pupil. The maximum difference, of £179 per pupil (or 19 per cent) occurs between Newham and North Yorkshire.

In contrast, the estimation of basic spending needs for Personal Social Services is far more complex. For example, the formula for children aged

5–17 is based on elaborate regression equations, which are presented in a fairly obscure way and involve 12 indicators and 25 regression coefficients, including an interaction term. But a single indicator dominates the equations, namely the estimated number of children aged 5–17 who are living in a lone-parent family: each such child accrues a thousand pounds. The average sum allocated for *every* child aged 5–17 by these children in single-parent families ranges from a minimum of about £100 to a maximum of just over £300; a range of £200. Each of the several other indicators used affects the total allocation per child by much less, with overall ranges of £12 to £18. A final adjustment procedure, involving four indicators, could alter the total amount by up to 30 per cent.

Once again, there is considerable imprecision in the various regression formulae used and in some of the indicators. This is dramatized in table 9.5, which presents the results of setting each coefficient at plus or minus two standard errors in order to illustrate the potential range of estimates for expenditure needs for an authority; it must be stressed that this simple procedure overstates the true variability, but we do not have available sufficient information to enable a better assessment. The starting point is an estimate of the nominal expenditure of £261 per child aged 5–17 that would be attracted by an average Borough in Inner London, simply on the basis of the estimated incidence of lone-parent families. If the regression coefficients for estimating the population 'at risk' of requiring Personal Social Services are set at plus or minus two standard errors, this estimated expenditure need might range from £167 to £356 per child aged 5–17. Secondly, the estimated number of children in lone-parent families is subject to considerable error, through under-counting in the Census and through the large sampling errors involved in grossing up (at the national level, which may in itself be inappropriate for individual Authorities) from the General Household

Table 9.5   Personal Social Services for children aged 5–17: contributions (in pounds per child aged 5–17) to GRE from lone-parent families, assessed at average values for Inner London

Source	At mean value (of risk)	Lower Bound[a]	Upper Bound[a]
Formula as used	261		
Estimates of population at risk	261	167	356
Lone parents (±15%)	222 to 300	142	410
Estimates of unit costs	199 to 324	108	509

[a] Lower and upper bounds are obtained by setting *all* regression coefficients to plus or minus two standard errors. Values in this column for successive rows include a combination of all previously identified sources of error.

Source: Review of Methodology on Personal Social Services, 1984, Local Government Working Group, LGF(G)(PSS)(84)R2.

Survey. As a rough and ready indication of the possible errors here, we allow for an error of 15 per cent in either direction, which may be conservative. On its own, this range of error could produce estimates of needed expenditure per child in an Authority of £222 to £300; if combined with the previous range of errors, the maximal errors might range from £142 to £410 per child. Finally, the regression equations used to assess unit costs also have large standard errors, which could lead to extreme estimates of £199 to £324, with other estimates at the mean. In the worst possible case, with all errors operating in the same direction and all being at plus or minus two standard errors (a most unlikely occurrence and an overstatement of the true joint confidence intervals), the estimated expenditure needs might range from £108 to £509 for every child aged 5–17. Such uncertainty in the allocation procedures (even if considerably overstated) is extremely worrying. But the approach used has considerable advantage in principle over the cruder system used for educational deprivation, since there is an attempt to relate expenditure needs directly to deprivation indicators, rather than adoption of an *ad hoc* procedure with little justification other than expediency.

A crucial issue in estimating groups at risk of needing a service and in predicting relative costs is the *choice of explanatory variables*. The desire to avoid using past expenditure in assessing need means that attention has often to be confined to those indicators which are easily available at the Local Authority level, but the choice often appears to be arbitrarily restricted. The indicators used are often extremely remote surrogates for true risk, and multiple deprivation is rarely treated as interactive rather than additive. All too often, resort is made to the standard measures of housing deprivation which are easily available from the Census, without any apparent consideration of whether these are sufficiently specific for the purpose at hand.

Many of the difficulties of timeliness, accuracy, reliability, specificity and of the construction and choice of indicators would be eased very considerably if Central Government were to institute a *very large continuing 'Resource Allocation' survey*, with a sample of perhaps two to ten per cent of the population in each year. Such a survey would probably serve to replace much of the need for a Decennial Census once established and would provide up-to-date estimates. An annual expenditure of some £3 million to £10 million might be involved, compared with about £40 million for the 1981 Census. Given that results would be used to allocate over £20 000 million per year, simply for the National Health Service and for the Block Grant, such a seemingly large expenditure would almost certainly be justified by improved efficiency in targeting expenditure.

An ongoing survey would be much more flexible, permitting more rapid introduction of new measures and much wider content than the Census. When questions, for example on morbidity, had been validated in the General Household Survey, it would be possible to include them in the

Resource Allocation Survey. More 'difficult' measures could be obtained periodically, but more frequently than once every ten years. Where necessary, the precision of estimates could be improved by using information from several successive years. Such a large Survey would of course serve many other governmental purposes. Widespread access by researchers would undoubtedly generate findings which could be used to improve the precision with which resources were targeted.

Broader Criteria for Resource Allocation Procedures

It is more or less impossible to consider formulae used for resource allocation without paying close attention to issues of *stability, equity, transparency and public accountability*. A system must work, in the sense of providing stable and predictable funding for individual Authorities, otherwise prudent planning is impossible to achieve. It must work well, in the sense of providing an equitable allocation, so that those in need really benefit. And it must be seen to work well, which requires the system to be transparent enough for public scrutiny to take place.

One problem is that these goals often conflict. For example, deprivation is associated with many factors, meaning that any equitable system loses transparency. If new research demonstrates a hitherto unknown link between needs and an available indicator, equity demands a change to the system, but this serves to undermine stability to an extent. But these criteria are also sometimes mutually reinforcing. For example, a just procedure may well require considerable complexity, but if it is stable over time, resources can be invested in making the procedure more transparent through better presentation of the justification for a formula and of the import of complex formulae and their inherent uncertainties in cash terms. Public accountability and transparency might be assisted by opening up the negotiation process between Central and Local government to participation by disinterested, knowledgeable parties and to non-expert advisors who could seek to ensure transparency, which is manifestly lacking in current procedures, particularly for the assessment of Grant Related Expenditure.

As was shown in table 9.2, Cleveland, Knowsley and Waltham Forest were all assessed as having similar expenditure needs for 1985/6, at about £500 per head of population; Hackney and Westminster have more or less equal assessments at about £670 per head. Is this *equitable*? Table 9.6 shows several indicators used in the derivation of GRE elements which are related to deprivation. By many indicators Knowsley is as deprived as Hackney and both Knowsley and Cleveland are more deprived than Waltham Forest. Yet the GRE figures do not reflect this.

London, especially Inner London, gains considerably from the heavy

Table 9.6 Some indicators of deprivation

	Surrey	Cleveland	Knowsley	Waltham Forest	Hackney	West-minster
GRE per head (£)	359	495	518	515	679	669
Household characteristics (per thousand persons) – 1981 Census						
Not self-contained	5	2	0	25	53	58
Lack amenity	20	29	19	80	88	82
Overcrowded	7	13	25	25	48	50
Lone parent	15	24	32	27	52	29
NCWP head	25	16	6	175	280	125
Lack car or van	15	39	52	36	57	56
Private rented accomod.	106	60	39	151	212	453
Economic (per cent)						
Unemployment benefit	2	10	12	5	10	7
Youth unempl.	3	17	23	8	(13)	(10)
Children 5–17 on SB	4	25	36	17	30	13
Children 5–17 low SEG	4	9	12	5	11	17
GRE indices						
Assessment of educational needs index	49	85	107	133	(158)	(158)
Area social conditions (£/head)	−17	−4	12	45	101	82
Density	16	32	30	63	103	113
Personal Social Services (£/head)	31	54	66	71	124	90

Source: Association of County Councils (1985)

weight given to population density and to a range of household characteristics derived from the Census, which are widely used in the redistributional
formulae. Scant weight is given to indices of economic deprivation, such as
unemployment levels and proportions of children or families in receipt of
Supplementary Benefit. Needs for Personal Social Services for children are
assumed to be predominantly determined by being in a lone-parent family,
regardless of the economic circumstances of the family.

Local Authority housing usually satisfies most of the basic criteria used to
assess housing deprivation in the Census, for example being self-contained,

having baths and inside toilets and avoiding overcrowding. Yet many of the poorest families, at risk of most forms of deprivation, are to be found in such housing. In particular, areas like Knowsley and Tower Hamlets, which contain vast tracts of the poorest council housing, do not show up as especially in need of redistributional funding under the formulae used in the assessment of GRE. In contrast, the privately rented, multiple-occupied flats of affluent young professionals in parts of Inner London (e.g. Camden or Kensington and Chelsea) would show up as deprived on several of the standard Census-based indicators. The lack of *specificity* in these indicators leads to manifest failure to achieve equity.

The use of better measures of (housing) deprivation, such as the Census-based ACORN (A Classification of Residential Neighbourhoods) or PIN-POINT schemes would undoubtedly be preferable to the current indicators. Table 9.7 illustrates this point. The five 'most deprived' Authorities are identified under several criteria. The first three are measures from the GRE assessment, all of which rely heavily on the 'standard' measures of housing characteristics from the Census. It is noteworthy that only London Authorities appear as most deprived by these criteria. The third item, which simply takes the sum of the four indicators most commonly used as measures of (housing) deprivation in the GRE formulae, identifies Kensington and Chelsea, Camden, and Hammersmith and Fulham as being among the five 'most deprived' Authorities in England: while these Boroughs contain pockets of deprivation and of poverty, it is clearly a nonsensical ranking.

The fourth item in table 9.7 shows the five Authorities identified as having the worst housing conditions under the ACORN scheme, which includes multiple criteria and identifies four mutually exclusive groups of housing areas associated with particular deprivation, each of which could be treated separately in the allocation of resources: poor terraced housing, the poorest Local Authority housing, areas with a high concentration of multiple-occupancy and of people of Asian origin, and areas with a high concentration of multi-let property with a significant proportion of people of Afro-Caribbean origin. The five 'most deprived' Authorities now include Liverpool and Knowsley and three of the poorest areas of Inner London. Even if this classification scheme could be improved upon, it clearly serves far better than the traditional indicators in identifying those areas most in need of extra resources, in order to compensate for poverty and deprivation, through educational and personal social service provision. Given that these indicators already exist for Local Authorities, it is surely indefensible to fail to explore their potential for improving the equity of resource allocation, and perhaps surprising that they have not yet been incorporated in the formulae for assessing GRE. Similar arguments might be advanced with respect to the measures of economic deprivation, which are presented as items five and six in table 9.7 and are given extremely low weight in the assessment of GRE,

Table 9.7   The five 'most deprived' Local Authorities according to several criteria

1   GRE, Assessment of Educational Needs
      Brent, Newham, Haringey, Ealing, ILEA
2   GRE, Personal Social Services (Pounds per head of population)
      Hackney, Lambeth, Hammersmith, Tower Hamlets, Islington
3   GRE, Housing indicators (lack amenity, density, not self-contained, lone-parent)
      Hammersmith, Kensington, Hackney, Camden, Newham
4   ACORN, Housing (poor terraced, poorest local authority, multi-occupied Asian, multi-let
      Afro-Caribbean)
      Hackney, Tower Hamlets, Knowsley, Liverpool, Southwark
5   Percentage receiving Unemployment Benefit
      Knowsley, Liverpool, Tower Hamlets, Hackney, Lambeth
6   Percentage of children aged 5–17 dependent on Supplementary Benefit claimants
      Tower Hamlets, Knowsley, Liverpool, Hackney, Lambeth
7   Department of the Environment 'Z-Scores'
      Hackney, Newham, Tower Hamlets, Lambeth, Hammersmith

Sources: Association of County Councils, 1985; Hayes, 1986

compared with the multiple use of housing indicators and of measures of ethnic origin.

The same points can also be made in the context of assessment of needs other than for the GRE. For example, the Department of the Environment makes heavy use of similar housing indicators to those used in assessing GRE and little use of economic indicators in deriving its 'Z-scores', presented as item seven in table 9.7, which are used to identify special areas. These suffer from the further problem of treating all deprivation as relative and scaling all measures to the same variance (as is also done for the index of an 'area's social conditions' used in the assessment of GRE). Clearly it is unreasonable to assume that being one standard deviation above the mean in terms of any indicator corresponds to the same amount of deprivation. If resources are being allocated in order to compensate deprivation, the absolute amount of deprivation must be relevant.

Stability has manifestly failed to be achieved in recent years for the allocation of the Rate Support Grant. The previous system was correctly abandoned in 1981 because of absurd instability (see Bennett, 1982) and a major goal of the new approach through the assessment of GRE was stability. Much turbulence has, of course, been introduced into Local Authority finance in recent years by frequent changes in the system for actual grant allocation, including tapering, claw-backs, targets, and rate-capping. But changes in the details of the assessment of basic expenditure needs through the GRE have also led to remarkable (and indefensible) instability over recent years. Since our concern here has been exclusively with assessment of Grant Related Expenditure and not with the subsequent use (and possible misuse) of these

Table 9.8   Changes in unit costs (per cent)

Indicator	83/4 to 84/5	84/5 to 85/6	85/6 to 86/7	83/4 to 86/7
GRE total	3.3	6.8	7.3	18.4
Primary pupil	8.6	11.1	11.9	35.0
Secondary pupil under 16	5.0	7.4	11.2	25.3
Domestic rate collection	−2.6	4.9	1.9	4.1
Planning applications	3.8	13.6	22.3	44.3
AEN-Secondary pupils	−6.3	6.7	11.7	11.7
Indictable offences	3.8	0.6	−6.8	−2.7
No. of fires	10.3	11.5	17.6	44.6
Areas of high fire risk	10.3	11.9	35.4	67.1

Source: Association of County Councils (1983, 1984, and 1985)

estimates in the actual allocations of money to Local Authorities, we shall concentrate on instability of the GRE.

In table 9.8 are shown some examples of the changes in unit costs which were used in the GRE formulae over the short period from 1983/4 to 1986/7. One reason that so few indicators can be shown is the all too frequent changes in the formulae used for allocation of elements of the GRE. The disparities in overall changes in assumed unit costs over a three-year period are quite remarkable. The unit costs associated with the fire service rose substantially (as did those for the police, which are harder to recover on a consistent basis over time within the GRE system, but responsible for far more expenditure). These changes reflected Government policy of increasing resources and wages for the police and fire service. Paradoxically, we might note that these services were responsible for a major portion of expenditure of the Metropolitan Authorities and the rises in expenditure incurred through policy of central Government were used as one of the rationales for dismantling these Authorities. Primary pupil costs also rose substantially during this three-year period. At the other extreme the unit costs associated with dealing with deprived secondary school pupils (AEN) were actually reduced in the first year shown here. The nominal costs of collecting domestic rates were also reduced between 1983/4 and 1984/5 and rose very little over the whole period. The unit costs used in assessing expenditure needs for indictable offences were reduced overall during the three year period.

Do these major differences in changes in assumed unit costs over time stem from a careful study of differential inflation and actual changes in expenditure? Studies based upon actual expenditure costs are ruled out in the context of the GRE, since these may reflect discretionary differences in service provision and efficiency. So where do the unit costs come from? For many services, these unit costs were undoubtedly determined by arbitrarily imposed cash limits, with the total target expenditure on the item being divided by the estimated client-group size (or other measure of amount of service provision). Such a procedure interferes with the inherently bottom-up nature of the GRE process. Some changes also probably represent deliberate tinkering with the formulae in order to reallocate funds between classes of authority, in accord with sometimes transient political priorities.

Table 9.9 shows the year-on-year percentage changes in the assessed GRE per head for each of the major classes of Local Authority and for several individual Authorities. Within each class of authority, the rank of each individual Authority's change is shown. Over the first year shown, Inner London fared relatively well, with an average overall increase in assessed expenditure needs of 7.2 per cent, and Outer London and the Shire Counties had relatively small increases overall (2.6 and 2.7 per cent respectively). For the following period, from 1983/4 to 1984/5, the Shire Counties did disproportionately well and Inner London and the Shire Districts fared badly. The

Table 9.9 Examples of instability in GRE per head

	Percentage change over period			Rank of change in class of authority		
	82/3 to 83/4	83/4 to 84/5	84/5 to 85/6	82/3 to 83/4	83/4 to 84/5	84/5 to 85/6
Inner London (12)	7.2	0.1	10.5			
Lewisham	2.0	0.4	19.9	12	6	1
Lambeth	5.3	2.6	4.7	9	2	12
Outer London (20)	2.6	1.2	5.1			
Bromley	−1.6	2.5	2.9	19	3 =	19
Newham	9.6	−0.7	7.2	2	20	4
Met Districts (36)	3.6	4.1	4.9			
Manchester	3.0	1.0	10.5	22 =	31	2
Gateshead	2.8	−2.2	7.4	24	36	4
Liverpool	0.9	0.6	11.4	31	33 =	1
N. Tyneside	0.4	3.6	3.7	35	6 =	33 =
Coventry	7.8	0.0	3.7	1	35	33 =
Shire Counties (39)	2.7	4.8	6.5			
Cumbria	1.4	1.3	9.3	33	38	3
Northumberland	0.6	0.3	10.0	38	39	1
Oxfordshire	4.2	2.2	3.8	2	37	30
Somerset	−0.8	6.0	9.0	39	4 =	5
Shire District Averages (39)	3.8	−4.2	3.1			
Beds.	10.3	−9.0	2.4	1	38	15
Cleveland	8.9	−13.2	20.8	2	39	1
Warwicks.	0.2	−2.6	0.9	37	4 =	28 =

Source: computed from Association of County Councils (1983, 1984, and 1985)

changes from 1984/5 to 1985/6 saw Inner London showing substantial relative rises in assessed expenditure needs again, with the Shire Districts again doing relatively poorly.

Why did costs of service provision for Inner London Boroughs go up relatively fast in the first and third periods and barely increase in the intermediate year? Clearly, this had nothing to do with real costs of service provision or true basic expenditure needs. On the contrary, the main alterations were driven by political considerations. In 1983/4 it was deemed important to redirect resources to inner-city areas, following the race riots (for example the weight given to the ethnic indicator in the assessment of educational needs for special remedial provision was doubled). This shift of resources caused a political outcry from the Shire Counties, so that formulae were then manipulated in order to appease this pressure. The following year it was the inner-cities' turn once again, especially Inner London. Externally imposed short-term alterations of this kind in the assessment of GRE clearly undermine prudent housekeeping by local government.

Let us now turn to examining the impact of these fluctuations upon individual Authorities. Within Inner London, Lewisham experienced the largest increase in GRE per head in the first period, an intermediate change in the next period, and the smallest increase in the third period. In contrast, Lambeth had one of the smaller changes in the first period, the second largest in the next, and the smallest increase in the third year.

Within Outer London, the experience of Bromley and of Newham are almost mirror images: Bromley did relatively badly in the first and third periods and well in the second, while Newham gained in the first and third periods, but had the smallest increase in the second.

Among the Metropolitan Districts, the experience of Liverpool, North Tyneside, and Coventry is most curious: each had relatively very small increases in two of the three years, combined with a relatively very large increase in one year. Furthermore, the year of relative glut was different in each case. It surely requires Machiavellian skills or gross incompetence to introduce such remarkable instability into formula funding, although some of the successive changes undoubtedly represent responses to the political pressure from those Local Authorities which suffered severe losses.

Shire Counties fared just as strangely, with both Cumbria and Northumberland being at the extreme low end of the ranking in change among these authorities for the first two years and yet requiring one of the largest increases in the third. This contrasts with Oxfordshire, which fared very well in the first period and very badly in the next two, and with Somerset, which had the smallest increase in the first period, followed by among the largest in each of the next two years.

Perhaps the most astonishing changes of all occur for the average changes for Shire Districts within each County. The Districts of Bedfordshire had the largest increase of any in the first period (10.3 per cent), followed by the second largest decrease (− 9.0 per cent) in the second period, and a middling change in the third. Cleveland's Districts suffered even more from the vagaries of the system, experiencing the second largest increase (8.9 per cent), followed by the largest decrease (− 13.2 per cent) and then the largest increase (20.8 per cent). In contrast, the Districts of Warwickshire experienced very little actual change in their assessed expenditure needs per head over the three years, with relatively small increases and decreases, although their ranking alters dramatically.

All of this instability, it must be emphasized, occurred in the supposedly 'objective' assessment of basic expenditure needs for Local Authorities. These assessments form a crucial input to the determination of the actual funding allocation to each Local Authority through Block Grant. Furthermore, these figures have been used in penalizing Local Authorities for exceeding expenditure targets set by central Government and for rate-capping. It is vital to maintaining a credible system of funding local government that absurd fluctuations in the most basic assessment of expenditure needs be avoided.

Conclusion

Somehow, a stronger system of checks and balances and of public scrutiny in order to ensure greater objectivity must be established. While central Government will certainly wish to exercise its rights to alter spending priorities from time to time, even their own goals will not often be achieved by fiddling with elements of an extremely complicated formula, which introduces unexpected as well as intended change. The assessment of *basic* expenditure needs should urgently be removed from the political arena. If, however, central Government wants to identify further, *discretionary* needs for Local Authority expenditure over and above this common core, funds can be provided explicity for such programmes in a more visible way.

Further instability in Local Government finance will undoubtedly be introduced through a shift to the 'community charge'. In *Paying for Local Government* (Department of the Environment, 1986b), we are promised a new, simpler set of formulae for the assessment of GRE, which will again have stability as a major goal. No doubt that shift will, once again, introduce severe anomalies in the continuity of assessed basic spending needs of individual Local Authorities. There is an opportunity for a subsequent improvement, if the system is freed from the worst effects of political interference, which should be made more explicit. If the formulae are simplified, it may become easier to maintain consistency and public scrutiny and, perhaps, to avoid unforeseen consequences of changes to the elements of the procedure.

Improving the quality and relevance of the inputs to the procedure is undoubtedly an important part of the process of achieving a better system of resource allocation. A major new Resource Allocation survey would help improve the stability, equity and transparency of the system, if combined with stronger checks against unforeseen conseqences of political interference.

Selected Key Reading

Bennett, Robert J. 1982: *Central Grants to Local Government*. Cambridge University Press.

Department of the Environment 1986b: *Paying for Local Government* (Cmnd. 9714). London; HMSO.

Jones, George and Stewart, John 1985: *The Case for Local Government* (2nd edn). London: George Allen & Unwin.

Mays, Nicholas and Bevan Gwyn 1987: *Resource Allocation in the Health Service: A Review of the Methods of the Resource Allocation Working Party (RAWP)*. LSE Occasional Paper on Social Administration no. 81, Bedford Square Press/ National Council of Voluntary Organisations.

10 The Changing Form of Women's Economic Dependency

Heather Joshi

Alongside the changes in the British family reviewed in chapter 3, there have been some dramatic changes during the twentieth century in British women's work. These changes in female employment are commonly supposed to have influenced rates of family formation and dissolution. Before such questions can be properly investigated, it is worth asking if the changes do really amount to a revolution in the economic roles of men and women. The negative answer proposed in this chapter raises some prior questions about policies intended to treat men and women as equals. If the presumption of wives' financial dependence on their husbands is not outdated in the 1980s, equitable treatment of the sexes in tax, pensions, social security and the financial arrangements on divorce may not be achieved by equal treatment. If the 'emancipation' of women has yet to run its full course, there should be limits to the extent one would expect it to have influenced demographic trends.

It is argued here that economic autonomy is still a long way off for most British women. Replacing the old presumption of financial dependence upon husbands with one of individual self-sufficiency would be justified if men and women had equivalent earning power. This would be going further than women have in fact come. There are financial handicaps to being female which keep most women either dependent on men or disadvantaged or both. Sex-blind treatment appeals to women's self-respect, and is fine for those who have successfully seized new opportunities in education and the labour market, but as long as equal treatment extends only to paid work, it does not give proper recognition to the contribution and needs of most women. They still subordinate their cash earning potential to the demands on their unpaid time and energy from their role in the family. Society still needs a large number of its adult citizens to give caring for others a higher priority than a conventional career. The expectation that such people will normally be female is self-fulfilling, but may be neither equitable nor efficient.

This chapter reviews the evidence about the changes and continuities in the role of women and men in the British economy, and summarizes research findings about the direct and indirect effect of gender on women's earning power. It concludes by drawing lessons for effective policy to bring about equality of opportunity for each sex, and by reviewing the evidence for effects of the changes to date on family formation in Britain.

Changes Over Time

Table 10.1 summarizes some of the changes in women's work, or at least its statistical visibility, over the twentieth century. At censuses before the Second World War, men outnumbered women in the paid workforce by more than two to one, by the mid-1980s the ratio approaches even numbers with women accounting for 40 per cent of the labour force at the 1981 census and, in 1987, 45 per cent of employees in employment.

Table 10.1   The trend in women's participation in the paid labour force in twentieth-century Britain

	Economically active women as % of all women aged 20–64				Women of all ages as % of labour force (men and women)
	Total labour force	of which Full-time	Part-time	Unemployed	
1901	33.9				29.1
1911	32.5				29.7
1921	30.6				29.5
1931	31.6				29.7
1941					
1951	36.3	30.3	5.2	0.8	30.8
1961	42.2	32.1	9.1	1.0	32.5
1971	52.3	32.8	18.0	1.5	36.5
1981	61.1	30.4	27.1	3.7	40.2

Source: Joshi, 1985. Census data have been adjusted along the lines advocated by Joshi and Owen, 1987.

The participation rate of women of working age doubled between the 1921 and 1981 (from 30.6 per cent to 61.1 per cent among those aged 20–64). For married women under 60 there was a five-fold increase from 12 per cent in 1931 to 57 per cent at the 1981 census.[1]

The contrasts sound even more spectacular if the changes are expressed in terms of experience over a lifetime. In the pre-war world which informed

[1] Sample surveys (which always tend to identify more women with jobs than the census; see Joshi and Owen, 1987) suggest that the trend in married women's economic activity rates levelled off in the first half of the 1980s. The General Household Survey put the activity rate of married women under 60 at 62 per cent in 1978, 1979 and 1985.

Beveridge's design for the Social Insurance system (Beveridge, 1942), a woman's labour force career usually ended upon marriage and work outside the home was normally treated as incompatible with domestic duty. During the post-war period women ceased to quit employment on marriage. Their withdrawal became temporary and increasingly associated with the presence of young children. Motherhood replaced marriage as the occasion for leaving paid work and seldom marked the end of a woman's labour force membership. The increased participation rates from the 1950s to the 1980s have been largely accounted for by reductions in the gaps in employment records around childbearing. Mothers of younger and younger children have been taking on the dual burden of paid work and child rearing (see Hunt, 1968; Martin and Roberts, 1984; Joshi, 1985).

The Limits to Change

Occupational segregation

There are also some respects in which little has changed. Men's and women's jobs remain largely separate. Women's employment has always been, and remains, concentrated in a few occupational categories (see Hakim, 1979: Joseph, 1983). At the 1981 Census three quarters of all female workers were in just four of the sixteen occupational orders, where they outnumbered men: personal services (e.g. cleaners, hairdressers); clerical; professional workers in education, health and welfare (i.e. school teachers and nurses); and selling (mainly shop assistants). The majority of female workers work only with other women – 63 per cent of women working with others in the 1980 Women and Employment Survey (Martin and Roberts, 1984, p. 28). Male workplaces are even more segregated (81 per cent of the husbands interviewed in the same survey in 1980 had no colleagues of the opposite sex doing the same type of work). There are some 'integrated' exceptions among the younger membership of some professions (see Crompton and Sanderson, 1986), but women are still very rare in 'top jobs'. For example, in 1984, fewer than 3 per cent of university professors were women. At that time a similar proportion of Members of Parliament were female. This nearly doubled to 6 per cent when 40 female MPs were returned in the 1987 General Election. Among those jobs classified as Social Class 1 by the Registrar General at the 1981 Census, only one in ten was held by women. There is, on the other hand, a remarkable concentration of female part-time employees in a few, mainly low-status occupations, seldom followed by men.[2]

---

[2] According to the Economic Activity Tables of the 1981 census it took just seven out of a possible 549 occupational categories to account for 64 per cent of all female part-time employees. These categories were: cleaners, shop assistants, certain clerks and cashiers, domestic and school helpers, secretaries, nurses, and assistants in catering.

Part-time Employment

Another qualification that should be made to the picture of a rising trend in women's paid work is that, as can been seen in figure 10.1, participation in full-time employment has not risen. All of the post-war increase in employment is accounted for by part-time jobs. This means that in aggregate, man-hours of paid work still outnumbered woman-hours by about two to one.[3]

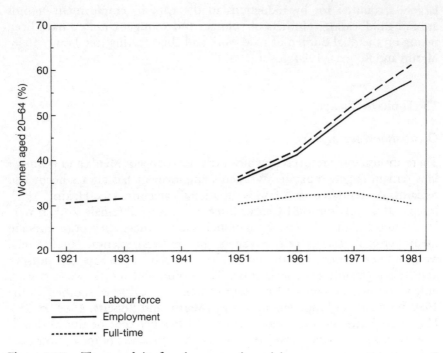

Figure 10.1   The trend in female economic activity rates among women aged 20–64, Great Britain, 1921–81
Source: Joshi (1985)

Unpaid Domestic Work

The picture about paid work must be set alongside that of the unpaid domestic work where the ratio of woman to man hours is reversed. Jonathan Gershuny's preliminary estimates of time spent in unpaid work (from the ESRC's time budget study in 1983/4, Gershuny et al., 1986, Table 2) are

[3] Zabalza and Tzannatos (1985, p. 116) offer an estimate of 0.52 for the ratio of woman hours to man hours employed in 1980.

that women averaged 16 hours per week more than men. The gap does seem to have been wider in the past (26 hours per week in 1961, for example) but these time budgets confirm common sense and findings from the Women and Employment Survey that women do more unpaid work than men. Even where both spouses do full-time paid work, wives generally do more of the housework, particularly child-care.

It is also noteworthy that the policy of community care of the handicapped relies almost exclusively on the unpaid caring work of wives, daughters and mothers (Equal Opportunities Commission, 1982; and Finch and Groves, 1983).

The Relative Economic Status of Men and Women

As with men's share of unpaid household work, indicators such as the ratio of women's to men's rates of pay, plotted in figure 10.2, and women's share in household earnings, have shown some changes but still display a gulf between the sexes. Taking data on all full-time manual workers, figure 10.2 shows that the ratio of women's hourly pay to men's suddenly rose in the mid-1970s from the level it seems to have previously held over recorded history, 60 per cent, to over 70 per cent in 1977, a level more or less maintained subsequently. The pattern of change over the 1970s and 1980s is similar if one considers different definitions of pay or broader classes of worker. This once-for-all

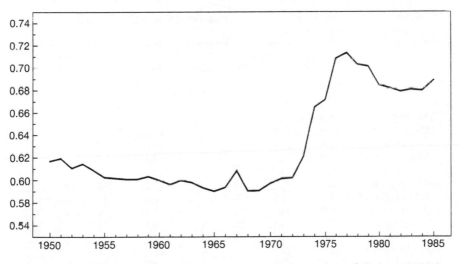

Figure 10.2 Women's wages relative to men's, hourly earnings, full-time manual jobs
Source: Department of Employment October Enquiry, All Industries

improvement in the relative wage of women coincided with the implementation of the Equal Pay Act, and this is generally thought to be more than a coincidence (see Zabalza and Tzannatos, 1985).

The contribution of wife's earnings to total household earnings showed some increase during the 1970s and then stabilized. Amongst non-retired married couples with an earning wife, she brought in, on average, around 30 per cent of their joint earnings – 37 per cent where there were no dependent children, or 25 per cent where there were children, according to the 1985 Family Expenditure Survey (FES). In 1980 the corresponding figures were 36 per cent and 23 per cent. There are of course a few cases where wives earn more than their husbands. This minority appears to have been on an upward trend (from 2 per cent of couples both of whom were employees in 1968 to 5 per cent in 1980 – Elias, 1983), but the conclusion of Lynne Hamill's study of the 1974 FES still stands. Breadwinner wives who are the couple's sole earners are a rarity, wives are typically joint but secondary earners.

Table 10.2 considers married couples in 1981 where at least one was economically active, i.e. it does not include couples who were both retired, or both students, for example. It shows that the most common arrangement – in 25 per cent of cases – was for the husband to be employed full-time while his wife was employed part-time. Two-earner couples with both employed full-time were almost as frequent – 23 per cent. In just over 40 per cent of cases the husband was, as traditional, the sole earner, and, in roughly equal numbers (5 per cent each) were cases where neither spouse earned, and cases

Table 10.2   The division of labour within couples with at least one economically active partner, England and Wales

	All such couples				Couples with children			
	1981		1971	1961	1981		1971	1961
	%	'000	'000		%	'000	'000	
All	100.0	9,635			100.0	5,387		
Two earners	48.8	4,700			44.0	2,371		
Man F-t, wife P-t	24.9	2,395			29.2	1,570		
", wife F-t	23.1	2,229			14.6	785		
Man P-t, wife P-t	0.5	52			0.2	9		
", wife F-t	0.3	25			0.1	7		
Wife sole earner	5.3	511	288		3.1	168	76	
Man out of work	2.7	256	123		2.4	127	52	
retired	1.6	156	108	51	0.2	10	8	4
student	0.1	13	20	5	0.1	5	6	5
other	0.9	86	37	6	0.5	25	10	2
Man sole earner	40.7	3,921			47.0	2,531		
No earner	5.2	504			5.9	316		

F-t = Full-time; P-t = Part-time

Source: Census of England and Wales: Household Composition Tables, 1981; and Hamill (1978).

where the wife was the sole earner. Perhaps because of disincentives built into the Supplementary Benefit system, the 'zero-earner couple' category is bigger than one would expect if the wives of unemployed men had the same economic activity rates as the wives of employed men (see Rimmer, 1987, p. 44 for a discussion of this phenomenon). Note also from table 10.2 (last figure in fifth row) that it is not totally unheard of for couples to share the rearing of their children by both working part-time, but the number involved was minute – 9000 in the whole of England and Wales in 1981.

Why Do Women Earn Less Than Men?

The lower level of wives' earnings is accounted for, in one sense, by women's lower hours of work and lower rates of pay per hour. These are in turn explained by two interacting factors, either of which is a sufficient condition for women's earnings to lag behind those of men: on one hand, the gendered division of family labour, and on the other, unequal treatment of men and women in the labour market. Both are probably deeply entrenched in our culture. Economists say that a labour market discriminates between the sexes if men and women of identical productivity are not identically remunerated. The conventional family division of labour not only reduces the number of hours a woman is available for paid work but also reduces the amount she could expect to earn per hour even in a non-discriminatory labour market. Interruptions in her employment experience, reductions in her mobility and labour market bargaining power are all ways in which family responsibilities reduce women's pay below what it might have been.

Does it Matter?

There are what economists call 'efficiency' reasons, in addition to the obvious grounds of equity, to be concerned about the relative economic weakness of women. The fashionable discussion of incentives usually overlooks what may be one of the more potent of the disincentives operating on the productivity of the British labour force: the anticipation of domesticity, discouraging young women from seeking training and employers and educational institutions from providing it, even to women who do not take on a family or a traditional role within one.

Although the force of custom and prevailing values may appear sufficient to account for traditional differences in the economic roles of spouses, and although people conforming to convention need not be aware of any financial motivation to do so, customary practice is reinforced by an economic rationale.

If, for whatever reason, a husband initially commands higher rates of pay than his wife it makes economic sense for him to 'specialize' in paid work and let her shoulder the brunt of the partnership's unpaid chores (Becker, 1981, 1985; for a critique see Owen, 1987). The erosion of a woman's earning potential perpetuates the double-bind of the double burden. Why should we worry about this if the marriage remains the harmonious institution for pooling resources which is normally assumed, in economic theory as elsewhere? Should it fail so spectacularly as to break up, the 'specialist in unpaid work' is left with depleted earning power. Old fashioned alimony can be justified on these grounds, and a new fashioned proposal is on the table in Australia that divorce settelments include a lump-sum compensation for sacrificed earning potential (Macdonald, 1986). Within an unknown number of marriages as yet unbroken, marital harmony cannot always be assumed. We probably don't need Jan Pahl's pioneering research to tell us how fragile conjugal consensus is. She shows that unequal access to cash is a source of friction, and that rows about money are a common cause of the domestic violence which is now coming to light (Pahl, 1983, 1985; see also Brannen and Wilson, 1987). The 'domestic bargain' (a phrase coined by Martin and Roberts, 1984) is not always a very 'good buy'. Cain (1985) argues that it is the unreliability of marriage, no longer, as we have seen in chapter 3, a contract of total sanctity, which constitutes the economic case for policy interventions to help women in the labour force. The financial hardship of most lone mothers (see chapter 4) bears witness to the casualties of women's weak position in the labour market.

Empirical Analysis of Women's Low Incomes

My own offering to the state of knowledge about the status of British women has been to investigate two particular questions. Firstly, how great are the effects of women's family responsibilities on their employment and pay. Secondly, how far can the low pay of women compared to men be explained by womens' domestic ties? On the first issue, I have taken evidence from a number of sources and some results are reviewed in Joshi, 1985, 1987a and b. This chapter therefore focuses more on the work I have done, with Marie-Louise Newell, on the question of comparing the pay of men and women.

There is evidence on both questions, from a unique and important data source: the MRC's follow-up study of the 1946 birth cohort, the National Survey of Health and Development, which also provided material for some of Kathleen Kiernan's research discussed in chapter 3. Roughly 4000 adults have been followed into adulthood from a sample of births in March 1946. The results of our investigations of sources of pay differentials are published in a monograph entitled *Pay Differentials and Parenthood* (Joshi and Newell, 1989). Marie-Louise Newell and I also used the survey to make a longitudinal study of occupational change after childbearing (Newell and Joshi, 1986; Joshi and Newell, 1987).

Although the most recent data available to us were collected in early 1978, just before the survey members reached the age of 32 in March 1978, their analysis should remain relevant in the 1980s in the light of the stagnation in the relative pay of men and women since then. The data given in figure 10.2 can be re-expressed in terms of the ratio of men's hourly pay to women's, which fell in the mid-1970s from the traditional level, around 1.67, to 1.45 in 1977 and after.

The Male–female Pay Gap Among Those Born in 1946

With the data on pay per hour collected for 26-year-olds in 1972 and 32-year-olds in 1978, we asked whether male and female rates of pay were affected to a similar degree by length of employment experience, and whether domestic responsibilities have a direct effect on pay. The survey data also allow us to explore whether, after allowing for other identifiable differences in the characteristics of male and female workers, the labour market during the 1970s appeared to discriminate against young women compared to their male contemporaries.

We used regression analyses to estimate and compare models explaining the variations in men's and women's pay. 'Human capital' variables such as education and employment experience help account for some, but not all, of the variation within and between the sexes. Information about job characteristics also helps explain pay variations within each sex, and to some extent between them.

In 1972, despite the fact that the women then in the labour force were the relatively well qualified (as those who were deferring childbearing were over-represented), men's pay exceeded women's, at the geometric mean,[4] by a factor of 60 per cent. Since the female workers were not in fact very much worse qualified or less experienced on average than the males, there was not much of the gap explained on these counts. The unexplained gap between the pay of 26-year-old men and women was 51 per cent allowing only for educational background and employment experience, or 38 per cent allowing also for information on job characteristics. The residual, that part of the earnings gap not explained by personal attributes, is conventionally taken as an indicator of discrimination. It is more debatable whether differences which are the outcome of different job characteristics are the outcome of unequal treatment or not.

In 1977, the average pay gap was still almost as large – 58 per cent at the

---

[4] Proportional pay differentials are analysed in terms of the logarithm of pay (per hour). The geometric mean is the value of pay at the average of these logarithms.

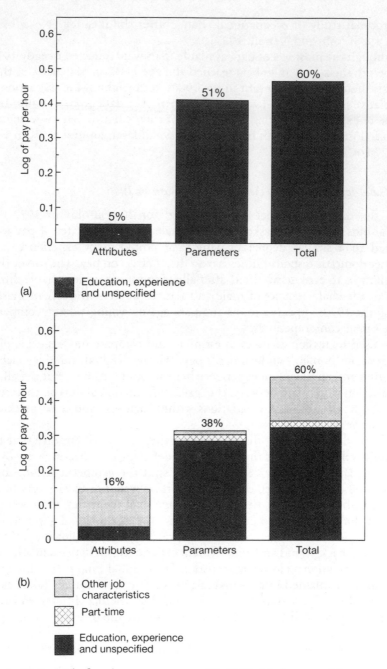

Figure 10.3 Male-female pay gap at age 26, 1972: (a) decomposition controlling for education and experience; (b) decomposition according to full model

Source: Joshi and Newell (1989) using MRC data on the 1946 birth cohort

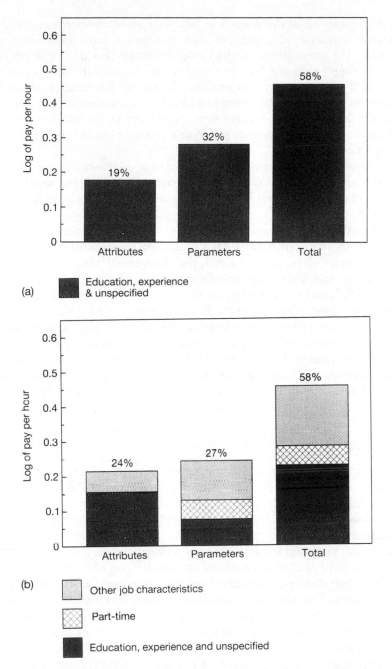

Figure 10.4 Male-female pay gap at age 32, 1978: (a) decomposition in controlling for education and experience; (b) decomposition according to full model
Source: As figure 10.3 *Note*: Labels express logs and percentages of female pay

geometric mean – but the women in jobs were more representative of their generation and more dissimilar to men in terms of work experience and education. The unexplained gap had indeed narrowed (to around 30 per cent for an 'average' woman) for the members of this cohort, even when the nature of the job is taken into account. (Including information about job characteristics improved the extent to which pay variance within the sexes was explained, but it did not explain very much more of the gap between the sexes since men and women in apparently similar sorts of jobs were being paid at different rates.)

Even after the Equal Pay Act had effected some narrowing of the pay gap, there was an unexplained excess of men's pay over women's pay worth about 30 per cent of that received by the average 32-year-old female employee in early 1978.

Another finding of these analyses worthy of note is the uneven incidence of sex discrimination (if that's what's explaining the otherwise unexplained gap). It appears to be much more severe for women with no educational qualifications and low occupational attainments than for those with sufficient qualifications to gain entry to the less-segregated non-manual (non-sales) sector of the labour market. The news may not be quite as good for female graduates either. There were perhaps too few such women in this social cross-section of the immediate post-war generation (3 per cent of the age group, 40 cases in the pay regression) for us to draw such conclusions, but similar analyses of a contemporary survey of graduates (Dolton and Makepeace, 1986) also indicates that male graduates in their early thirties were doing considerably better than women.

Effects of Family Responsibility on Pay

When we looked at the additional explanatory power brought to these models by information about the worker's family responsibilities we found that parenthood had little effect on men's labour force participation or pay. It was, however, a strong determinant of women's employment participation and experience. Though we found no direct effects on pay, holding other things equal, we found indirect effects of motherhood on pay. We estimated that the consequences of motherhood lowered the pay of employed mothers relative to their childless contemporaries through factors such as lost employment experience, downward occupational mobility and the low rates paid for part-time work. These three factors each accounted for similar proportions of combined effect on average pay of around 15 per cent. Note that this is only half the apparent pay advantage the average woman would reap from being paid like a man. That both sources of pay differential exist may come as no surprise, their relative size was not anticipated.

In examining the pay advantage of married men over bachelors, we tentatively concluded that for men, but not women, acquiring a spouse leads to higher pay, and perhaps productivity – an indirect contribution to the economy of a wife's domestic work.

Occupational Change After Childbearing

A separate analysis that Marie-Louise Newell and I have done on the employment histories of women born in 1946 looked for evidence of occupational downgrading associated with childbearing (Newell and Joshi, 1986; Joshi and Newell, 1987). Close examination of these histories found similar patterns to those reported by other researchers, such as Dex (1987), Elias and Main (1982), and Stewart and Greenhalgh (1984). Around three in ten of those who reported paid work within 10 years of their first birth had returned to a different type of job that was likely to have been worse paid than the one they last held before the maternity. Mothers who had left jobs in the middle

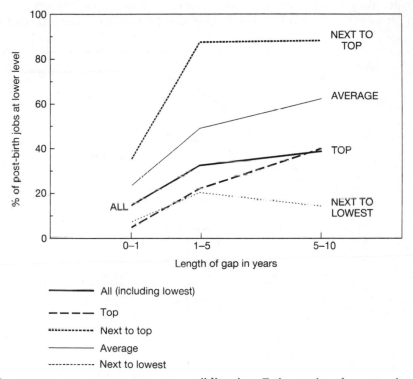

Figure 10.5 Job downgrading after childbearing. Estimates based on experience up to age 32, mothers born in 1946, by economic level of job before first child
Source: Newell and Joshi (1986)

of the socio-economic spectrum were most exposed to the risk of falling back on the ladder, particularly if they left a long gap in their employment record. Women with paper qualifications were more successful at re-entering their original occupation than employees of banks and public administration whose skills we surmise were more specific to the employer. It may also be that such employers were, at least in the early 1970s, less prepared to make the organizational adjustments which make it feasible for mothers to combine paid work with responsibility for young children.

Lifetime Earnings Profiles

The Opportunity Cost of Child-rearing

A synthesis of my two strands of research is attempted for an illustrative 'typical' case in figure 10.6. This traces the simulated lifetime earnings of a person who leaves school at age 17 and faces an earnings profile of 'average' shape, rising with age and experience until a plateau somewhere around age 45 for a continuous worker. The level of this profile, for a woman, is set to

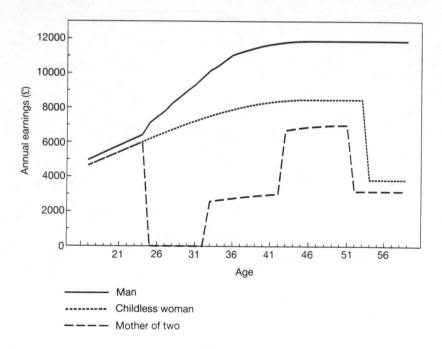

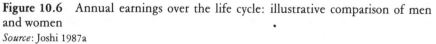

Figure 10.6 Annual earnings over the life cycle: illustrative comparison of men and women
Source: Joshi 1987a

pass through £6000 at age 24. Part-time employment is assumed at all times to involve a 10 per cent pay penalty reflecting the 'crummy job effect' on the pay of those with current domestic constraints. It is hypothetically assumed that if a woman marries but remains childless, she would work continuously in a full-time job until switching to part-time employment, set somewhat arbitrarily at age 54, the age when the majority of her employed contemporaries are in part-time jobs. If she has a break of, in this illustration, eight years out of employment to rear to children, and works part-time for most of the years when they are still at school, the lifetime earning profile is given by the lower line. The difference between the bottom two lines represents, for this example, the lifetime earnings forgone as a result of having children, and amounts to £135 000.

The top line on the picture is even more speculative, but informed by the analysis of 32-year-olds discussed above, it traces what the person would earn with identical characteristics other than that of being male and staying throughout in full-time employment. The area between the top two profiles is the totally hypothetical cost of being female; it is the same order of magnitude as the hypothetical cost of a woman becoming a mother. (Each about 46 per cent of the total lifetime earnings of a woman who remains childless.) The numbers involved are also set out in table 10.3. The area

Table 10.3   Simulated annual earnings at selected ages for an illustrative case

Age	Man	Woman No child	Woman Two children
	£	£	£
19	5,891	5,035	5,035
24	7,020	6,000	6,000
29	8,622	6,897	0
34	10,403	7,649	2,628
39	11,384	8,184	2,891
44	11,750	8,447	6,770
49	11,781	8,469	6,979
54	11,781	3,828	3,159
59	11,781	3,828	3,159
Total earnings *from ages 17 to 59*	428,000	293,000	158,000
Index numbers Woman with two children is 100:	271	185	100
Childless woman is 100:	146	100	54

The advantage of being male is set at 17% up to age 26, passing through 32% at age 32 and fixed at 40% from age 36 onwards. The participation, hours and wage profiles for women are derived from data on women of all ages up to 59 collected in the 1980 Women and Employment Survey.

between the top and bottom lines roughly corresponds with the average gaps between couples' earnings which we can observe in totally independent data like the Family Expenditure Survey discussed above.[5]

Socio-Economic Variations

One of the many caveats I want to make about these still-experimental calculations is that they are not typical at all socio-economic levels. The less education a woman has, the less important are the delayed costs on later rates of pay of current absence from the labour market, but the higher is the 'cost of being female' relatively speaking. Women with more education have more to lose from becoming mothers, and perhaps less from just being women. This could well explain the fact that the trend since 1970 towards deferring first births has largely been confined to women with more education (see Joshi, 1985). The growing population of 'Dinkie' couples (dual-income no kids) was also noted in chapters 7 and 8 as providing a booming market of house purchasers. The younger mothers in council housing probably face lower opportunity costs to childbearing but a stronger need to supplement family income with a low-paid part-time job.

Looking Forward

Are these findings of the obstacles women face out of date? One might hope so, but the picture in figure 10.2 does not immediately support such optimism. Later generations of women have been catching up with their male contemporaries as far as the acquisition of paper qualifications is concerned. Most of them also expect to form families. Will these families be more symmetrical as far as the allocation of unpaid work is concerned? Will enlightened employer practice prevail to preserve skills of workers who are also rearing children? Or will a new generation of qualified women, some of whom are still keeping open their options, decide that the economic penalties of motherhood outweigh its attractions? Does it still 'pay' to be male as much as our estimates suggest?

New Research

The evidence necessary to answer such a question would need to combine information on pay with life history. Among possible sources of such infor-

---

[5] This does not mean that all of the gap between men's actual incomes and women's is due to their gender alone. The illustrative female case is based upon a non-manual occupation, which is typical for women. Men in non-manual occupations have earnings profiles considerably above those for all men, who include a majority in lower-paid manual jobs.

mation is the proposed follow-up in their early thirties of a sample of people born in 1958 – the members of the National Child Development Study, another national cohort study similar to that of the 1946 generation described above. Another such source is the material collected in 1987 for the ESRC's studies of Economic Change and Social Life.

We know that women without male 'breadwinners' are over-represented among the statistically visible poor – the lone mothers and the lone elderly women. What we do not yet know is how women's changing opportunities for paid work have affected their relative risk of poverty. The implication of sex differences in economic activity for economic inequality are among the questions that are being pursued in my current research with John Ermisch and other colleagues. We are also looking into implications for inequality in the future of the social differentials in current demographic trends. Another important area of research is attempting to uncover female poverty that is hidden within households (Brannen and Wilson, 1987).

Policy Implications

The policy implications which I have drawn from the analyses mentioned above have been set out at greater length elsewhere (Joshi, 1986). The journey to Equality of Opportunity for women has not yet been completed. Progress is still needed to reduce the sex segregation of jobs, the low pay ghettoes that it permits, and the waste of potential female skills that it entails. Such progress will run into the familiar obstacles if measures are not also taken to recognize, support and share the unpaid tasks needed to maintain and reproduce the population.

Measures to improve women's access to education, training and remunerative jobs need to be complemented by measures to give families more choice about the management of their unpaid responsibilities. Examples of measures to support parents would be increases and improvements in childcare, for pre-school children and those of school age; to make parental leave available to parents of both sexes; to recognize childcare as a legitimate work expense for tax and benefit purposes; and to encourage the participation of fathers in child-rearing. This last suggestion might be taken more seriously as the working week gets shorter and if the pay penalties for devoting time to caring were reduced. I have an even more fanciful suggestion that we challenge the age segregation of modern society which keeps young children, and their attendants, out of the adult sphere. As Charlotte Höhn remarked (in her address to the 1987 European Population Conference), modern cities are not 'kinder-freundlich'. It is time at least for the English language to take on the concept of child-friendliness.

Women, on the whole, have not achieved an equal economic footing with men in British society and they will not achieve it universally overnight. Meanwhile, it would be a mistake for legislation on divorce, tax or pensions to assume that they had. Equitable treatments must be devised that recognize economic sacrifices (whether they've been made by men or women) as well as economic achievements. For example, the Home Responsibility Protection of pension rights under the current version of the State Earnings Related Pension Scheme (SERPS) recognizes that valuable work is being done by women who are not earning enough to pay contributions, but does not allow for the fact that the low pay of some who are contributing reflects their domestic responsibilities as well. British women are still taking better care of their families than their pension rights. It should not be beyond the wit of woman (and man) to devise more adequate forms of compensation. The research described here should inform and stimulate the policy debate.

The Economic Role of Women and Demographic Change

The slowly evolving British family leaves a much more easily discernible impact on women's employment in Britain than the possible reverse influence of women's earning opportunities on family formation and dissolution. There is some evidence of modest influences, among many others, of the female labour market on family building patterns. The research reported by John Ermisch in chapter 4 has shown that a woman's earning power is positively associated with her chances of both divorce and remarriage. Máire Ní Bhrolcháin (1986a and b) has investigated the association of employment and birth spacing in life history data, including some from the 1946 birth cohort. She concludes that during the 1950s and 1960s the prospect of returning to the labour market gave women an incentive to compress their childbearing, thus shortening intervals between births and accelerating the tempo of fertility. She also suggests that this mechanism was reversed in the 1970s, by which time more mothers were taking up employment between births, which would be likely to encourage longer gaps between babies.

In a series of studies using time series data on fertility and female employment (Joshi, Layard and Owen, 1985; De Cooman, Ermisch and Joshi, 1987 and 1988; Ermisch, 1987) the following account has emerged. An upward trend in the labour force attachment of successive generations accounts, statistically, for rising female employment (primarily of middle-aged married women) during the 1950s and 1960s, when fertility was also high and rising. The effects of this trend weakened in the 1970s but the numbers of economically active women were by that time swollen by the fall in the numbers of children and by the fall in the numbers of women entering motherhood in their twenties. This growth in women's propensity to take paid work probably has both economic and social origins, but our analyses of fertility suggest that it is not an important explanatory factor in the 'baby bust'. Cultural and social forces are also likely to be important in explaining the fall in fertility, but among economic factors the ratio of women's to men's pay emerges as having contributed to falling birth rates during the 1970s. In contrast, this ratio does not seem to have played much of a direct role in explaining rising aggregate labour supply. The once-and-for-all improvement in women's relative pay associated with the enactment of equal pay legislation seems to have affected the female labour force indirectly by encouraging the deferment of childbearing in the mid-1970s. These preliminary results suggest the desirability of looking beyond the female labour market for an adequate characterization of economic influences on fertility.

Conclusion

It is not at all clear that further progress towards improving the economic status of womem would precipitate the demise of the British family or the dreaded (by some) 'twilight of parenthood'. Effective progress for women involves changes which recognize the family responsibilities of paid workers of both sexes. This should, if anything, strengthen the family and encourage childbearing. It is arguable that the Swedish policy of support for parents in the labour force, as well as similar measures in Eastern Europe, have put a brake on fertility decline and perhaps reversed it.

Acknowledgement

The author's research described here has been funded by the ESRC, both when the Centre for Population Studies was a Designated Research Centre and under Programme Grant No. G00222005: Economic Inequalities Gender and Demographic Differentials. She is also grateful to the MRC's National Survey of Health and Development for permission to use their data.

Selected Key Reading

Joshi, Heather 1985: Motherhood and employment: change and continuity in post war Britain. In British Society for Population Studies, *Measuring Socio-Demographic Change*, OPCS Occasional Paper No. 34. London: OPCS, 70–87.
Glendinning, Caroline and Millar, Jane (eds) 1987: *Women and Poverty in Britain*. Brighton: Wheatsheaf Books.
Henwood, Melanie, Rimmer, Lesley and Wicks, Malcolm 1987: *Inside the Family: Changing Roles of Men and Women*. Occasional Paper 6. London: Family Policy Studies.

For Internationally Comparable Information

OECD 1985: *The Integration of Women into the Economy*. Paris: OECD.

For an American Perspective

England, Paula and Farkas, George 1986: *Households, Employment and Gender: A Social, Economic and Demographic View*. New York: Aldine.

11 Demographic Patterns among Britain's Ethnic Groups

Ian Diamond and Sue Clarke

Introduction

As befits a traditionally seafaring nation, Britain has always been a multi-ethnic society. Immigrants have been motivated by pull factors such as demand from Britain for labour or push factors such as the need to escape religious persecution. Accurate data on the number of immigrants in the population first became available in the mid nineteenth century through the inclusion of country of birth on the census. This source has permitted the identification of a number of significant migrations. Immigrations in the mid nineteenth century were characterized first by a large Irish component – around 750 000 of a total population of 26 million in 1871 – and subsequently by Russians, particularly Jews fleeing from an anti-semitic policy.

Although immigration continued in the early part of the twentieth century there were no major arrivals and the main pattern was of small communities establishing themselves particularly around port cities. For example, Ng (1968) chronicles the development of the Chinese community in London, and there were black communities in cities such as Liverpool and Cardiff. The 1930s were notable for a further influx of Jews, this time escaping persecution in Nazi Germany. Holmes (1982) states that around 50 000 arrived between 1933 and 1939.

However, such immigrations were small compared with those which have occurred since the Second World War. These have been predominantly from the New Commonwealth and Pakistan whose numbers have dwarfed those from the traditional sources of Ireland and Europe. In addition, there have been notable smaller migrations – often from groups such as Chileans, Ugandan Asians and Iranians escaping persecution.

The focus of this chapter will be on these later migrants because first, recent migrants have contributed significantly to the changing demographic structure of Britain's population and second, data are more readily available on these groups. Until recently there has been little systematic attempt to estimate the size of ethnic populations or their assimilation with the resident population, as data have traditionally been collected only on country of birth which excludes second and subsequent generations.

The chapter will start by describing the extent of post-Second-World-War immigration by identifying trends in the demographic and socio-economic characteristics of the migrants and their regional distribution. It then discusses recent patterns of nuptiality, fertility, morbidity and mortality within different ethnic communites. Throughout, the chapter will concentrate on ethnic groups from the New Commonwealth, Pakistan, Africa and Asia. The major omission is that of the Irish. This is because first, recent flows of Irish migration have tended to be to countries such as the USA, Canada and the Antipodes; second, regulations regarding Irish–British movement make the extent of migration hard to quantify, as in particular the proportion of seasonal workers at any time can be difficult to identify; third, the length of time that there has been a significant Irish community means that comparisons between first and subsequent generations can prove irrelevant. However, where the demographic characteristics of recent Irish immigrants are notable – such as with regard to fertility – they will be highlighted.

It should also be stressed that the ethnic groups used in this paper are necessarily broad. Immigrants to Britain do not form a representative sample of the population from which they came. For example, Indian and Pakistani immigrants are predominantly from the Punjab (Smith, 1976). A full description of the origins of British immigrants is beyond the scope of this chapter; Clarke (1984) provides an excellent review.

Levels of Immigration Since 1960

Size and Characteristics of Ethnic Groups

Immigration since the 1960s has been greatly influenced by three factors: first, demand for labour in Britain which influenced many immigrants in the 1960s; second, government policy, in particular the Immigration Act of 1971 and its associated changes of rules; third, events elsewhere in the world leading to the arrival of particular groups, for example Ugandan Asians in 1972 and South Africans in 1985. The main effect of the rule changes to the 1971 Act has been to limit immigration to the dependents of those already resident and to those with work permits – the 1971 Act made workers from the New Commonwealth subject to the same restrictions as those from other non-European Economic Community (EEC) countries in that they have to

Table 11.1   Flows of immigration to the United Kingdom by country of last residence (thousands)

Year	All[a] countries	Aust., NZ and Can.	India, Bangladesh, Sri Lanka	Caribbean	Other Common- wealth	Pakistan	Other
66	219	36	27[b]	15	35	–	77
71	200	52	24[b]	5	36	–	82
76	191	40	15	4	36	12	84
81	153	20	18	3	26	9	66
82	202	20	17	2	28	11	113
83	202	32	13	5	35	12	92
84	201	28	15	2	30	10	100
85	232	31	13	3	32	9	129
86	250	30	16	5	29	10	145

[a] Excludes Irish Republic
[b] Includes Pakistan

Source: OPCS (1987)

renew their work permit annually. The 1987 Immigration Bill will introduce a new barrier by additionally requiring husbands to show that they can support their incoming families financially, both on entry and on subsequent applications.

These changes are partially reflected in Table 11.1 which gives the numbers of immigrants coming in over the period 1966 to 1986. It shows that until 1985 the overall numbers remain fairly constant at around 200 000, the decline in Caribbean immigration being compensated by increases in those from outside the Commonwealth and Pakistan. These latter immigrants have been primarily from the EEC and very recently from the Republic of South Africa which sent a new inflow of 29 000 between 1985 and 1986 (OPCS, 1987).

However, to understand the effects of the legislation fully it is necessary to subdivide the immigrants by sex. Table 11.2, taken from Brown (1984), for a nationally representative sample of ethnic groups, gives the distribution of immigrants by their time of arrival. The ratios of women to men for these data are illustrated in figure 11.1 which shows a steady increase in the proportion of women immigrants.

With the exception of the African Asian group, immigration was initially a male phenomenon while recent arrivals have predominantly been women joining their husbands. The African Asian group differ in many respects as they primarily comprise Ugandans who were forced to leave Uganda as a result of the policies of the Amin Government. As a result they migrated as families. There has been criticism of the manner in which immigration officials have treated these new arrivals in that many wives have been

Table 11.2   Patterns of immigration by sex: percentage of residents 1982 arriving in a particular time period

Date of Settlement	WI			India			Pakistan			Bangladesh			Africa, Asia		
	M	(%)	F	M	(%)	F	M	(%)	F	M	(%)	F	M	(%)	F
Pre-1956	16		6	6		4	2		–	2		–	1		–
56–57	22		20	7		3	9		2	8		–	2		–
60–June 62	32		28	11		6	20		3	9		–	2		1
July 62–64	9		15	13		11	13		8	30		4	5		4
65–Mar. 68	8		12	22		22	22		15	11		9	15		11
Apr. 68–72	6		9	16		21	18		21	21		21	35		38
73–77	1		3	14		18	9		31	13		28	28		32
78–82	1		1	7		9	5		18	5		37	7		9
Don't Know	4		7	4		6	2		2	2		1	5		5
Total number not born in UK	1203		1362	1349		1139	1042		741	362		248	924		709

These data come from a nationally representative sample and are not population figures.

Source: Brown (1984)

rejected. McKie (1988) describes the results of a confidential Home Office inquiry into the use of DNA fingerprinting which conducted a small survey of 40 cases involving 89 children and found that around 80 per cent of the children were the true sons and daughters of men resident in Britain. A number of these had previously had their applications rejected. It would appear that the use of DNA fingerprinting has the potential to ensure that immigration legislation is conducted fairly. It is likely, however, that there will be a reduction in the numbers of immigrants who are joining their husbands resident in Britain as the proportion of British residents with dependents overseas will decline.

British migration in the past twenty years has not only been characterized by immigration, for there have also been many emigrants. In fact it was not until 1983 that there was a systematic net immigration. Between 1966 and 1982 there were typically more emigrants. The favourite destinations of these emigrants were Australia, New Zealand and Canada who in the late 1960s and early 1970s received around 50 per cent of British emigrants. This proportion has reduced steadily and in 1986 the most popular destination became the European Community, excluding the Irish Republic (OPCS, 1987).

There are few systematic data on return migration. However, since 1976 net migration to and from the Caribbean has been around zero, while emigration to India, Bangladesh and Sri Lanka has remained constant at around 20 per cent of immigration. There has been little notable emigration to Pakistan in this period.

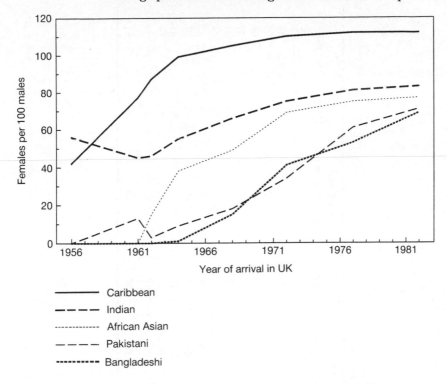

Figure 11.1 Sex ratio of 1982 UK resident immigrants by year of arrival in UK
Source: Derived from Brown (1984)

The most comprehensive source of the size of Britain's ethnic groups is the Labour Force Survey (LFS) which since 1981 has asked individuals to report to which of ten ethnic groups they consider themselves to belong.[1] These data suggest that between 1984 and 1986 the size of the ethnic minority populations in Britain was around 2 400 000 which constituted 4.5 per cent of the total population. Of these 40 per cent were born in the United Kingdom. The percentage distributions of ethnic groups for age and sex from 1985 LFS are contained in table 11.3 and the average proportions for 1984–1986 are illustrated in figure 11.2. All non-white ethnic groups have younger populations than whites. This is not surprising as immigrants are predominantly young and will not have been in this country long enough to have grown old. Comparisons with the white population are least marked among the

[1] The ten ethnic groups are White, West Indian or Guyanese, Indian, Pakistani, Bangladeshi, Chinese, African, Arab, Mixed Origin and Other. Respondents reporting themselves in the last two groups were asked for further specification.

Table 11.3 Population of Great Britain in 1985 by ethnic group, age and sex

	Number (thousands)	Under 16 %	16–29 %	30–44 %	45–64 men 45–59 women %	Males %	Females %
White	50,798	20	22	20	19	49	51
West Indian and Guyanese	547	26	33	15	22	46	54
Indian	689	32	26	24	15	51	49
Pakistani	406	43	25	18	12	53	47
Bangladeshi	99	51	18	14	16	56	44
Chinese	122	27	25	30	14	53	47
African	102	28	28	36	7	57	43
Arab	61	17	48	21	11	73	27
Mixed	232	55	25	11	7	53	47
Other	117	24	26	34	12	46	54
Not stated	637	31	23	17	16	48	52
All	54,325	21	22	20	19	49	51

Source: OPCS, 1986a

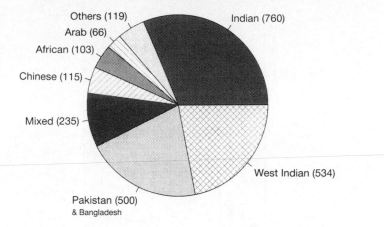

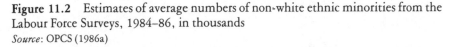

Figure 11.2   Estimates of average numbers of non-white ethnic minorities from the Labour Force Surveys, 1984–86, in thousands
Source: OPCS (1986a)

West Indian, Chinese and African groups and most marked among the Bangladeshi, Pakistani and Mixed groups. The Mixed group will, of course, be particularly young as they will be predominantly second or higher generation offspring of racial intermarriages. The age distributions of ethnic groups are also reflected in the distributions by sex. The predominance of women in the white group is a result of excess male mortality at older ages which will not yet have affected the ethnic communities. Other than the West Indian and Arab communities there is little variation in the distribution by sex with a little over 50 per cent of each ethnic group being male. With respect to the West Indian community it has been suggested (Brown, 1984; Coleman, 1985) that young West Indian males consistently have high non-response rates and so this distribution may be a little biased in favour of the proportion of women.

The LFS also permits an analysis of the regional distributions of ethnic groups by metropolitan area (OPCS, 1986a). In the main, ethnic minorities[2] are concentrated in particular areas (table 11.4). This results from two components of immigration to Britain. First, chain migration where new migrants will be influenced in their decision to migrate by those already in Britain and will tend to go to the same areas. For example, St. Vincentians are concentrated in High Wycombe, Leeward Islanders in Leicester and Punjabis congregate in Hounslow, Ealing, Southall and Gravesend (Simmons, 1981). Second the pull factors inherent in recent British immigration are manifested

---

[2] In the rest of this chapter ethnic minority is used to refer to non-white ethnic groups.

Table 11.4 Regional distribution of residence of ethnic group

	Number (thousands)	% living in district						% born in UK
		Gt. London	Gt. Man.	W. Mid.	W. Yorks	Other metrop.	Non-metrop.	
West Indies	530	57	4	14	3	2	19	50
India	760	39	4	19	5	1	32	35
Pakistan	380	14	10	24	16	4	31	40
Bangladesh	90	54	5	12	5	3	22	30
Africa	100	64	3	2	2	5	24	35
China	110	33	4	3	2	8	49	20
Mixed	210	36	7	7	3	6	42	75
Other	160	51	3	4	2	4	36	19
Total population		12	5	5	4	7	67	

Source: OPCS 1986a

in the regional distribution of immigrants. For example, the Wolf Rubber Factory in Southall recruited directly in the Punjab (Peach, 1984).

Household Structure

The household structure of ethnic groups is comprehensively described by Brown (1984) who shows that there are considerable differences between ethnic groups (table 11.5). Smith (1976) had previously observed this and reasoned that it could, in part, be explained by the smaller proportion of elderly amongst the ethnic minorities as, particularly among the groups who had immigrated most recently, the population has not had time to mature. For example, it is hardly surprising that Brown (1984) finds a much lower percentage of pensioner-only households among non-whites when one considers that 33 per cent of whites are aged 55 and over compared with only 13 per cent of West Indians and 10 per cent of Asians.

Brown (1984) also reports significant differences between West Indian and Asian households: only 5 per cent of Asian households consisted of one adult alone compared with 13 per cent of West Indian and 20 per cent of white households. Furthermore, West Indians have as high an incidence of households consisting of one adult with or without children as whites – one quarter of all households. However, these white households consist mainly of pensioners while the West Indian households contain many more young single adults and lone-parent families (Brown, 1984). This is largely a

Table 11.5   Household type in the United Kingdom by ethnic origin

	White	WI	Asian	Indian	Pakistani	Bangla-deshi	African, Asian
Pensioner(s)[a] only	29	2	2	2			3
Vertically or horizontally extended	4	8	18	15	21	18	21
Lone parent with children	3	18	4	4	3	7	3
Others with children	26	36	56	56	63	61	43
Lone adult (not pens.)	6	11	4	3	5	8	3
Adults without children	32	25	17	20	9	6	27

All figures are percentages of each column
[a] A pensioner is defined as a person over pensionable age (60 women, 65 men)

Source: Brown, 1984

function of the different patterns of marriage and parenthood amongst the West Indian population, where women commonly have children in early adulthood but wait much longer before marriage or cohabitation – a common form of relationship in the Caribbean being the 'visiting relationship' with the partners not sharing a common address (Clarke, 1984).

In Brown's survey the average household size of whites (2.6 persons) is much smaller than that of West Indians (3.4) or Asians (4.6), although, in those households with children the average number of children per household is similar for West Indians (1.7) and whites (1.6). However, 57 per cent of West Indian households contain children compared with only 31 per cent of white households. Asian households are much more likely than any others to contain children, 73 per cent of them doing so, with an average of 2.6 children per household. The higher fertility of Asian households will be discussed in further detail below.

West Indian women appear to play a more dominant role in the household structure than do women from the other main ethnic groups. Brown (1984) defines the head of household as 'the person in whose name the house or flat was held; if the dwelling was held jointly the head of household was taken to be the person who knew most about the housing costs and payments' (p. 38). Under this definition one third of West Indian households were headed by a woman compared with a quarter of white and less than one tenth of Asian households. Further, whereas amongst the white female heads over half are widows, West Indian female heads of households are more likely to be lone parents, single women without children or women, with or without children, living with their husbands. Such married or cohabiting West Indian women are much more likely to be classed as heads of the household (10 per cent) than white (4 per cent) or Asian (3 per cent) women.

There is a little information on dependency ratios for different ethnic groups. Smith (1976) calculates dependency ratios – defined as the average number of dependants/average number of adults who were working. Unfortunately, he used only those households with a male head which excluded a disproportionate number of West Indian households, many of which will be lone-parent families. Also as these were calculated from census data taken from the 1971 census, only country of origin is used. This will further exclude those ethnic minority households headed by UK-born men.

Smith's ethnic minority households tend to have a higher number both of working adults and of dependents. However, there are greater differences in the numbers of dependents and consequently the dependency ratios for all ethnic minority households are greater than those for whites. Again, there are significant differences between the different ethnic groups, with Indian households having the highest ratio of dependents per earner at 1.87, followed by Pakistani and Bangladeshis (1.72), African Asians (1.65) and West Indians (1.49), compared with 1.17 for white households.

When we further consider the small proportion of elderly amongst many of the minority groups, we can expect that if fertility rates do not change then as more people from minority groups move from being working adults to dependants as a result of retirement, these dependency ratios will become even more diverse.

Due to the relative recency of Asian immigration in particular, there has not been sufficient time for some ethnic groups to establish the type of extended household structure that they may consider desirable. Smith (1976) found that 7 per cent of Asian households contained people from all three main age ranges (0–15, 16–54, 55 +) compared with only 3 per cent of white and 2 per cent of West Indian households.

Since at that time only 7 per cent of Asians in the United Kingdom were aged 55 and over, compared with 33 per cent of the total UK population, this shows a very clear tendency for older Asians to live with their children and grandchildren in a vertically extended family.

Employment

In order to understand fully the demography of Britain's ethnic groups it is important to describe differentials in employment. Every study has shown that ethnic minorities have higher proportions in unskilled and semi-skilled occupations and a higher rate of youth unemployment than the white population. The Runnymede Trust (1980) argue that this reflects a number of factors: racial discrimination; recent migrants lacking skills and language; and the age structure of ethnic minority groups – young people are generally more likely to be unemployed. In addition, the pull factors leading to recent immigration play a part. For example, it is well known that London Transport recruited operators directly in Jamaica.

Smith (1976) and Brown (1984) both report that the Pakistanis and Bangladeshis were around three times more likely to be in unskilled or semi-skilled occupations than whites while Indians and West Indians were around twice as likely. Furthermore, when the occupations of men with degree standard qualifications were compared, whites were much more likely to be in occupations commensurate with these qualifications. The one ethnic minority group with a significant proportion in professional and managerial posts are the African Asians. This is because the Ugandan Asian immigrants, in particular, were mostly from the middle classes. They have subsequently achieved high educational qualifications and achieved occupations in the managerial and professional classes. However, the Department of Employment (1987) show that the African Asians with high qualifications still do less well than comparably qualified whites.

Data from the 1985 LFS demonstrate that these patterns remain. The Department of Employment (1987) states that 'the relative position of the different ethnic groups has remained broadly the same'. These data do indicate additionally that Asians are more likely to be self-employed, and that among women West Indians were the most likely to be economically active.

With regard to qualifications, it is interesting that among men aged 16–24, Indians and 'other non-whites' had markedly larger proportions with higher qualifications[3] than whites – 13 per cent and 15 per cent respectively compared to 5 per cent. This could be due to a combination of the propensity of Indians in Britain to study and a 'brain drain' of highly qualified Indians to Britain. On the other hand, West Indian, Pakistani and Bangladeshi men aged 16–24 are less likely to have gained higher qualifications. This is also reflected in lower economic activity rates for Indians as they are more likely to stay in education. Clearly there are important implications for future upward social mobility if these two groups continue to achieve high qualifications – but only if they have access to employment commensurate with their qualifications.

To turn to unemployment, rates were much higher for ethnic minorities, particularly amongst those aged 16–24 among whom over 30 per cent were unemployed compared with 16 per cent for whites. Furthermore, considering the population aged 16–24 it is notable that unemployment rates for those with higher qualifications are much higher for Asian minorities than for any other groups, so it is possible that Asians with higher qualifications may be forced either into lesser occupations or into unemployment.

In summary, there is little evidence of an upturn in the economic position of ethnic minorities. On the contrary, relative underachievement among those of West Indian origin may lead to continuing high levels of unemployment and employment in unskilled and semi-skilled occupations.

Marriage and Intermarriage

The vast majority of marriages and cohabiting relationships in the United Kingdom are between partners from the same ethnic group, but as ethnic groups become more established it is possible that there will increasingly be marriage between them. There is very little work on intermarriage apart from that of Coleman (1985). He shows that, for whites, 99.1 per cent of women and 99.2 per cent of men are in a white/white relationship although this is, to a large extent, inevitable as whites make up 95 per cent of the total UK population. This factor will also be a major contributor to the proportion of

---

[3] Higher qualifications are those requiring advanced post-school study. They include all degrees or degree level qualifications as well as Higher National Certificates and Diplomas, Teaching and Nursing Qualifications.

mixed marriages involving a white partner, which is 87 per cent of all mixed marriages. Amongst the larger ethnic minority groups, West Indians are the most likely to intermarry, with 24 per cent of men and 13 per cent of women in mixed marriages (22 per cent of West Indian men and 10 per cent of West Indian women having a white partner). Ethnic minority men consistently have a higher rate of intermarriage than do the women, with 12 per cent of Indian, Pakistani and Bangladeshi men in mixed marriages (8 per cent of men from both groups being married to a white woman) compared to 7 per cent of Indian women and 9 per cent of women from Pakistan and Bangladesh (4 per cent of Indian and 2 per cent of women from Pakistan and Bangladesh having a white husband with a further 6 per cent of these women being married to Indian men). The historical imbalance between the sexes, with men outnumbering women in the early years of migration for all ethnic groups, is one likely explanation. Additionally, 'men have traditionally been freer to explore new territory and new social relationships than women' (Bagley, quoted by Smith, 1976), which would include the freedom to marry outside their own ethnic group. In Coleman's sample 48 per cent of married African men and 27 per cent of married African women were married outside their own group. However, in many of the marriages between Africans and Indians or Pakistanis, the African partner came from East Africa and so is likely to be of Asian origin. This would bring the proportion of Africans in mixed marriages closer to the West Indian mixed marriage rate of 19 per cent.

As would be expected, the 'mixed origin' group, being the least homogeneous, have a very high rate of marriage with other groups, only 22 per cent taking a partner also of 'mixed origin'. A total of 61 per cent of the women from this group, and 72 per cent of the men, take a white partner. As we have already shown that the greatest number of mixed marriages involve one white and one non-white partner, it is likely that a large proportion of the mixed origin group results from a white/non-white union, and are marrying back into the ethnic group of one of their parents. However, in South Asia there is a long history of mixed marriages, and within the mixed origin group approximately one in five marriages with at least one partner of mixed South Asian/white descent were between husbands and wives both of South Asian/white descent.

To turn to the incidence of marriage, a total of 69 per cent of men and 64 per cent of women are married, while of the 36 per cent of women unmarried almost half are widowed or divorced as opposed to only one sixth of the men. The highest proportions married in the population aged 16 and over are Pakistanis and Bangladeshis (77 per cent), closely followed by Indians (73 per cent). The next most married group is the whites (67 per cent) followed by both Chinese and Africans (61 per cent), Arabs (57 per cent), West Indians (53 per cent) and finally those of mixed origin (46 per cent).

The reasons for these differentials are predominantly cultural as the norms within the Asian communities are much more geared towards marriage than those of other groups. In particular, recent trends in marriage and cohabitation – described by Kiernan in chapter 3 above – and the traditional role of the visiting relationship in Caribbean society will result in higer proportions unmarried amongst whites, mixed and West Indian groups.

Fertility

This section is restricted to births to mothers born overseas, and does not consider births to all ethnic minority mothers as there are few data. This will cause some distortions from the true situation, especially amongst the earlier immigrants such as the Caribbeans, where UK-born mothers play a significant part in the total fertility. Some data are available from the Labour Force Survey but the particularly high non-response rate from UK-born Caribbeans makes the data too scarce to be useful (Thompson, 1982). It is to be hoped that future work using data from the OPCS Longitudinal Study will prove illuminating.

Although many of the ethnic minority groups in the UK exhibit very distinct fertility patterns, there is some evidence to suggest a trend towards convergence of minority-group fertility towards that of the host nation. In the ten years from 1971 to 1981 this particularly applies to the fertility of women born in the Caribbean, Irish Republic, and the Far Eastern and Mediterranean Commonwealth (Yusuf and Werner, 1987). There is also some evidence of assimilation amongst Sikhs whom Smith (1976) found to be the largest of the Indian religious groups. Simons (1982) describes a survey of immigrant Sikhs in London which found that among women married shortly before the survey, there were similar levels of fertility and use of modern methods of contraception as in the UK-born population. Between 1981 and 1986 the Total Period Fertility Rate (TPFR) for UK-born women has remained constant at 1.7, lower than the rate for any of the ethnic minority groups. The TPFR for non-UK-born women fell from 2.5 in 1981 to 2.4 in 1983. Amongst the minorities, those with the highest rates have shown the greatest change, with steady reductions over the period (table 11.6).

Women born in Pakistan and Bangladesh have by far the highest fertility rates, with a 1986 TPFR over three times the national average, and almost twice as high as that of any other ethnic group. This is due not only to extremely high fertility at younger ages, but also to a significantly higher rate of childbearing at older ages for these women (Thompson, 1982). However, between 1981 and 1986 the TPFR for this group has fallen by almost 1, from 6.5 to 5.6.

Table 11.6   Total Period Fertility Rates in England and Wales by birthplace of mother

Birthplace of mother	1981	1982	1983	1984	1985	1986
Total	1.8	1.8	1.8	1.7	1.8	1.8
United Kingdom[a]	1.7	1.7	1.7	1.7	1.7	1.7
Total outside UK	2.5	2.5	2.4	2.5	2.5	2.4
New Commonwealth and Pakistan	2.9	2.9	2.8	2.8	2.9	2.9
India	3.1	3.0	2.8	2.8	2.9	2.9
Pakistan and Bangladesh	6.5	6.3	6.1	5.7	5.6	5.6
East Africa	2.1	2.1	2.0	2.1	2.1	2.0
Rest of Africa	3.4	3.3	3.1	2.9	3.0	2.8
Caribbean	2.0	2.0	1.8	1.8	1.8	1.8
Far East[b]	1.7	1.9	1.9	2.0	2.0	1.9
Mediterranean[c]	2.1	2.2	2.1	2.2	2.2	2.1
Rest of New Commonwealth	2.3	2.3	2.4	2.3	2.3	2.3
Rest of World	2.0	1.9	1.9	2.0	2.0	1.9

[a] Including Isle of Man and Channel Islands
[b] Hong Kong, Malaysia and Singapore
[c] Cyprus, Gibraltar and Malta
The TPFR summarizes age-specific fertility rates as the number of children that would be born per women if that year's rates were to be obtained over the 30-year span of childbearing ages. In chapter two this is called the Total Fertility Index.

Source: OPCS, 1986b

Figures 11.3–11.5 show the age specific fertility rates for different groups for 1971, 1981 and 1986. The pattern of high and extended fertility for Pakistani and Bangladeshi women is clearly seen. However, it is also clear that fertility at all ages for these women has fallen substantially between 1971 and 1986 particularly at ages over 25. The relatively late arrival in the UK of this ethnic group, and particularly of females, may have some bearing on this decline. Although among all Asian groups it has been the men who led the migration, the lag between male and female migration is far greater for Pakistanis and Bangladeshis than for Indians or African Asians (Brown, 1984). As over two thirds of female immigrants over the age of 15 at the time of immigration have said that they came to Britain to join their husbands or other family (Smith, 1976), it is possible that the higher fertility of the Pakistani and Bangladeshi women at older ages is in part a result of delayed parenthood due to separation from their husbands earlier in the marriage (or, in some cases, delayed marriage due to separation).

There is further evidence to suggest that many women in the older age groups resumed childbearing, first started overseas, after a period of separation from their husbands (Thompson, 1982). This may suggest a period effect as those women now in their twenties will complete their fertility earlier than their contemporaries in their thirties with a consequent reduction

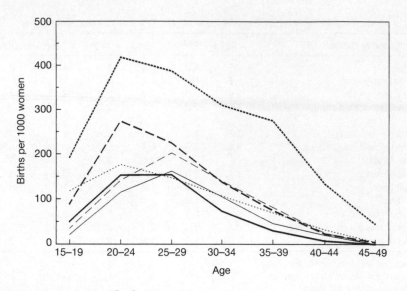

Figure 11.3 Age-specific fertility rates by mother's place of birth, England and Wales, **1971**
Source: Yusuf and Werner (1987)

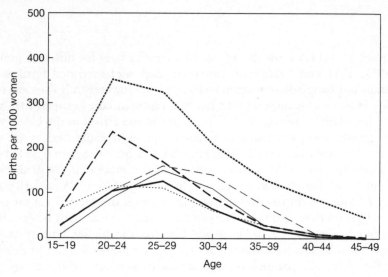

Figure 11.4 Age specific fertility rates by mother's place of birth, England and Wales, **1981**
Source: Birth Statistics 1981

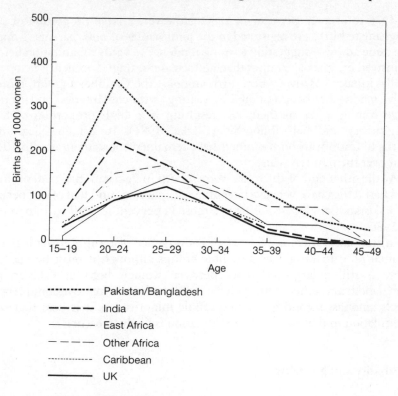

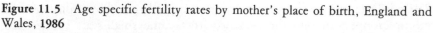

Figure 11.5 Age specific fertility rates by mother's place of birth, England and Wales, **1986**
Source: Birth Statistics 1986

in the TPFR. Thompson (1982) further shows that first births tend to follow soon after marriage for women born in the Indian subcontinent, with the average age at marriage for mothers from Pakistan and Bangladesh being 21, compared to an average for Indians of 22, and a national average of 23. Caribbean-born women tend to marry later (the average age at marriage of Caribbean-born mothers having their first birth in marriage in 1979 being 25). This is almost certainly a function of the West Indian culture where marriage frequently comes after childbearing.

Turning to trends in illegitimacy, these are illustrated in figure 11.6. Over the past decade, there has been a marked increase amongst both UK-born women and those born in the 'Rest of Africa' rising from around 10 per cent in 1976 to over 22 per cent in 1986. However, a large proportion of such illegitimate births are registered in the joint names of both parents, living at the same address, suggesting a strong tendency towards cohabitation before, or instead of, marriage rather than an increase in single mothers.

Illegitimacy has always been high amongst the Caribbean group. Historically, mating has been initiated by visiting, with cohabitation and/or marriage coming after motherhood, resulting in a high proportion of birth illegitimacy and half-siblingship (Clarke, 1984). In Britain, illegitimate births to Caribbean-born mothers have remained constant at around 50 per cent over the past ten years.

At the other end of the scale, women born in Pakistan/Bangladesh, India and East Africa have very low rates of illegitimacy, around half of one per cent for Pakistan/Bangladesh, rising to almost 34 per cent for East African women in 1986.

In summary, there is evidence of convergence of fertility towards that of women born in Britain by all ethnic groups although it must be said that there is still a large difference between women born in Pakistan and Bangladesh and other ethnic groups. It will be interesting to monitor fertility levels amongst second generation ethnic minorities as it is here that most assimilation to that of the white population is likely to occur.

Morbidity and Mortality

There is little systematic work on levels of morbidity and mortality between ethnic groups although the evidence from some small-scale studies does suggest that there are higher incidences of ill health among ethnic minorities than among the white population. It is essential to establish the extent to which such differentials can be explained by adverse social conditions experienced by ethnic minorities in comparison with the white population. For example, it is well known that mortality amongst unskilled manual workers is higher than among those in non-manual occupations, and the Black Report (Townsend and Davidson, 1982) reports that unskilled manual workers (Social Class V) comprise around 5 per cent of British-born workers as opposed to around 15 per cent of those born in India and Pakistan.

Even after controlling for such factors it is likely that there may be special demands for health provision from ethnic groups as a result of cultural or language differentials. Examples include dietary requirements or the need for female doctors. It has been argued that such demands form the main reasons for excess ill health among ethnic minorities compared with whites with similar demographic and social characteristics. Norman (1985) quotes Pearson (1984) in this context:

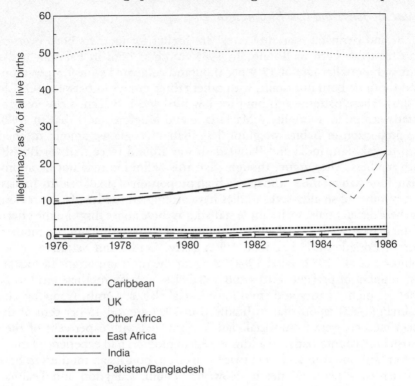

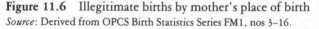

Figure 11.6 Illegitimate births by mother's place of birth
Source: Derived from OPCS Birth Statistics Series FM1, nos 3–16.

The overwhelming majority of health problems faced by ethnic minorities in Britain are different in degree, but not in kind from those experienced by the rest of the population. Social factors contributing to ill health, and the general health care experience of the NHS are often intensified for the ethnic minority users by racism and racial prejudice, cultural insensitivity and language differences.

This is supported by the Open University (1985) who describe the concept of 'institutional racism' which means that 'racist beliefs are accepted as factual evidence for differences between ethnic groups'. As a result these views determine the behaviour of the health practitioners. The Open University (1985) argue that differences in the health status of ethnic groups are almost entirely due to social factors, reinforced by a racist social structure.

Infant Mortality and Low Birthweight

Infant and perinatal mortality rates[4] are higher for mothers born overseas than for those born in Britain. In 1985, mothers born in Pakistan had a perinatal mortality rate of 17.9 per thousand compared with 9.5 per thousand for those born in Britain, with other ethnic groups in between (OPCS, 1986b). These patterns also hold for low birthweight which is closely associated with infant mortality – Macfarlane and Mugford show that in 1980, the proportion of babies weighing less than 2500 grams[5] among mothers born in Pakistan, India and Bangladesh was around twice that for British-born mothers. They argue, though, that this definition may not be appropriate for Asian mothers who have a high proportion of small healthy babies.

A number of smaller-scale studies have attempted to identify the reasons for these differentials; such simple statistics as those above disguise the effects of the demographic, social and environmental characteristics of the mothers (Lumb, Congdon and Lealman, 1981; Terry, Cordie and Settatree, 1980; Robinson et al., 1982; Patel 1984). Among the most important factors are age, number of previous births and social class – Asian mothers tend to be older, of higher parity and from lower social classes. Lumb, Congdon and Lealman (1982) report that in Bradford in 1977 around 45 per cent of the Asian mothers were from social class V compared with 6 per cent of their British born counterparts. In addition, Asian mothers had experienced much shorter birth intervals and were twice as likely as non-Asian mothers to have experienced a perinatal death. However, Lumb, Congdon and Lealman (1981), Terry, Cordie and Settatree (1980) and Robinson et al. (1982) all found that even after controlling for age, sex and social class there was still an 'ethnic effect'; but Patel (1984) was able to explain this by controlling for length of antenatal supervision – Asian mothers were less likely to have experienced a long period of medical care in pregnancy.

The policy implications are clear. Mothers from ethnic minorities should be encouraged to seek antenatal supervision. This requires improved communication of the benefits of such care which may need the influence of religious and community leaders as well as the production of more literature in minority languages and the availability of interpreters, child care and transport to the clinic.

---

[4] The infant mortality rate is the number of deaths to infants aged less than one year per thousand live births. The perinatal mortality rate is the number of stillbirths and deaths to infants aged less than 7 days per thousand livebirths and stillbirths.
[5] Below 2500 grams is the World Health Organization definition of a low birthweight baby.

Morbidity and Mortality in Later Life

There has been some work on diseases specific to ethnic groups such as sickle cell anaemia. However, such diseases do not constitute a high proportion of the morbidity of ethnic groups and in the main there appear to be few differences between the types of illnesses experienced by ethnic minorities and those of whites, but there does tend to be evidence of higher incidences of ill health among ethnic minorities. Norman (1985) reports a study of the elderly in Birmingham by Blakemore (1982) which shows that Afro-Caribbeans, particularly women, were more likely to have been to a doctor or hospital than those of Asian or white origin. Norman (1985) argues that the relatively low use of hospital services by Asians is due to the fears that many elderly Asians have of hospital.

With regard to mortality, Adelstein, Marmot and Bulusu (1983) show that mortality among immigrants from the Indian sub-continent from common cancers such as the stomach, large intestine and breast is markedly low whereas those for the buccal cavity, liver and oesophagus is high, as is tuber-culosis. Among other common causes of death, Caribbean and African immigrants have very high levels of mortality from hypertension and strokes.

The importance of improving health care for ethnic groups will become increasingly important as these groups grow older. The ageing of ethnic minority populations will require some definitive policy initiatives. Norman (1985) provides a comprehensive review of this important area, arguing that the elderly in ethnic minority populations are in 'triple jeopardy' – 'at risk because they are old, because of the physical conditions and hostility under which they have to live, and because services are not accessible to them'. She calls for specific actions by ethnic minority groups, general practitioners, health authorities and by central government to improve the knowledge of and accessibility to health care by ethnic minorities in Britain.

Conclusions

This chapter has described the variety of demographic patterns and trends among Britain's ethnic groups and assessed the extent of assimilation. It has of necessity been largely confined to those born abroad. The need for a census question on ethnicity is paramount if initiatives, particularly for health care, can be directed at those most in need, and progress monitored.

Fertility is declining among those born overseas, largely perhaps as a result of the ageing of some of these groups. The very high fertility of those born in Pakistan and Bangladesh may well be a period effect caused by the separation of husbands and wives. The importance of taking into account cultural influences is very clear in this area as types of relationships vary greatly among different groups.

The continued assimilation of the fertility patterns of non-white ethnic groups to those of the white population will mean that there will not be a massive explosion in the size of the non-white ethnic groups. Recent estimates suggest that they comprise around 4.5 per cent of the population and it is forecasted that this proportion will rise slowly to around 5.4 per cent in 1991 (OPCS, 1986a). While this proportion will continue to increase slowly it seems unlikely, given current immigration policies and demographic patterns, that it will exceed 7 per cent.

Although the non-white ethnic population will never be the major component in the size of Britain's population, the clear social and economic disadvantages outlined in this chapter may continue to prove an important social problem. The extent to which this can be ameliorated will depend very much on continued assimilation, both demographically and socially; a reduction in the extent to which race is a source of disadvantage; and, crucially, the evolution of a social structure in which there are equal opportunities for all – not simply statements of policy but agendas for action.

Selected Key Reading

Brown, Colin 1984: *Black and White Britain – The Third PSI Survey*. London: Heinemann Educational Books.
Clarke, Colin, Ley David, and Peach Ceri, (eds) 1984: *Geography and Ethnic Pluralism*. London: Gorge Allen & Unwin.

Bibliography

Abrams, Mark 1978: *Beyond Three Score Years and Ten: A First Report on the Survey of the Elderly*. Mitcham: Age Concern.

Adelstein, Abraham, Marmot, Michael and Bulusu, Lak 1983: Immigrant mortality in England and Wales 1970–78. *Population Trends*, 33, 14–17.

Adler, Michael and Bondi, Liz 1988: Delegation and community participation: a new approach to the problems created by falling primary school rolls. In Bondi and Matthews (eds), *Education and Society*. London: Croom Helm (forthcoming).

Adler, Michael and Raab, Gillian 1988: Exit, choice and loyalty: The impact of parental choice on admissions to secondary schools in Edinburgh and Dundee. *J. Educational Policy*, 3.

Association of County Councils 1983: *Block grant indicators 1983/4*. Reading: Society of County Treasurers.

Association of County Councils 1984: *Block grant indicators 1984/5*. Reading: Society of County Treasurers.

Association of County Councils 1985: *Block grant indicators 1985/6*. Reading: Society of County Treasurers.

Association of University Teachers 1983: *The Real Demand for Student Places*. London: AUT.

Atkins, Elizabeth A., Cherry, Nicola, Douglas, James W. B., Kiernan, Kathleen E. and Wadsworth, Michael E. J. 1981: The 1946 British birth cohort study. In S. A. Mednick and A. E. Baert (eds), *An Empirical Basis for Primary Prevention: Prospective Longitudinal Research in Europe*. Oxford: Oxford University Press, 25–30.

Audit Commission 1986: Report by Her Majesty's Inspectors on the effects of local authority expenditure policies on education provision in England – 1985. London: Department of Education and Science.

Bagley, Christopher 1974: Interracial marriage in Britain – some statistics. *New Community*, 1, 4, 24–32.

Bagrit, Leon 1965: *The Age of Automation*. BBC Reith Lectures. London: Weidenfeld.

Becker, Gary S. 1981: *A Treatise on the Family*. Cambridge, Mass.: Harvard University Press.

Becker, Gary S. 1985: Human capital, effort and the sexual division of labour. *Journal of Labor Economics*, 3, S33–S58.

Becker, Gary S., Landes, Elizabeth M. and Michael, Robert T. 1977: An economic analysis of marital instability. *Journal of Political Economy*, 85, 1141–87.

Begg, Iain and Eversley, David 1986: Deprivation in the inner city: social indicators from the 1981 Census. In V. A. Hausner (ed.), *Critical issues in urban economic development*, vol. 1. Oxford: Oxford University Press, 50–88.

Bennett, Robert J. 1982: *Central grants to local government*. Cambridge: Cambridge University Press.

Beveridge, William 1942: *Social Insurance and Allied Services* Cmd. 6404, London: HMSO.

Birth Statistics Series FM. Office of Population Censuses and Surveys. London: HMSO.

Blacker, C. P. S. 1933: Population prophecies: Unsigned review in *The Lancet*, 480–1.

Blakemore, Ken, 1982: Health and illness among the elderly of minority ethnic groups living in Birmingham – some new findings. *Health Trends*, 14, 3, 69–72.

Bondi, Liz and Matthews, M. H. (eds), *Education and Society*. London: Croom Helm (forthcoming).

Bone, Margaret 1985: *Family Planning in Scotland in 1982*, (OPCS). London: HMSO.

Bosanquet, Nicholas 1975: *New Deal For The Elderly*. London: Fabian Society.

Bosanquet, Nicholas 1978: *A Future for Old Age*. London: Temple Smith/New Society.

Brannen, Julia and Wilson, Gail (eds) 1987: *Give and Take in Families: Studies in Resource Distribution*. London: Allen & Unwin.

Brant, John 1984: Patterns of migration from the 1981 Census. *Population Trends*, 35, 23–30.

Brass, William 1983: Birth projections based on births by order. Unpublished note. London School of Hygiene.

Breheny, Michael, Hall, Peter and Hart, Douglas 1987: *Northern Lights: A Development Agenda for the North in the 1990s*. Preston and London: Derrick, Wade and Walters.

Breheny, Michael, Hart, Douglas and Hall, Peter 1986: *Eastern Promise: Development Prospects for the M11 Corridor*. London: Derrick, Wade and Walters.

Briault, Eric 1986: Education provision and demographic change in England and Wales. In W. T. S. Gould and R. Lawton (eds), *Planning for Population Change*. London: Croom Helm, 163–80.

British Society for Population Studies 1983: *The Family*. OPCS Occasional Paper 31. London: OPCS.

British Society for Population Studies 1985: *Measuring Socio-demographic Change*. OPCS Occasional Paper 34. London: OPCS.

Brittan, Sam 1986: The great housing barrier. *Financial Times*, 27 November.

Britton, Malcolm 1986: Recent population changes in perspective. *Population Trends*, 44, 33–41.

Britton, Malcolm and Birch, Frances 1985: *1981 Census Post-enumeration Survey*. London: HMSO.

Brown, Audrey 1986: The family circumstances of young children. *Population Trends*, No. 43, 18–23.

Brown, Colin 1984: *Black and White Britain - The Third PSI Survey*. Aldershot: Gower.

Buck, Nick, Gordon, Ian and Young, Ken (eds) 1986: *The London employment problem*. Oxford: Clarendon Press.

Burnhill, Peter 1985: Contribution to Discussion on Projections of Student Numbers in Higher Education. *J. Royal Statistical Society Series A*. 148, 199–203.

Burnhill, Peter, Garner, Cathy and McPherson, Andrew 1987: Social class, parental schooling and the demand for higher education. DHE/68 Centre for Educational Sociology, University of Edinburgh.

Burnhill, Peter, Garner, Cathy and McPherson, Andrew 1988: Social change, school attainment and entry to higher education 1976– 1986. In D. Raffe (ed.), *Schooling and Scheming: Education and the Youth Labour Market*. Lewes: Falmer Press (forthcoming).

Busfield, Joan and Paddon, Michael 1977: *Thinking about children* Cambridge: Cambridge University Press.

Cain, Glen 1985: Welfare economics of policies toward women. *Journal of Labor Economics*, 3, S375–S396.

Cambridge Econometrics 1987: *Regional economic prospects: analysis and projections to the year 2000*. Cambridge and Belfast: Cambridge Econometrics and Northern Ireland Economic Research Centre.

Campbell, Beatrix 1984: *Wigan Pier Revisited*. London: Virago Press.

CES Ltd 1985: *Outer Estates in Britain: A Framework for Action*. London: CES. Paper 28.

Challis, David and Davis, Bleddyn 1983: Long-term care for the elderly: the Community Care Scheme. *British Journal of Social Work*, 15, 6.

Champion, Tony 1981a: Counterurbanization and rural rejuvenation in Britain: an evaluation of population trends since 1971. Newcastle upon Tyne: University of Newcastle, Department of Geography, Seminar Paper 38.

Champion, Tony 1981b: Population trends in rural Britain. *Population Trends*, 26, 20–3.

Champion, Tony 1983: Population trends in the 1970s. In Goddard and Champion (eds), *The Urban and Regional Transformation of Britain*. London: Methuen, 187–214.

Champion, Tony 1987a: Momentous revival in London's population. *Town and Country Planning*, 56, 80–2.

Champion, Tony 1987b: Recent changes in the pace of population deconcentration in Britain. *Geoforum*, 18, 379–401.

Champion, Tony, Clegg, Kathy and Davies, Ross 1977: *Facts about the new towns: a socio economic digest*. Corbridge: Retailing and Planning Associates.

Champion, Tony and Congdon, Peter 1988: An analysis of the recovery of London's population change rate. Unpublished paper, Newcastle University.

Champion, Tony, Coombes, Mike and Openshaw, Stan 1984: New regions for a new Britain. *Geographical Magazine*, 56, 187–90.

Champion, Tony and Green, Anne 1987: The booming towns of Britain: the geography of economic performance in the 1980s. *Geography*, 72, 97–108.

Champion, Tony and Green, Anne 1988: *Local Prosperity and the North-South divide: winners and losers in 1980s Britain.* Coventry: Institute for Employment Research, University of Warwick.

Champion, Tony, Green, Anne and Owen, David 1987: Housing, labour mobility and unemployment. *The Planner*, 73 (4), 11–17.

Champion, Tony, Green, Anne, Owen, David, Ellin, David and Coombes, Mike 1987: *Changing places: Britain's demographic, economic and social complexion.* London: Edward Arnold.

Charles, Enid 1936: *The Menace of Under-population: a Biological Study of the Decline of Population Growth.* London: Watts and Co. (Previously published as *The Twilight of Parenthood.*)

Charness, Neil (ed.) 1985: *Ageing and Human Performance.* Chichester and New York: Wiley & Sons.

Clarke, Colin 1984: Pluralism and plural societies: Caribbean perspectives. In Clarke, Ley and Peach (eds), *Geography and Ethnic Pluralism.* London: George Allen & Unwin, 51–86.

Clarke, Colin, Ley, David and Peach, Ceri (eds) 1984: *Geography and Ethnic Pluralism.* London: George Allen & Unwin.

Cole, Dorothy (Wedderburn) and Utting, John 1962: *The Economic Circumstances of Old People.* London: Bell & Co.

Coleman, David 1985: Ethnic intermarriage in Great Britain. *Population Trends,* 40, 4–9.

Coleman, David A. (ed.) 1982: *Demography of Immigrant and Minority Groups in the UK.* London: Academic Press.

Collins, P. M. D. 1983: Demographic trends and future university candidates. Working Paper. Royal Society, London.

Committee of Vice-Chancellors and Principals 1983: Office note on full-time student numbers in universities up to 1999/2000. VC/83/90(b).

Craig, John and Broad, Pat 1982: The evolution of population estimates in England and Wales. *Population Trends* 29, 4–7.

Crompton, Rosemary and Sanderson, Kay 1986: Credentials and careers: some implications of the increase in professional qualifications amongst women. *Sociology,* 20, 1, 25–42.

Damesick, Peter and Wood, Peter (eds) 1987: *Regional Problems, Problem Regions and Public Policy in the United Kingdom.* Oxford: Clarendon Press.

De Cooman, Eric, Ermisch, John and Joshi, Heather 1987: The next birth and the labour market: a dynamic model of births in England and Wales. *Population Studies,* 41, 237–68.

De Cooman, Eric, Ermisch, John and Joshi, Heather 1988: Econometric modelling of the birth rate. Centre for Economic Policy Research Discussion Paper 213. London: CEPR.

Debré, Michel 1978: Opinion page of *Le Monde,* quoted in Dirk J. Van de Kaa, 1987: Europe's second demographic transition. *Population Bulletin,* 42, no. 1, 46–7.

Department of Education and Science 1977: Falling numbers and school closures. Circular 5/77. London: HMSO.

Department of Education and Science 1978: *Higher Education into the 1990s: a discussion document.* London: HMSO.

Department of Education and Science 1981: School Closures. Circular 2/81. London: HMSO.

Department of Education and Science 1982: Pupil numbers and school leavers: future numbers. London: HMSO.

Department of Education and Science 1983: Future demand for higher education in Great Britain. Report on Education, no. 99. London: HMSO.

Department of Education and Science 1984a: Future demand for higher education in Great Britain. Report on Education, no. 100. London: HMSO.

Department of Education and Science 1984b: D.E.S. technical report to Report on Education, no. 100. London: HMSO.

Department of Education and Science 1985: *Statistical Bulletin 5/85*. London: Department of Education and Science.

Department of Education and Science 1986a: Projections of school population. Unpublished report. Schools Projection Team, Statistics Branch.

Department of Education and Science 1986b: Projections of future student numbers. London: HMSO.

Department of Education and Science 1987: International statistical comparisons in higher education. *Statistical Bulletin 4/87*. London: HMSO.

Department of Employment 1985: *Employment: the challenge for the nation*, Cmnd. 9474. London: HMSO.

Department of Employment 1987: Ethnic origin and economic status. *Employment Gazette*, 18–26.

Department of the Environment 1980: *Homeless Households Reported by Local Authorities in England: Statistics for the First Half of 1979*. London: Department of the Environment.

Department of the Environment 1985: *Rate support grant 1985/6*. London: HMSO.

Department of the Environment 1986a: *1983 Based Estimates of Numbers of Households in England, the Regions, Counties, Metropolitan Districts and London Boroughs 1983–2001*. London: Department of the Environment.

Department of the Environment 1986b: *Paying for local government*, Cmnd. 9714. London: HMSO.

Department of the Environment 1987: *Local Authorities' Action Under the Homelessness Provision of the 1985 Housing Act: England. Results for the Fourth Quarter 1986. Supplementary tables*. London: Department of the Environment.

Department of Health and Social Security 1976a: *Priorities for Health and Social Services in England: A Consultative Document* London: HMSO.

Department of Health and Social Security 1976b: *Sharing Resources for Health in England: Report of the Resource Allocation Working Party*. London: HMSO.

Department of Health and Social Security 1980: *Social Security Statistics 1980*. HMSO.

Department of Health and Social Security 1983: *Health Care and its Costs*. London: HMSO.

Department of Health and Social Security 1984: *Population, Pension Costs and Pensioners' Incomes*. London: HMSO.

Department of Health and Social Security 1985: *Reform of Social Security: Programme for Change*, Cmnd. 9518. London: HMSO.

Department of Health and Social Security 1986: *Social Security Statistics 1986*. HMSO.

Derbyshire, Michael E. 1987: Statistical rationale for Grant Related Expenditure Assessment (GREA) concerning personal social services (with discussion). *J. Royal Statistical Society A*, 150, 309–33.

Devis, Tim 1983: People changing address. 1971 and 1981. *Population Trends*, 32, 15–20.

Devis, Tim 1984: Population movements measured by the NHS Central Register. *Population Trends*, 36, 18–24.

Dex, Shirley 1987: *Women's Occupational Mobility*. London: Macmillan.

Diamond, Ian 1985: Invited contribution to 'Projections of Student Numbers in Higher Education'. *J. Royal Statistical Society Series A*, 148, 189–4.

Diamond, Ian 1987: The student number debate. *AUT Bulletin*, no. 150, 6–7.

Diamond, Ian 1988: Loglinear and proportional odds models of educational achievement in Scotland. University of Southampton: Department of Social Statistics.

Diamond, Ian and Smith, Fred 1982: Whither mathematics? Comments on the report by Professor D. S. Jones. *Bull. Institute of Mathematics and its Applications*, 18, 189–92.

Diamond, Ian and Smith, Fred 1984: Demand for Higher Education. *Bull. Institute of Mathematics and its Applications*, 20, 124–5.

Dolphin, Anthony M. 1981: The demand for higher education. *Department of Employment Gazette*, 302–5.

Dolton, Peter and Makepeace, Gerry 1986: Sample selection and male–female earnings differentials in the graduate labour market: *Oxford Economic Papers*, 38, 2, 317–41.

Donnison, David 1967: *The Government of Housing*. Harmondsworth: Penguin.

Donnison, David and Soto, Paul 1980: *The Good City*. London: Heinemann.

Duesenberry, James 1960: Comment on 'An economic analysis of fertility' by Gary S. Becker. In R. Easterlin (ed.), *Demographic and Economic Change in Developed Countries*. Princeton: Princeton University Press.

Duncan, Greg J., and Hoffman, Saul D. 1985: Economic consequences of marital instability. In T. Smeeding and M. David (eds), *Horizontal Equity, Uncertainty and Well-being*. National Bureau of Economic Research, Income and Wealth Conference. Chicago: University of Chicago Press, 429–70.

Dunnell, Karen 1979: *Family Formation 1976*. London: HMSO.

ESRC 1987: *Horizons and Opportunities in the Social Sciences*. London: Economic and Social Research Council.

Eeklaar, John and Maclean, Mavis L. 1986: *Maintenance after Divorce*. Oxford: Oxford University Press.

Eldridge, Sandra M. and Kiernan, Kathleen E. 1985: Declining first marriage rates in England and Wales: a change in timing or rejection of marriage? *European Journal of Population*, 1, 327–45.

Elias, Peter 1983: The changing pattern of employment amongst married couples. *EOC Research Bulletin* no. 8, Winter 1983–4, 1–16.

Elias, Peter, and Main, Brian 1982: *Women's Working Lives: Evidence from the Nation Training Survey*. Coventry: Institute for Employment Research, University of Warwick.

England, Paula and Farkas, George 1986: *Households, Employment and Gender: A Social, Economic and Demographic View*. New York: Aldine.

English House Condition Survey Part 1 1982: Department of the Environment. London: HMSO.

Equal Opportunities Commission 1982: *Caring for the Elderly and Handicapped: Community Care Policies and Women's Lives*. Manchester: Equal Opportunities Commission.

Erickson, Eugene P., Kadane, Joseph B. 1985: Estimating the population in a Census year: 1980 and beyond (with discussion). *Journal of the American Statistical Association*, 80, 98–131.

Ermisch, John 1983: *The Political Economy of Demographic Change*, London: Policy Studies Institute/Heinemann.

Ermisch, John 1985: Economic implications of demographic change. Centre for Economic Policy Research Discussion Paper 44. Also published, in 1986, by the Manchester Statistical Society.

Ermisch, John 1986: Economics of the family: applications to divorce and remarriage. Discussion Paper 140, Centre for Economic Policy Research, London.

Ermisch, John 1987: Econometric analysis of birth rate dynamics. National Institute of Economic and Social Research Discussion Paper no. 127. London: NIESR.

Ermisch, John, Jenkins, Stephen and Wright, Robert, E. 1987: Analysis of the dynamics of lone parenthood: socio-economic influences on entry and exit rates. Report to the Directorate of Manpower, Education and Social Affairs. Paris: OECD.

Ermisch, John and Joshi, Heather 1987: Demographic change, economic growth and social welfare. In *European Population Conference 1987: Issues and Prospects. Plenaries*. Helsinki: Central Statistical Office of Finland, 329–86. Also available as Centre for Economic Policy Research Discussion Paper 179.

Evandrou, Maria, Arber, Sara, Dale, Angela and Gilbert, G. Nigel 1986: Who cares for the elderly? Family care provision and receipt of statutory services. In C. Phillipson, M. Bernard, P. Strang (eds), *Dependency and Inter-Dependency in Old Age*. Beckenham: Croom Helm, 150–66.

Eversley, David 1972: Rising costs and static incomes: some economic consequences for regional planning in London. *Urban Studies*, 9, 347–68.

Eversley, David 1983: The family and housing policy: the interactions of the family, the household and the housing market. In British Society for Population Studies, *The Family*, 82–95.

Eysenck, Hans J. 1958: A short questionnaire for the measurement of two dimensions of personality. *Journal of Applied Psychology*, 42, 14–17.

Falkingham, Jane 1987: Britain's ageing population: the engine behind increased dependency? Suntory Toyota International Centre for Economics and Related Disciplines, Discussion Paper 17. London School of Economics.

Farahani, Mahmood Mahmoodi Hajdabadi 1981: *A Model of Fertility by Birth Order and Duration of Marriage*. Ph.D. thesis, University of London.

Fielding, Tony 1986: Counterurbanization. In Michael Pacione (ed.), *Population Georgraphy: Progress and Prospects*. London: Croom Helm, 224–56.

Fildes, Robert 1985: Contribution to discussion of 'Projections of student numbers in higher education'. *J. Royal Statistical Society Series A*, 148, 209–11.

Finch, Janet and Groves, Dulcie (eds) 1983: *A Labour of Love: Women, Work and Caring*. London: Routledge and Kegan Paul.

Flowerdew, Robin and Salt, John 1979: Migration between labour market areas in Great Britain, 1970–1971. *Regional Studies*, 13, 211–31.

Flynn, Peter 1986: Urban deprivation: what it is and how to measure it. *Public Money*, 6, 37–41.

Forrest, Ray and Murie, Alan 1983: Residualization and council housing: aspects of the changing relations of housing tenure. *Journal of Social Policy* 12, 453–68.

Fox, A. John and Goldblatt, Peter 1982: *Socio-economic Differentials in Mortality from the OPCS Longitudinal Study*. Office of Population Censuses and Surveys. London: HMSO.

Fry, Vanessa C. 1984: Inequality in family earnings. *Fiscal Studies* 5, 54–61.

Garner, Cathy 1988: Deprivation and educational attainment. In Bondi and Matthews (eds), *Education and Society*. London: Croom Helm (forthcoming).

General Household Survey (annual): Social Survey Division. Office of Population Censuses and Surveys. London: HMSO.

Gershuny, Jonathan, Miles, I., Jones, S., Mullings, C., Thomas, G. and Wyatt, S. 1986: Time budgets: preliminary analyses of a national survey: *Quarterly Journal of Social Affairs*, vol. 2, 13–39.

Gilbert, Nigel et al. 1989: Resources in old age: ageing and the life course. In Jeffreys (ed.) *As Britain Ages*. London: Routledge.

Gleave, David and Palmer, David 1980: The relationship between geographic and occupational mobility in the context of regional economic growth. In Hobcraft and Rees (eds), *Regional Demographic Development*. London: Croom Helm, 188–210.

Gleave, David and Sellens, Rowena 1984: *An investigation into British labour market processes*. London: Economic and Social Research Council.

Glendinning, Caroline and Millar, Jane (eds) 1987: *Women and Poverty in Britain*. Brighton: Wheatsheaf.

Glennerster, Howard 1985: *Paying for Welfare*. Oxford: Basil Blackwell.

Goddard, John B. and Champion, Tony (eds) 1983: *The Urban and Regional Transformation of Britain*. London: Methuen.

Goddard, John B. and Gillespie, Andrew E. 1987: Advanced telecommunications and regional economic development. In Brian T. Robson (ed.), *Managing the city*. London: Croom Helm, 84–109.

Goldstein, Harvey 1988: *Multi-level Modelling*. London: Griffin.

Gould, W. T. S. and Lawton, R. (eds) 1986: *Planning for Population Change*. London: Croom Helm.

Grant, Gordon 1986: Older carers, interdependence and the care of mentally handicapped adults. *Ageing and Society*, 6, 333–51.

Green, Anne 1986: The likelihood of becoming and remaining unemployed in Great Britain, 1984. *Transactions. Institute of British Geographers,* New Series, 11, 37–56.

Green, Anne 1988: The North–South divide in Great Britain: an examination of the evidence. *Transactions. Institute of British Geographers'* New Series, 13.

Green, Anne, Owen, David, Champion, Tony, Goddard, John and Coombes, Mike 1986: What contribution can labour migration make to reducing unemployment?

In P. E. Hart (ed.), *Unemployment and labour market policies*. Aldershot: Gower, 52–79.

Groves, Dulcie M. 1986: Women and Occupational Pensions, 1870–1983: an exploratory study. Unpublished Ph.D. thesis, University of London.

Groves, Dulcie M. 1987: Occupational pension provision and women's poverty in old age. In Glendinning and Millar (eds), *Women and Poverty in Britain*. Brighton: Wheatsheaf, 199–217.

Groves N. S. 1986: Letter to the chairman of the governors of Altwood School. In submission to the Secretary of State by the Governors of Altwood School, Maidenhead.

Grundy, Emily 1985: Divorce, widowhood, remarriage and geographic mobility among women. *Journal of Biosocial Science*, 17:4, 415–35.

Grundy, Emily 1986: Ageing: age-related change in later life. Paper to British Society for Population Studies Conference: Population Research in Britain. University of East Anglia. In Hobcraft and Murphy (eds), *Population Research in Britain*. Oxford: Oxford University Press (forthcoming).

Guy, Catherine 1983: *Asking about marriage*, London: National Marriage Guidance Council.

Hakim, Catherine 1979: *Occupational Segregation*. Research Paper, no. 9, London: Department of Employment.

Hall, Peter (ed.) 1981: *The inner city in context*. London: Heinemann.

Hall, Peter 1986: From the unsocial city to the social city. *The Planner*, 17(3), 17–24.

Hall, Peter, Breheny, Michael, McQuaid, Ronald and Hart, Douglas 1987: *Western Sunrise: The Genesis and Growth of Britain's Major High Technology Corridor*. London: Allen & Unwin.

Hall, Peter, Thomas, Ray, Gracey, Harry and Drewett, Roy 1973: *The Containment of Urban England*. London: George Allen & Unwin (2 vols).

Hamill, Lynne 1978: Wives as sole and joint breadwinners, Government Economic Service Working Paper no. 13.

Hammond, A. 1984: What the Department of Education and Science collects and why. In 'Forecasting pupil numbers' Report of one-day workshop, Local Education Authorities Research Group. London: ILEA.

Hamnett, Chris 1984: Housing the two nations: socio-tenurial polarization in England and Wales. *Urban Studies*, 43, 389–405.

Hamnett, Chris 1986: The changing socio-economic structure of London and the South East 1961–1981. *Regional Studies*, 20, 391–406.

Hamnett, Chris and Randolph, Bill 1982: How far will London's population fall? A commentary on the 1981 census. *The London Journal*, 8, 95–100.

Hamnett, Chris and Randolph, Bill 1983a: The changing structure of the Greater London housing market, 1961–81. *The London Journal*, 9, 153–64.

Hamnett, Chris and Randolph, Bill 1983b: The changing population distribution of England and Wales, 1961–81: clean break or consistent progression? *Built Environment*, 8, 272–80.

Hamnett, Chris and Williams, Peter 1980: Social change in London: a study in gentrification. *The London Journal*, 6, 51–66.

Hankins, Frank H. 1932: Has the reproductive power of Western peoples declined? In Pitt-Rivers, G. H. L. F. (ed.), *Problems of Population. Being the Report of the*

Proceedings of the Second General Assembly of the International Union for the Scientific Investigation of Population Problems. London: George Allen & Unwin, 181–8.

Hannah, Leslie 1986: *Inventing Retirement*. Cambridge: Cambridge University Press.

Harlem Brundtland, Gro 1983: Statement as Chairman of the European Population Conference, 1982. In *Proceedings of the European Population Conference, 1982*. Strasbourg: Council of Europe, 13–19.

Harper, Sarah and Thane, Pat 1989: Ageing, Work and Retirement 1945–1965. In Jeffreys (ed.), *Growing Old in Twentieth-Century Britain*. London: Routledge.

Haskey, John 1983: The chances of divorce: the influence of marital status and age at marriage. *Population Trends*, 32, 4–14.

Haskey, John 1984: Social class and socio-economic differentials in divorce in England and Wales. *Population Studies*, 38, 419–38.

Haskey, John 1986: One-parent families in Great Britain. *Population Trends*, 45, 5–13.

Haskey, John 1987a: One-person households in Great Britain: living alone in the middle years of life. *Population Trends*, 50, 23–31.

Haskey, John 1987b: Social Class differences in remarriage after divorce. *Population Trends*, 47, 34–42.

Hayes, Michael G. 1986: Liverpool's relative position: a technical study. *Urban Decline and Deprivation Report No. 1*, City of Liverpool.

Henry, Louis 1953: *Fécondité des Mariages: Nouvelle Méthode de Mesure*. Travaux et documents, Cahier No. 16, Institut National d'Etudes Démographiques. Paris: Press Universitaires de France.

Henwood, Melanie, Rimmer, Lesley and Wicks, Malcolm 1987: *Inside the Family: Changing Roles of Men and Women*. Occasional Paper 6. London: Family Policy Studies Centre.

Herbert, David 1972: *Urban Geography*. Newton Abbot: David and Charles.

Herington, John 1984: *The Outer City*. London: Harper & Row.

HM Treasury 1986: *The Government's Expenditure Plans 1986-7 to 1988-89*, vol. 11, London: HMSO.

Hobcraft, John 1985: Measuring demographic change and its consequences. In British Society for Population Studies, *Measuring Socio-demographic Change*, 39–50.

Hobcraft, John (forthcoming): Population and resource allocation. In Hobcraft and Murphy (eds), *Population Research in Britain*. Oxford: Oxford University Press.

Hobcraft, John and Rees, Philip (eds) 1980: *Regional Demographic Development*. London: Croom Helm.

Holmans, Alan 1981: Housing careers of recently married couples. *Population Trends*, 24. London: HMSO.

Holmes, Colin 1982: The promised land? Immigration into Britain 1870–1980. In Coleman (ed.), *Demography of Immigrant and Minority Groups in the UK*. London: Academic Press, 1–21.

HBF 1985: *Homes, jobs, land: the eternal triangle*. London: House Builders Federation.

Housing and Construction Statistics (various): Department of the Environment. London: HMSO.

Hughes, Gordon and McCormick, Barry 1981: Do council housing policies reduce migration between regions? *Economic Journal*, 91, 918–37.

Hughes, Gordon and McCormick, Barry 1985: Migration intentions in the UK. Which households want to migrate and which succeed? *Economic Journal Conference Papers Supplement*, 95, 113–23.

Hughes, Gordon and McCormick, Barry 1987: Does migration reduce differentials in regional unemployment rates? Paper presented at the International Conference on Migration and Labour Market Efficiency, October, mimeo (Edinburgh/Southampton University, Dept of Economics).

Hunt, Audrey 1968: *A Survey of Women's Employment*. London: HMSO.

IMS 1987: *Relocating managers and professional staff*. Brighton: Institute of Manpower Studies, University of Sussex. IMS Report no. 139.

Jeffreys, Margot (ed.) 1989: *Growing Old in Twentieth-Century Britain*. London: Routledge.

Jenkins, J. and Walker, J. R. 1985: School roll forecasting. In J. R. England (ed.), *Information Systems for Policy Planning in Local Government*. London: Longman, 63–84.

Johnson, James H., Salt, John and Wood, Peter A. 1974: *Housing and the migration of labour in England and Wales*. Farnborough: Saxon House.

Johnson, James H. and Salt, John 1980: Employment transfer policies in Great Britain. *Three Banks Review*, 126, 18–39.

Johnson, Malcolm L. 1982: The implications of greater activity in later life. In M. Fogarty (ed.), *Retirement Policy: The Next Fifty Years*. NIESR, PSI, RIPA. Joint Studies in Public Policy 5. London: Heinemann, 138–56.

Johnson, Paul 1987: The structured dependency of the elderly: a critical note. Centre for Economic Policy Research, Discussion Paper 202.

Jones, Douglas S. 1981: Whither mathematics? *Bull. Institute of Mathematics and its Applications*, 17, 194–195.

Jones, Gill 1987: Leaving the parental home: an analysis of early housing careers. *Journal of Social Policy*, 16, 49–74.

Jones, George and Stewart, John 1985: *The Case for Local Government* (2nd edn). London: George Allen & Unwin.

Jones, Huw, Caird, J., Berry, W., and Dewhurst, J. 1986: Peripheral counter-urbanization: findings from an integration of census and survey data in northern Scotland. *Regional Studies*, 20, 15–26.

Joseph, George, 1983: *Women at Work*. Deddington: Philip Allan.

Joshi, Heather 1984: *Women's Participation in Paid work: Further analysis of the Women and Employment Survey*. Department of Employment Research Paper, no. 45. London: Department of Employment.

Joshi, Heather 1985: Motherhood and employment: change and continuity in post-war Britain. In British Society for Population Studies, *Measuring Socio-demographic Change*, 70–87.

Joshi, Heather 1986: The domestic division of labour and gender inequality in the labour market. In P. Nolan and S. Paine (eds), *Rethinking Socialist Economics*. Cambridge: Polity Press, 258–69.

Joshi, Heather 1987a: The cost of caring. In Glendinning and Millar (eds), *Women and Poverty in Britain*. Brighton: Wheatsheat, 112–33.

Joshi, Heather 1987b: The cash opportunity costs of childbearing: An approach to estimation using British data. Centre for Economic Policy Research, Discussion Paper 208.

Joshi, Heather, Layard, Richard and Owen, Susan 1985: Why are more women working in Britain? *Journal of Labor Economics*, 3, S147–S176.

Joshi, Heather and Newell, Marie-Louise 1989: *Pay Differentials and Parenthood:* In M. Uncles (ed.), *London Papers in Regional Science 18. Longitudinal Data Analysis: Methods and Applications*. London: Pion, 89–102.

Joshi, Heather and Newell, Marie-Louise 1988: *Pay Differentials and Parenthood: Analysis of Men and Women Born in 1946*. Coventry: Institute for Employment Research, University of Warwick. Also available as CEPR Disscussion Papers nos 156 and 157.

Joshi, Heather and Owen, Susan 1987: How long is a piece of elastic? *Cambridge Journal of Economics*, 11, 54–74. (Also appeared as Centre for Economic Policy Research Disscusion Paper no. 31.)

Karn, Valerie, Kemeny, Jim and Williams, Peter 1985: *Home Ownership in the Inner City: Salvation or Despair? Studies in Urban and Regional Policy 3*. Aldershot: Gower.

Kaufman, Georgia 1984: Unwanted children? Recent trends in illegitimacy in England and Wales with special reference to London from 1970–83. Unpublished M.Sc. thesis, London School of Economics.

Kennett, Stephen R. 1983: Migration within and between labour markets. In Goddard and Champion (eds), *The Urban and Regional Transformation of Britain*. London: Methuen, 215–38.

Kiernan, Kathleen E. 1980a: Patterns of family formation and dissolution. In British Society for Population Studies, *The Implications of Current Demographic Trends in the UK for Social and Economic Policy*. OPCS Occasional Paper, 19/2, London: OPCS, 20–35.

Kiernan, Kathleen E. 1980b: Teenage motherhood: associated factors and consequences. *Journal of Biosocial Science*, 12, 393–405.

Kiernan, Kathleen E. 1983: The structure of families today: continuity or change? In British Society for Population Studies, *The Family*, 17–36.

Kiernan, Kathleen E. 1986a: Leaving home: living arrangements of young people in six West-European countries. *European Journal of Population*, 2, 177–84.

Kiernan, Kathleen 1986b: Teenage marriage and marital breakdown: a longitudinal study. *Population Studies*, 40, 35–54.

Kiernan, Kathleen E. 1986c: Transitions in young adulthood. Paper presented at the British Society for Population Studies 1986 Conference on Population Research in Britain. National Child Development Study, Working Paper no. 16. London: The City University, and in Hobcraft and Murphy (eds), *Population Research in Britain*. Oxford: Oxford University Press (forthcoming).

Kiernan, Kathleen E. 1987: Demographic experiences in early adulthood: a longitudinal study. Ph.D. thesis, University of London.

Kiernan, Kathleen E. and Diamond, Ian 1983: The age at which child bearing starts – a longitudinal study. *Population Studies*, 34, 363–80.

Kiernan, Kathleen E. and Eldridge, Sandra M. 1985: A demographic analysis of first marriages in England and Wales 1950 to 1980. Centre for Population Studies Research Paper, 85–1. London School of Hygiene.

Kiernan, Kathleen E. and Eldridge, Sandra M. 1987: Inter- and intra-cohort variation in the timing of first marriage. *British Journal of Sociology*, 38, 44–65.

Kitson, Gay C. and Raschke, Helen J. 1981: Divorce research: what we know: what we need to know. *Journal of Divorce*, 4, 1–37.

Kleinman, Mark and Whitehead, Christine 1987: Local variations in the sale of council houses in England, 1979–1984. *Regional Studies*, 21, 1–12.

Knox, Paul L., 1982: *Urban social geography: an introduction*. London/New York: Longman.

Labour Force Survey 1983 and 1984 1986: Office of Population Censuses and Surveys. London: HMSO.

Laslett, Peter and Wall, Richard 1972: *Household and Family in Past Time*. Cambridge: Cambridge University Press.

Law, C. M. and Warnes, A. M. 1976: The changing geography of the elderly in England and Wales. *Transactions, Institute of British Geographers, New Series*, 1, 453–71.

Lawton, Richard 1982: People and Work. In John W. House (ed.), *The UK Space*. London: Weidenfeld and Nicolson, 103–203.

Lawton, Richard 1986: Planning for people. In Gould and Lawton (eds), *Planning for Population Change*. London: Croom Helm, 9–38.

Le Bras, Henri and Roussel, Louis 1982: Retard ou refus du mariage: l'évolution récente de la première nuptialitè en France et sa prévision. *Population*, 37, 1009–44.

Lesthaeghe, Ron 1983: A century of demographic and cultural change in Western Europe: an exploration of underlying dimensions. *Population and Development Review*, 9, 411–35.

Lesthaeghe, Ron and Meekers, Dominique 1987: Value changes and the dimensions of familism in the European Community. *European Journal of Population*, 2, 225–68.

Lumb, K. M., Congdon, P. J., Lealman, G. T. 1981: A comparative view of Asian and British born maternity patients in Bradford 1974–1978. *Journal of Epidemiology and Community Health*, 35, 106–9.

McCormick, Barry 1983: Housing and unemployment in the UK. In C. A. Greenhalgh, P. R. G. Layard, and A. J. Oswald (eds), *The Causes of Unemployment*. Oxford: Clarendon Press, 283–305.

McCrone, Gavin 1969: *Regional policy in Britain*. London: George Allen & Unwin.

Macdonald, Peter (ed.) 1986: *Settling Up: Property and Income Maintenance on Divorce in Australia*. Sydney: Prentice Hall.

Macfarlane, Alison and Mugford, Miranda 1984: *Birth Counts*. London: HMSO.

McKie, Robin 1969: *The Observer*, 31 January.

McPherson, Andrew and Willms, Doug 1987: Equalisation and improvement: some effects of education in Scotland. *Sociology*, 21, 509–39.

Macura, Milos and Malacic, Janez 1987: Population prospects for Europe. In *European Population Conference 1987: Issues and Prospects. Plenaries*. Helsinki: Central Statistical Office of Finland, 1–45.

Madge, Janet and Brown, Colin 1981: *First Homes: a Survey of the Housing Circum-stances of Young Married Couples*. London: Policy Studies Institute.

Main, Brian 1985: Women's hourly earnings: the influence of work histories on rates of pay. University of Edinburgh, Department of Economics Discussion Paper VIII.

Maitland, Nan 1987: Community care: a consumer model. Unpublished, Bexley Housing Department.

Mao Qing and Mar Molinero, Cecilio 1986: Non-compulsory education in South-ampton. Research Paper. Department of Accounting and Management Science, University of Southampton.

Mar Molinero, Cecilio 1988: Southampton: a quantitative approach to school loca-tion, closure and staffing. *J. Operational Research Soc.* (forthcoming).

Martin, Jean and Roberts, Ceridwen 1984: *Women and Employment: A Lifetime Perspective*. London: HMSO.

Martin, Ron 1986: In what sense a 'jobs boom'? Employment recovery, government policy and the regions. *Regional Studies*, 20, 463–72.

Martin, Ron 1987: Mrs. Thatcher's Britain: a tale of two nations. *Environment and Planning A*, 19, 571–4.

Massey, Doreen 1979: In what sense a regional problem? *Regional Studies*, 13, 233–44.

Mays, Nicholas and Bevan, Gwyn 1987: *Resource Allocation in the Health Service: A Review of the Methods of the Resource Allocation Working Party (RAWP)*. LSE Occasional Paper on Social Administration no. 81. London: Bedford Square Press/National Council of Voluntary Organisations.

Meredith, Paul 1984: Falling rolls and the reorganisation of schools. *J. Social Wel-fare Law*, 43, 208–21.

Millar, Jane 1987: Lone mothers: In Glendinning and Millar (eds), *Women and Poverty in Britain*. Brighton: Wheatsheaf, 159–77.

Minford, Patrick 1985: *Unemployment: cause and cure* (2nd edn). Oxford: Basil Blackwell.

Minford, Patrick, Ashton, Paul and Peel, Michael 1987: The effects of housing distortions on unemployment. Centre for Economic Policy Research Discussion Paper 191.

Moser, Claus and Layard, Richard 1964: Planning the scale of higher education in Britain: some statistical problems. *J. Royal Statistical Society Series A*, 127, 473–526.

Moser, Katherine, Fox, A. J. and Jones, D. R. 1984: Unemployment and mortality in the OPCS longitudinal study. *Lancet* 2, 1324–8.

Moser, Katherine et al. 1987: Unemployment and mortality: a comparison of the 1971 and 1981 longitudinal census samples. *British Medical Journal* 294, 86–90, 39–50.

Munro, Moira 1986: Housing and labour market interactions: a review. Discussion Paper 12. Glasgow: University of Glasgow Centre for Housing Research.

Murphy, Michael 1984: The influence of fertility, early housing-career and socio-economic factors on tenure determination in contemporary Britain. *Environment and Planning A*, 16, 1303–18.

Murphy, Michael 1985: Demographic and socio-economic influences on recent British marital breakdown patterns. *Population Studies*, 39, 441–460.

Murphy, Michael (forthcoming): Modelling households: a synthesis. In Hobcraft and Murphy (eds), *Population Research in Britain*. Oxford: Oxford University Press.

Murphy, Michael and Sullivan, Oriel 1983: Housing tenure and fertility in post-war Britain. Centre for Population Studies Research Paper 83–2, London School of Hygiene.

Murphy, Michael and Sullivan, Oriel 1985: Housing tenure and family formation in contemporary Britain. *European Sociological Review* 1, 230–43.

Murphy, Michael and Sullivan, Oriel 1986: Unemployment, housing and household structure among young adults. *Journal of Social Policy* 15, 205–22.

National Research Council, Working Group on Population Growth and Economic Development, Committee on Population 1986: *Population Growth and Economic Development: Policy Questions*. Washington DC: National Academy Press.

NBS 1986: *Are first-time buyers being prevented from entering the owner-occupied housing market?* London: Nationwide Building Society.

Newell, Colin 1986: Spatial variations in fertility and nuptiality in Britain: an historical perspective. Centre for Population Studies Research Paper 86–1, London School of Hygiene.

Newell, Marie-Louise and Joshi, Heather 1986: The next job after the first baby: occupational transition among women born in 1946. Centre for Population Studies Research Paper 86–3, London School of Hygiene.

Ng, Kwee Choo 1968: *The Chinese in London*. Oxford: Oxford University Press.

Ní Bhrolcháin, Máire 1986a: Women's paid work and the timing of births: longitudinal evidence. *European Journal of Population*, 2, 43–70.

Ní Bhrolcháin, Máire 1986b: The interpretation and role of work-associated accelerated childbearing in post-war Britain. *European Journal of Population*, 2, 135–54.

Ní Bhrolcháin, Máire 1987: Period parity progression ratios and birth intervals in England and Wales, 1941–1971: a synthetic life table analysis. *Population Studies* 41, 103–25.

Nichol, A. W. 1985: Contribution to discussion of 'Projections of student numbers in higher education'. *J. Royal Statistical Society Series A*. 148, 208.

Norman, Alison 1985: *Triple Jeopardy*. London: Centre for Policy on Ageing.

OPCS 1980: Estimating local authorities' populations. *Population Trends*, 20, 12–16.

OPCS 1983: *Recently moving households: a follow-up study to the 1978 national dwelling and housing survey*. London: HMSO.

OPCS Monitor 1984: Conceptions inside and outside marriage, 1969 to 1981. FM/1 84/6. London: OPCS.

OPCS 1984: *Census 1981: Key statistics for local authorities – Great Britain*. London: HMSO.

OPCS 1986a: Ethnic minority populations in Britain. *Population Trends*, 46, 18–21.

OPCS 1986b: Birthweight Statistics 1985. OPCS Monitor DH3 86/2.

OPCS 1987: Migration in 1986. *Population Trends*, 50, 32–38.

OPCS 1988: Mid-1985-based population projections for local authority areas in

England. London: Office of Population Censuses and Surveys, Monitor PP3 88/1.

Ogilvy, Audrey A. 1980: *Interregional Migration since 1971: an appraisal of data from the National Health Service Central Register and labour force surveys*. Occasional Paper 16. London: OPCSs.

Ogilvy, Audrey A. 1982: Population migration between the regions of Great Britain 1971–79. *Regional Studies*, 16, 65–73.

O'Higgins, Michael 1986: Public spending: the pressure is off. *New Society*, 21 November, 20–1.

Open University 1985: *The Health of Nations*. Milton Keynes: Open University Press.

OECD 1985: *The Integration of Women into the Economy*. Paris: OECD.

Owen, Susan J. 1987: Household production and economic efficiency: arguments for and against domestic specialisation. *Work, Employment and Society*, 1, 157–78.

Pahl, Jan 1983: The allocation of money and the structuring of inequality within marriage, *Sociological Review*, 31, no. 2, 237–62.

Pahl, Jan (ed.) 1985 *Private Violence and Public Policy*. London: Routledge & Kegan Paul.

Parsons, David 1987: Recruitment difficulties and the housing market. *The Planner*, 73(1), 30–4.

Patel, Bharat 1984: A statistical study of ethnic differences in perinatal mortality. Unpublished M.Sc. thesis, Southampton University.

Payne, Joan 1987: Does unemployment run in families? Some evidence from the General Household Survey. *Sociology*, 21, 199–214.

Peach, Ceri 1984: The force of West Indian island identity in Britain. In Clarke, Ley and Peach (eds), *Geography and Ethnic Pluralism*. London: George Allen & Unwin, 214–30.

Peach, G. C. K. 1982: The growth and distribution of the black population in Britain 1945–80. In Coleman (ed.), *Demography of Immigrant and Minority Groups in the UK*. London: Academic Press, 23–42.

Pearson, Maggie 1984: An insensitive service. In A. Harrison and J. Gretton (eds), *Health Care UK 1984: An Economic, Social and Political Audit*. London: Chartered Institue of Public Finance and Accounting, 122.

Piachaud, David 1985: *Round about Fifty Hours a Week: The Time Costs of Children*. Poverty Pamphlet 64. London: Child Poverty Action Group.

Pifer, Alan 1987: Our Ageing Society. Lecture to the Royal Society of Arts, London.

Pifer, Alan and Bronte L. (eds) 1986: *Our Ageing Society*. New York: W. W. Norton.

Pissarides, Christopher A. 1981: Staying on at school in England and Wales. *Economica*, 48, 345–63.

Pissarides, Christopher A. 1982: From school to university: the demand for post-compulsory education in Britain. *Economic Journal*, 92, 654–67.

Platek, R., Rao, John N. K., Sarndal, Carl E. and Singh, M. P. 1987: *Small Area Statistics*. London: Wiley.

Population Projections, Population Estimates (various): Office of Population Censuses and Surveys. London: HMSO.

Raab, Gillian and Adler, Michael 1987: A Tale of Two Cities: the impact of parental choice on admissions to primary schools in Edinburgh and Dundee. *Research Papers in Education*, 2, 157–76.

Raffe, David 1984: School attainment and the labour market. In Raffe (ed.), *Fourteen to Eighteen: The Changing Pattern of Schooling in Scotland*. Aberdeen: Aberdeen University Press, 194–213.

Rayner, Derek 1981: *Government Statistical Services*, Cmnd. 8236. London: HMSO.

Raynor, J. et al. 1974: *The Urban Context*. Milton Keynes: Open University.

Redpath, Bob and Harvey, Brenda 1987: *Young People's Intentions to Enter Higher Education*. London: HMSO.

Rees, Philip H. 1977: The measurement of migration from census and other sources. *Environment and Planning A*, 9, 247–72.

Rees, Philip H. 1986: A geographical forecast of the demand for student places. *Trans actions of the Institute of British Geographers*, 11, 5–26.

Rex, John and Moore, Robert 1967: *Race, Community and Conflict*. Oxford: Oxford University Press.

Rhind, David (ed.) 1983: *A Census User's Handbook*. London: Methuen.

Rice, Patricia 1985: Household investment in post-compulsory schooling in the UK. Research paper, Department of Economics, University of Sussex.

Rimmer, Lesley 1987: Paid work. In Henwood, M., Rimmer, L. and Wicks, M., *Inside the Family: Changing Roles of Men and Women*. London: Family Policy Studies Centre, 37–48.

Robbins, Lionel 1963: *Higher Education*, Cmnd. 2154. London: HMSO.

Robert, S. and Randolph, W. 1983: Beyond decentralisation: the evolution of population distribution in England and Wales, 1961–81. *Geoforum*, 14, 75–102.

Robertson, G. 1979: Housing tenure and labour mobility in Scotland. ESU Discussion Paper 4. Edinburgh: SEPD.

Robinson, M. J., Palmer, S. R., Avery, A., Jones, C. E., Benyon, J. L. and Taylor, R. W. 1982: Ethnic differences in perinatal mortality – a challenge. *Journal of Epidemiology and Community Health*, 36, 22–6.

Royal Statistical Society 1984: Projections of Student Numbers in Higher Education. Report of a Working Party, Royal Statistical Society.

Royal Statistical Society, 1985: Symposium on projections of student numbers in higher education. *J. Royal Statistical Society Series A*, 148, 175–213.

Rudd, Ernest 1987: The education qualifications and social class of the parents of undergraduates entering British universities in 1984. *J. Royal Statistical Society Series A*, 150, 346–72.

Runn_cymede Trust 1980: *Britain's Black Population*. The Runnymede Trust and the Radical Statistics Race Group. London: Heinemann Educational Books.

Salt, John 1986: Labour force and employment in western Europe. In Gould and Lawton (eds), *Planning for Population Change*. London: Croom Helm, 39–63.

Salt, John and Flowerdew, Robin 1980: Labour migration from London. *The London Journal*, 6, 36–50.

Simmons, I. 1981: Contrasts in Asian residential segregation. In P. Jackson and S. J. Smith (eds), *Residential Segregation*, Special Publication no. 12. London: Academic Press for the Institute of British Geographers, 184–90.

Simons, John 1982: Attitudes to family size among immigrant Sikhs in London. In

Coleman (ed.), *Demography of Immigrant and Minority Groups in the UK*. London: Academic Press, 169–92.

Simons, John 1986a: Culture, economy and reproduction in contemporary Europe. In D. Coleman and R. Schofield (eds), *The State of Population Theory*. Oxford: Basil Blackwell, 256–78.

Simons, John 1986b: How conservative are British attitudes to reproduction? *Quarterly Journal of Social Affairs*, 2(1), 41–54.

Simpson, Stephen 1984: Pupil forecasts: Survey of other authorities' practice. In 'Forecasting Pupil Numbers', report of one-day workshop. Local Education Authorities Research Group. London: ILEA.

Simpson, Stephen 1987: School roll forecasting methods: a review. *Research Papers in Education*, 2, 63–77.

Smith, David J. 1976: *The Facts of Racial Disadvantage*. London: PEP.

Smith, Fred 1985: Invited contribution to projection of student numbers in higher education. *J. Royal Statistical Society Series A*, 148, 184–9.

Social Trends (annual): Central Statistical Office. London: HMSO.

Sparks, Janet 1986: Marital condition estimates 1971–85: a new series: *Population Trends*, 45, 18–25.

Spence, Nigel A., Gillespie, Andrew E., Goddard, John B., Kennett, Steve R., Pinch, Steve P., and Williams, Allan M. 1982: *British Cities: Analysis of Urban Change*. Oxford: Pergamon.

Stewart, Mark and Greenhalgh, Christine 1984: Work history patterns and the occupational attainment of women. *Economic Journal*, 94, 493–519.

Stillwell, John C. H. 1985: Migration between metropolitan and non-metropolitan regions in the United Kingdom. In P. E. White and B. van der Knaap (eds), *Contemporary Studies in Migration*. Norwich: Geo Books, ch. 2.

Stillwell, John C. H. 1986: The analysis and projection of inter-regional migration in the United Kingdom. In R. Woods and P. H. Rees (eds), *Population Structures and Models*. London: Allen & Unwin, 160–202.

Stones, Michael J. and Kozma, Albert 1985: Physical performance. In Charness (ed.), *Ageing and Human Performance*. Chichester and New York: Wiley, 210–31.

Sullivan, Oriel 1984: Family formation and housing circumstances in contemporary Britain. Unpublished Ph.D. thesis, University of London.

Sullivan, Oriel 1986: Housing movements of the divorced and separated. *Housing Studies*, 1, 35–48.

Sullivan, Oriel and Falkingham, Jane (forthcoming): Unemployment: family circumstances and childhood correlates among young people in Britain. In Hobcraft and Murphy (eds), *Population Research in Britain*. Oxford: Oxford University Press.

Sullivan, Oriel and Murphy, Michael 1987: Young outright owners in Britain. *Housing Studies*, 2, 177–91.

Terry, P. B., Cordie, R. G. and Settatree, R. B. 1980: Analysis of ethnic differences in perinatal statistics. *British Medical Journal*, 2, 1307–8.

Thane, Pat (forthcoming): The debate on the declining birth-rate: the menace of an ageing population in Britain, 1920–1950. In Debra Thom and Joan Austocker (eds), *The Declining Birth-Rate in Europe 1900–1950*. Cambridge: Cambridge University Press.

Thatcher, Roger 1985: Contribution to discussion. *Journal of the Royal Statistical Society A*, 148, 307.

Thompson, Jean H. 1982: Differential fertility among ethnic minorities. In Coleman (ed), *Demography of Immigrant and Minority Groups in the UK*. London: Academic Press, 71–82.

Thomson, David 1987: Incomes in old age – rising or falling? Unpublished paper, Rank Xerox Unit. Cambridge: University of Cambridge.

Thornes, Barbara and Collard, Joan 1979: *Who Divorces?* London: Routledge and Kegan Paul.

Timaeus, Ian M. 1986: Family and households of the elderly population: prospects for those approaching old age. *Ageing and Society*, 6, 271–93.

Tinker, Anthea 1981: *The Elderly in Modern Society*. London: Longmans.

Todd, Jean and Griffiths, D. 1986: *Changing the Definition of a Household: Report by the Social Survey Division*, Office of Population Censuses and Surveys. London: HMSO.

TCPA 1987: *North–South divide: a new deal for Britain's regions*. London: Town and Country Planning Association.

Townsend, Alan R. 1983: *The Impact of Recession: On Industry, Employment and the Regions, 1976–1981*, London: Croom Helm.

Townsend, Alan R. 1986: The location of employment growth after 1978: the surprising significance of dispersed centres. *Environment and Planning A*, 18, 529–45.

Townsend, Peter and Nick Davidson (eds) 1982: *The Black Report: Inequalities in Health*. Harmondsworth: Penguin.

Townsend, Peter et al. 1987: *Poverty and Labour in London*. London: Low Pay Unit.

Tyler, Peter and Rhodes, John 1986: South East employment and housing study. Cambridge: Department of Land Economy, Discussion Paper 15.

Universities' Central Council for Admissions 1986: Statistical Supplement to the 23rd Report. Cheltenham.

Walker, Alan and Carol (eds) 1987: *The Growing Divide*. London: Child Poverty Action Group.

Wall, Richard 1984: The living arrangements of the elderly in contemporary Europe. Paper presented at the IUSSP Workshop on the later stages of life cycle, Berlin.

Wall, Richard 1988: Leaving home and living alone: an historical perspective. Centre for Economic Policy Research Discussion Paper 211.

Warnes, A. M. and Law, C. M. 1984: The elderly population of Great Britain: location trends and policy implications. *Transactions of the Institute of British Geographers*, New Series, 9, 37–59.

Welford, A. 1985: Changes in performance with age: an overview. In Charness, N. (ed.), *Ageing and Human Performance*. Chichester and New York: Wiley, 36.

Werner, Barry 1982: Recent trends in illegitimate births and extra-marital conceptions. *Population Trends*, 30, 9–15.

Werner, Barry 1985: Fertility trends in different social classes: 1970–83. *Population Trends*, 41, 5–13.

Werner, Barry 1986a: Family building intentions of different generations of women: results from the GHS 1979–83. *Population Trends*, 44, 17–23.

Werner, Barry 1986b: Trends in first, second, third and later births. *Population Trends*, 45, 26–33.

Werner, Barry and Chalk, Susan 1986: Projections of first, second, third and later births. *Population Trends*, 46, 26–34.

Westoff, Charles 1986: Perspective on nuptiality and fertility. *Population and Development Review*, vol. 12 Supplement, 155–70.

Whitehead, Margaret 1987: *The Health Divide: Inequalities in Health in the 1980s*. London: Health Education Council.

Whitelegg, John 1986: Planning for health care provision in Britain: the local dimension. In W. T. S. Gould and R. Lawton (eds), *Planning for Population Change*. London: Croom Helm, 132–62.

Williams, Pat (Thane) 1970: The development of old age pensions policy in the United Kingdom, 1878–1925. Unpublished Ph.D. thesis, LSE, University of London.

Willis, Kenneth 1974: *Problems in migration analysis*. Farnborough: Saxon House.

Willis, Paul 1984: Youth unemployment 2: Ways of living. *New Society*, 5 April, 13–15.

Willms, Doug and Kerr, Peter 1987: Changes in sex differences in Scottish examination results since 1976. *J. Early Adolescence*. (forthcoming).

Yusuf, Farhat and Werner, Barry 1987: Immigrant fertility and differentials in England and Wales, 1971–1981. European Population Conference, 1987.

Zabalza, Antonio and Tzannatos, Zafiris 1985: *Women and Equal Pay: The Effects of Legislation on Female Employment and Wages in Britain*. Cambridge: Cambridge University Press.

The Contributors

WILLIAM BRASS was Professor of Medical Demography and Director of the Centre for Population Studies at the London School of Hygiene until 1988. His research has been in methodological and epidemiological aspects of population studies, including estimates of basic demographic measures from limited and indirect data. He is currently the President of the International Union for the Scientific Study of Population.

TONY CHAMPION is Lecturer in Geography at the University of Newcastle upon Tyne. His research interests are in recent changes in population distribution in advanced Western societies, particularly trends in metropolitan deconcentration and re-urbanization. He is co-author of *Facts about the New Towns* and *Changing Places: Britain's Demographic, Economic and Social Complexion*, and also co-editor of *The Urban and Regional Transformation of Britain* and *The Future for the City Centre*.

SUE CLARKE is a Lecturer in the Department of Actuarial Mathematics and Demography at Macquarie University, Sydney, having previously worked in the Department of Economics at the University of Southampton. Her research interests include differential patterns of mortality and the dynamics of population growth.

IAN DIAMOND is a Senior Lecturer in Demography at the University of Southampton and a CEPR Research Fellow. He is currently Honorary Secretary of the British Society for Population Studies. His research interests include the causes of recent fertility decline in the United Kingdom and the relationship between population change and government policy, particularly in education.

JOHN ERMISCH is a Senior Research Officer at the National Institute of Economic and Social Research, a visiting Senior Research Fellow at Birbeck College and Co-Director of the Programme on Human Resources in Britain since 1900 at CEPR. His writing on economic demography and housing economics includes *the Political Economy of Demographic Change*. He is President of the European Society for Population Economics.

JOHN HOBCRAFT is Professor of Population Studies at the London School of Economics and a CEPR Research Fellow. He is currenly President of the British Society for Population Studies and a joint editor of *Population Studies:* He has published on both methodological and substantive topics, spanning both developing and developed countries. He has co-authored *Demographic Estimation for Developing Societies*, and co-edited *Regional Demographic Development* and *Reproductive Change in Developing Countries*.

HEATHER JOSHI is a Senior Research Fellow of Birbeck College and a visiting lecturer at the Centre for Population Studies at the London School of Hygiene, where she was based at the time of working on this book. She was then also Co-Director of CEPR's Programme on Human Resources in Britain since 1900. She was formerly an economic adviser in DHSS and has written on questions relating to paid work and family formation. She directs the only economic demography research team in Britain.

KATHLEEN KIERNAN is Deputy Director of the Social Statistics Research Unit at The City University, and a CEPR Research Fellow. Previously she was a Senior Research Fellow at the Centre for Population Studies. She is a social demographer who has published on a range of topics relating to the family, including leaving home, cohabitation, marriage, divorce, fertility and celibacy.

MICHAEL MURPHY is a Senior Lecturer in Population Studies. He joined the London School of Economics and Political Science in 1980 after working as a statistician in the Central Statistical Office, and as a research fellow at the London School of Hygiene and Tropical Medicine. His work interests are in both developed and developing countries and include technical demography, families and households and socio-economic influences on fertility. He is a CEPR Research Fellow.

PAT THANE is Principal Lecturer in the Department of Social Science and Administration, University of London, Goldsmiths College and a CEPR Research Fellow. She has written extensively on the history of the British Welfare State since the later nineteenth century including on the history of provision for the elderly.

The Centre for Economic Policy Research

The Centre for Economic Policy Research is a registered charity with educational purposes. It was established in 1983 to promote independent analysis and public discussion of open economies and the relations among them. Institutional (core) finance for the Centre has been provided through major grants from the Economic and Social Research Council, the Leverhulme Trust, the Esmée Fairbairn Trust and the Bank of England. None of these organizations gives prior review to the Centre's publications nor do they necessarily endorse the views expressed therein.

The Centre is pluralist and non-partisan, bringing economic research to bear on the analysis of medium- and long-run policy questions. The research work which it disseminates may include views on policy, but the Board of Governors of the Centre does not give prior review to such publications, and the Centre itself takes no institutional policy positions. The opinions expressed in this volume are those of the authors and not those of the Centre for Economic Policy Research.

Index